How
the Tiger
Lost Its
Stripes

Jan 17, 99

For Rena + Henry,

.. Both of whom have
loved animals since they
were cubs themselves!

Best Wishes,

How
the Tiger
Lost Its
Stripes

*An Exploration into the
Endangerment of a Species*

Cory J Meacham

Harcourt Brace & Company
New York   San Diego   London

Requests for permission to make copies of any part of the work should be mailed to:
Permissions Department, Harcourt Brace & Company, 6277 Sea Harbor Drive,
Orlando, Florida 32887-6777.

Library of Congress Cataloging-in-Publication Data
Meacham, Cory J.
How the tiger lost its stripes: an exploration into the
endangerment of a species/Cory J Meacham. — 1st ed.
p.   cm.
Includes bibliographical references and index.
ISBN 0-15-100279-7
1. Tigers.   2. Endangered species.   3. Wildlife conservation.
I. Title.
QL737.C23M43   1997
333.95´975616 — dc21   96-39845

The text was set in Electra LH.
Designed by Geri Davis
Printed in the United States of America
First Edition

A B C D E

For my sire and dam

Gilbert Herrick Meacham

and

Elinor Natsuko Glover Meacham

Contents

∿

Preface

❦

THE TIGER IS IN NO DANGER OF EXTINCTION.

If that observation surprises you, you are not alone. And whatever distrust you might feel for research that supports such a claim is reasonable, considering the amount of evidence to the contrary. Few animals are advertised so conspicuously as the tiger in the global campaign to raise awareness for the plight of endangered animals.

But the fact remains, unchallenged by science, that the animal we call the tiger is in no greater danger of extinction than the common house cat. They breed so readily, in fact, that adults are regularly separated to thwart their promiscuity and contraceptives are used to stanch the issue of cubs. When those measures fail, healthy tigers all over the world are killed, legally. The advantage of such fecundity is that you and your descendants shall have ample opportunity to view living representatives of the species *Panthera tigris*. No question about it.

There is, of course, a catch. The tigers to which you and your descendants are guaranteed a view will be, in one form or another, captive animals—zoo tigers, or tigers that do tricks. Your progeny might have the luxury of watching tigers romp through comparatively vast spaces, but perimeter boundaries of some kind will stand not too far in the distance, and the prey on which those tigers feed will be either carefully managed or stocked outright. More significantly, such exotic displays will be exceptional. Anything closer to a truly wild situation is far from guaranteed. And *that* is the point. At the core of every discussion about the extinction of the tiger is an issue that can be summed up in a single word: wildness.

Everyone involved in the conservation of the tiger clamors for greater awareness among the general public, and that is what I hope to achieve through this book. I am not an activist, nor am I a scientist, a politician, or a big-game hunter. I'm a writer. I don't work for a corporation, or a government, or even for the tiger. I work for you. My goal is simply to present, not to persuade. Nevertheless, I am mindful of my responsibility to draw informed conclusions, and I am quite aware that people are sick of simply being shown problems. We want solutions, or at least options. I have striven to present those, too.

I am also mindful that much of what is written about endangered animals these days is seen only by readers who have already made up their minds without ever reaching the people who are still trying to decide. "Preaching to the choir," as the metaphor goes. To avoid that, I have aimed this book at the widest possible audience, writing not for the scientific community but rather for the lay public. Less can be covered in such a book, and what can be covered must be dealt with fundamentally. I apologize for what some readers may see as oversimplifications, but I defend myself with the pledge that I have not knowingly condensed anything in this book with bias. Speaking of bias, and considering the nature of the subjects addressed in this book, you deserve to know that its author once lived in Taiwan and its publisher once owned Sea World. Fortunately, neither fact affects the product.

Some of the information in this book is brutally time-sensitive. Certain details may have changed before you even read this page.

People switch jobs, voluntarily or not, and the policies they champion go with them. Laws are amended or rewritten or revoked. Funding dries up. Entire governments crucial to the stability of certain tiger habitats may fall. (One government both crucial to the tiger and visited frequently herein will endure an extraordinary transformation at the very stroke of midnight on June 30 in the same year this book makes its debut.) But every effort has been made to supply the latest available information, and many aspects of the analysis presented here will retain their value historically, regardless of what changes may occur. Many aspects are not subject to the vicissitudes of time at all.

Much of what I learned while conducting my research for this book came as a surprise to me, including the reality shared in the first sentence of this preface. Until I started working on this book I was under the impression that every time I looked at a tiger—even one in a cage—I was looking at something fantastically rare. I suspect that's the case with many people. Another common misperception involves the tiger's native habitat. Fully a third of the people who learned of my work on this book congratulated me on the opportunity I would surely have to visit Africa. But there are no wild tigers in Africa. There never have been. Explaining that fact often evoked a grimace of embarrassment on the face of my well-wisher, just as it may now be conjuring a similar look on your face, for which I have a quick remedy: I myself was under that misperception, too, until just a few years ago. Naïveté, however, is an asset for writers, I feel. It helps us remember what our job is, and who we're doing it for. Since when were we all expected to have memorized the geobiotics of every animal species? What is *not* known about the tiger outweighs what is known by many orders of magnitude. The world's most experienced and respected felid scientists went out of their way to make that point clear to me. In that realm, this book will make little progress, for this is not a book about the tiger. It's a book about the endangerment of the tiger.

Tigers are perfect examples of what biologists call "charismatic megafauna"—read: "attractive big animals." Elephants and rhinos qualify, too, along with many other instantly recognizable beasts. But tigers hold a special fascination for many people, perhaps due to the animal's mysterious and predatory nature, perhaps because they have miniature cousins who share homes with us. Maybe it's just because tigers are such impossibly beautiful creatures. Whatever the reason, the animal inspires powerful emotions, which would not be a problem if the questions surrounding tigers had clear-cut answers. Passion is a valid, useful motivator. But several of the strategies available in the "fight" to "save" the tiger are emotionally loaded, diametrically opposed, mutually exclusive, or all three, which leads, quite often, to what I call conflict paralysis. Few topics are so divisive as those involved in tiger conservation. Even abortion and gun control withstand comparison. (Both, in fact, are remarkably apropos, as shall become clear.) Comembers of tiger conservation teams, both scientific and political, disagree trenchantly among themselves on many critical points. Conversely, strange alliances abound. There are, in fact, no clear-cut answers when it comes to tigers.

One technical note: Any book that deals with either science or politics will feature a disproportionate share of arcane language. This book deals with both. To fight the confusion that so much gobbledygook cannot help but incite, an acronym glossary has been included. Even that, however, won't defend you against a set of terminology quirks so unlikely they can only be described as bizarre. For starters, the words "field" and "felid" both figure prominently and essentially into the text. Confusing them will lead to hazardous misunderstandings. Then, certain unavoidable acronyms in this book differ in letters but still rhyme in sound, one instance of which involves two different languages. Other phonetic oddities occur with unwelcome frequency, the most uncanny of which, perhaps, arose at a conference in Indonesia where two of the twelve people in attendance were named Sarah, two were named Doug, and two were surnamed Christie—and one of the Sarahs was one of the Christies. Even the

two most elemental adjectives in the book—"wild" and "captive"—
are laden with etymological baggage. Every effort has been made to
decipher undecipherables and to render the results clearly. And regarding the Chinese terms used in this book, except in cases where
established international usage dictates otherwise, the Yale system of
transliteration has been used to convert all Chinese words into English. In certain cases involving a person's name, however, his or her
individual preferences for transliteration have been used.

According to the Chinese calendar, 1998 is the next "year of the
tiger." Rich ironies will make that occasion simultaneously rewarding
and ominous for the celebrants, the observers, and even for the animal
itself. By the end of that year, several people quoted in this book will
be either endorsed or invalidated depending upon how accurately
their forecasts have played out. This is an important time. We might
not get other chances, and some of the choices that face us are irrev-
ocable and incompatible. The stripes on a tiger's coat provide it with
uniquely effective camouflage. Tucked amid reeds and grasses, it can
easily remain undetectable from even a few yards away. That advantage helps the animal compete, affording it close range to prey and
concealment from foes. Without its stripes, the tiger cannot long
survive.

—Cory Meacham
San Diego, California

*How
the Tiger
Lost Its
Stripes*

༈

❧

CHAPTER 1

A Tiger Is
Not a Tiger
Is Not a Tiger

I N THE SWELTERING HEAT OF A FEBRUARY AFTERNOON on the island of Sumatra, Dr. Douglas Armstrong puts a blowgun to his lips and sends a syringe-tipped dart sailing into the flank of a crouching Sumatran tiger. The animal charges him, flinging itself against the bars of its enclosure and splitting the air with a spectacular roar. Over the next half hour, Armstrong, a staff veterinarian on leave from the Henry Doorly Zoo in Omaha, Nebraska, darts the seething animal again several times, administering a careful mix of drugs necessary to knock it out gradually but completely. When at last the tiger lays motionless, Armstrong slips into its cage and confirms the depth of the animal's anesthesia before inviting the rest of his team to join him.

An hour later in a makeshift laboratory nearby, Dr. Onnie Byers, a reproductive physiologist with an organization called the Conservation Breeding Specialist Group, sets a small wooden board atop a brick of dry ice and leans down hard on it with the heels of her hands. The smoking white block whines and sputters in protest as rows of blunt metal pegs on the bottom of the board find purchase. "You'd think I was hurting it," Byers observes, hovering for a moment with her elbows locked. When she backs off, a neat grid of pea-size depressions dots the crystalline surface of the ice. Swapping the pegboard for a pipette, Byers moves quickly over the ice, tapping at the concave dots like a confectioner decorating a cake. Into each hollow she deposits a glistening genetic gem, collected from Armstrong's anesthetized cat: a pearl of tiger semen.

Seated a few feet away at a fold-up table, Minnesota Zoo conservation biologist Kathy Traylor-Holzer works the keyboard of her laptop computer, grooming what is known in her field as a studbook: a comprehensive database of animal genealogy and vital statistics—kept mostly on-line these days—which must be updated continuously to reflect changes in the population of the animals it represents. Without such a record, so the theory goes, the animals can't be managed effectively. At the moment, Traylor-Holzer is focusing on the body weight of the sleeping tiger. "Much too big," she complains, pulling her hands away from the keyboard and shaking her head.

On this February day in 1995, five recognized subspecies of tiger still walk the earth. Three additional subspecies survived well into the century, including two that accompanied the Sumatran tiger along the Indonesian archipelago. But they're gone now. None in the wild. None in zoos. It is with intentions of preventing a similar fate for the Sumatran tiger that Armstrong, Byers, and Traylor-Holzer have come to Sumatra, along with a corps of researchers who represent zoos from Australia and England in addition to the United States.

Sumatran tigers are the smallest of the surviving subspecies, averaging 110 kilograms (243 pounds) for males and 95 (209 pounds) for females. The sleeping cat tips the scales at 125 kilograms (276 pounds), a troubling bulk because it hints at a possibility that would significantly devalue his semen—that he's a hybrid, that somewhere in his bloodline lurks an ancestor from a different, larger subspecies. If indeed that's the case, he becomes, by some standards, more of a threat than a value.

"It is becoming increasingly difficult to find a home for a non-pure tiger," explains Sarah Christie, the Conservation Programmes' coordinator at the London Zoo and a member of the Sumatra team. To many laypeople, a tiger is a tiger is a tiger. But conservation biologists are significantly more particular. "The only homes you can find for hybrid tigers these days," Christie continues, "are either in private hands, in circuses, in the zoos of very underdeveloped areas of the world, or sometimes in safari parks that just want the animals for exhibit and aren't really bothered about whether they're contributing to a conservation effort. As zoos buy into the conservation ethic, they want to obtain pure subspecies animals."

With those comments, Christie tugs at threads connected to several of the most volatile and divisive concepts churning through the uneasy landscape of tiger conservation. Premier among them is the role that zoos will play. In conventional terms, a zoo is the very definition of captivity—the nemesis for every wild thing. Bars and moats represent the removal of animals from their native habitats as surely as they hold back the people who come to visit. But some zoos are changing, and while the more visible expression of that change has taken the form of spacious enclosures and "enriched" environments for the animals, a development of greater significance is taking place behind the scenes.

"The expertise available in zoos to assist wild conservation is huge," says Christie. "As you're going to have to manage the wild, the techniques you're going to need to manage the animals *in* the wild have all been developed in zoos. The personnel with the skills have all been trained in zoos, and most of them still work in zoos." Despite her professional bias and her casual juxtaposition of the words "management" and "wild" (a relationship to be analyzed meticulously later), Christie's point is undeniable: Zoos are rich depositories of skills and knowledge. To ignore such resources while striving to engineer any viable conservation strategy would be a mistake.

Not everyone is comfortable with this newly broadened role for zoos. Field researchers, ceding a degree of kinship in the overall discipline of science, often discount zoos as "captive only" or "out of touch with the wild." On a different level, activists driven by concern for the environment or for animal welfare dismiss zoos altogether on political and emotional grounds. Despite such enmity—none of it necessarily invalid or unimportant—the distinctions that once estranged zoos from the origins of their inhabitants are disappearing faster than a traditional box-cage display. Conservation is now a salable concept in the environmentally aware First World, and zoos are touting their efforts to safeguard the homelands of their charges. Visitors like the thought that their gate fees support such work. The big winners in this evolution, Christie and her colleagues submit, are the animals, with none benefiting more readily than the tiger, and no tiger more readily than the Sumatran.

⤳

When the beads of tiger semen have frozen solid, Dr. Byers plucks them from their icy nest, rinses them in a bath of liquid nitrogen, ladles them into clearly marked plastic vials, and transfers them to a portable cryogenic vault. In addition to semen from other tigers, the contents of the vault include samples of tiger tissue and tiger blood. Ultimately, the contents of the vault will make their way to the United States for genetic analysis—the same kind of scientific scrutiny used in law-enforcement laboratories around the world to determine the identity of criminals. Such investigation has become commonplace in its application to humans, but tigers are new to the tests.

The purpose behind analyzing their DNA is twofold: If unique genetic "markers" can be found to distinguish one subspecies of tiger clearly from another, then hybrids can be identified readily and unambiguously. A simple premise, perhaps, and it may indeed play out simply; early results indicate that markers are in fact present. But the implications are far-reaching and complex, and they strike at the very identity of the animal in question.

"What *is* a subspecies?" asks Christie, noting that genetics is not her expertise. "Before all this DNA technology there was a kind of rule-of-thumb definition of separate species as being two relatively similar animals that either would not breed together, or if they did breed together would not produce fertile offspring. A mule, for example. However, as we have come to know more about the actual genetic makeup of animals, this rule-of-thumb distinction no longer seems to be valid. When it comes down to subspecies, we've never really *had* a valid distinction."

Despite that deficiency, eight "types" of tiger, including those now extinct, are formally and consistently referenced by every branch of animal science. The differences between the sets are sometimes self-evident. Stand a Siberian tiger—the largest—beside a Sumatran, and even untrained eyes can easily distinguish between the two. Insert a Bengal between them and the distinctions quickly merge. Remove those three and place a South China tiger beside an Indochinese and even experts will shrug. In addition to size, a handful of subtle physical characteristics are commonly used to differentiate the subspecies, including such things as darkness of fur, width and pattern of stripes, and length of neck ruff. But anomalies abound, overlap is common, and the definitions themselves change. More than one subspecies classification of tigers recognized in the past has been quietly abandoned. "These taxonomic distinctions are not laid in stone," Christie cautions. "They are not of divine origin. Nature hasn't decided to have different subspecies; *we're* the ones who've decided. It's only valid insofar as it fits the animal for its environment."

That last point is key. Far more significant than the physical dissimilarity between the tigers are their geographic ranges, as evidenced by their regionally specific common names: Sumatran, Indochinese, South China, Bengal, and Siberian, in addition to the now-extinct Javan, Bali, and Caspian tigers. Range-oriented categories were more than adequate so long as tigers remained plentiful; unequivocal identification only surfaced as an issue when the salvation of the animal came into question and the application of scarce resources available to achieve that salvation commenced. We must now decide if we can afford to save all five surviving subspecies. If not, should they be interbred to save as many of their genes as possible? (This technique is known in zoological circles as "lumping.") Or should they be kept separate? ("Splitting.") What seemed like the perfect means to settle those questions handily introduced itself with the advent of molecular genetics.

In 1979 Dr. Dave Wildt, who would eventually head the department of reproductive physiology at the Smithsonian National Zoo, moved to Washington, D.C., from Texas. Accompanying him on the move were several domestic lab cats with which he was conducting early research into feline reproductive physiology. His cats ended up housed beside those of Dr. Stephen J. O'Brien, a geneticist with the National Institutes of Health who was observing his own set of cats for insights into the connection between feline and human leukemia. "Our cats were sharing the same room," Wildt recalls, "so we started visiting. Eventually, Steve said, 'Geez, you know people at the zoo? I'd love to get my hands on some tiger blood. . . .' So we developed this long relationship."

That relationship has played an increasingly active role in the dynamics of big-cat conservation biology. Shortly after his initial connection with O'Brien, Wildt traveled to Africa to study wild cheetah. As part of his research, he sent blood samples from more than fifty of the cats back to O'Brien for analysis under the newly developed rigors of DNA typing. The results were startling. "They looked like inbred mice," Wildt says of the cheetah. "Steve called us and said, 'You're kiddin' me here. What did you guys do, take one blood sample and divide it fifty ways?' We said no. Fifty different cheetahs." O'Brien retested the samples, analyzed his results, and submitted his theory:

Some ten thousand years ago, roughly during the last ice age, the cheetah had passed through what geneticists call a bottleneck—a severe reduction in the size of the population of all the animals of a single species alive on the planet at any given time.

Genetic bottlenecks are not rare, but O'Brien's tests (still disputed by a colleague or two) indicate a constriction so tight that the animals from whom Wildt had collected blood all looked to be descended from a common ancestor—a single pregnant female, perhaps, who wandered into an ice cave just before the storm that killed all the rest of her kind. "That stimulated my interest in the loss of genetic diversity," Wildt observes, underplaying his role in a discovery that guarantees him a place in the history of felid biology.

Working with a third colleague, veterinarian Mitch Bush, Wildt and O'Brien refined their cheetah research and applied it to other animals. The step from cheetah to tiger was but a genus away, and, partly in an effort to take advantage of this new technology, the guardians of tiger studbooks approached Wildt and O'Brien with something of a quest: a true genetic baseline for tigers, against which all future evaluations could be confidently judged. Such a standard, everyone realized, was only possible if the source materials (blood, skin, semen, etc.) were collected from an animal that was incontestably a bona fide representative of its subspecies—what Steve O'Brien calls a "voucher specimen." Starting with a hybrid would be disastrous, forever skewing the baseline.

The easiest method to achieve such veracity, of course, is simply to spot the desired animal roaming through its native habitat and collect from it the necessary samples. Fine, if you're dealing with field mice. Tigers tend to be somewhat more elusive and less cooperative. The candidates most readily available for anything near conventional methods of sample collection, therefore, are captive. But animals in cages can be moved away from their native habitats and mingled with other transplanted specimens, often resulting in offspring who themselves can be shuffled and subsequently bred. Ancestry among captive animals gets murky in a hurry. That is why—completing an ironic circle—studbooks are kept.

~

Though DNA typing has revolutionized the study of genetics, scientists have known for centuries the liabilities of mating closely related members of the same family. As zoos took advantage of the tiger's proclivity to reproduce, captive populations of the animal quickly expanded. A method for tracking their ancestry became necessary not so much to avoid hybridizing as to combat the more onerous threat of inbreeding.

This is the other edge of the genetic sword when it comes to managing captive animals for conservation purposes. Genetic variety produces robust, adaptable organisms. Genetic uniformity puts them at risk. "Variation is good," Steve O'Brien explains, "because it provides a moving target for pathogens—viruses that overcome defenses. It provides flexibility of the species to adapt to changes." Enriching the gene pool is handily accomplished by breeding the two most distantly related specimens available—but not so distant as to transgress the boundaries of subspeciation if you're concerned about producing a hybrid. Complicate that task by reducing the overall number of parents from which you may choose, and you face essentially the same dilemma now bedeviling the people who hope to coordinate the captive breeding of endangered species.

Sarah Christie, in addition to her responsibilities at the London Zoo, is the captive breeding coordinator for the Europäisches Erhaltungszucht Programm—or EEP—one of the largest zoological associations in the world. Based on recommendations Christie issues after analyzing the studbooks, zoos across Europe make decisions regarding how to move, breed, and even euthanize their Sumatran and Siberian tigers. (Formal captive-breeding programs for the other three surviving subspecies have yet to be organized in Europe.) Counterparts to Christie—only a handful in all—make similar recommendations to the zoos in other regions of the world. Ideally, from the coordinator's point of view, every captive tiger would be registered in a studbook and the animal's breeding activity would be governed by an informed, responsible coordinator. Hybridization and inbreeding among all the captive tigers in the world could then be intimately monitored.

Reality could hardly be further removed. Captive tigers of unknown origin are strewn around the globe, their fates determined by people whose interests range from playing with the animals to slaughtering them. Circuses, safari parks, and magic acts raise tigers selectively for size and beauty, routinely mixing subspecies and inbreeding the animals on purpose. Wealthy private citizens keep tigers as pets, often just as content with a "mutt" as a purebred, not unlike many dog owners. Farmers who raise tigers for their bones—a practice we shall investigate at length—are more concerned with volume than certifiable ancestry. Even some of the most progressive zoos in the most developed countries of the world have ignored the recommendations of the tiger-breeding coordinators, who hold no direct authority. In consequence, only a portion of the world's captive tiger population is formally registered in studbooks—an inventory that hovers around a total of twelve hundred animals. (Roughly that many more are suspected to be kept without records in a hazy status referred to by studbook keepers as "lost to follow-up." Nobody knows the exact worldwide grand total of captive tigers.) Of those, perhaps a quarter can be considered "incontestably" pure, but even in those cases the animal's provenance relies on faith in eyewitness accounts either of the beast's own extraction from the wild or the extraction of all its ancestors.

This is the Holy Grail in conservation breeding: pristine, genetically uniform but still robust "founder stock." The consecrated progenitors from whom all descendants of a given subspecies may spring healthy and undefiled. To those pursuing such unicorns, a simple, reliable genetic test floats like a tantalizing lifeboat in an ocean of uncertainty. Got a tiger? Send in some blood or tissue—maybe even just a bit of fur—and get a complete genetic profile. No more exhaustive genealogical investigations. No more finger-crossing reliance on historical studbook entries. DNA typing will end the controversy. . . .

So it would seem. But enhanced specificity gives rise to new options, which require new considerations, which may actually lead to new confusion. "You've got to remember," warns Christie, "that subspecies and species, looked at over thousands of years, are constantly changing. We are here in 1995 and we've kind of drawn a line across the evolutionary tree and said, OK, this one is distinct from that one. You go back down the evolutionary tree and it could be millions of years ago that the lines diverged or it could just be a few thousand years. It's like a value judgment."

Precisely such a value judgment now faces the tiger. The Bali and the Javan subspecies are currently recognized as discrete, but there is little doubt that those animals, at some point in history, were one and the same with the ancestors of what is now recognized as the Sumatran tiger. Either tigers walked across the land bridges exposed ten thousand years ago during the last ice age, or they subsequently swam the gaps. (Tigers are indeed avid swimmers, even in deep water.) If genetic tests on pelts that remain from the Javan and Bali subspecies were to reveal no differences between them and the Sumatran tiger, should the three be reclassified as one? If significant differences show up, should similar variations be sought among the now-separated tiger populations on Sumatra? If such variations occur, should those animals be newly reclassified and then staunchly segregated to avoid producing what would have to be identified as a new type of hybrid? The only "official" boundary between the Bengal and Indochinese subspecies is the Irrawaddy River in Myanmar (formerly Burma); who believes this liquid thread has kept the two clans apart? Someone has to decide exactly how many black bars must materialize on a DNA fingerprint before we start calling animals by different names. Otherwise, indefinite segmentation will render every individual a subspecies.

"If there is a unit that can be recognized," offers Steve O'Brien, "it's at the species level. Everything else is just file keeping." Nevertheless, he is quick to point out how valid arguments can be made both for and against the preservation not only of subspecies, but even of hybrids, too. "[At one point] the decision was made [in the scientific community] not to protect hybrids because that would defeat the idea of keeping the purity of the species. Makes perfect sense, right? The problem with that is that as you began to apply molecular techniques to some of these populations, you began to discover natural integrations. For example, we discovered that wild coyotes and wolves hybridize naturally when things get a little rough. . . . So, what are you gonna do?"

With respect to tigers, such quandaries may be limited to academia. Certain aspects of conservation biology are beyond the grasp of science. "Politics and national pride will come into it," says Christie. "You cannot take people and their preferences out of the equation. Indians have their tiger, and the Indochinese have *their* tiger. They will *want*, for reasons of nationalism and politics, to maintain that. I doubt that it will go so far that the Thais will say that their tiger is different from the Cambodian tiger, but I suspect that the range countries are proud of having their own tigers and will want to conserve them. And indeed we need to use that feeling as a motivation for conservation."

O'Brien agrees. "The fact that you have the different range countries, and the fact that you have an extremely charismatic, popular animal, means there's no way, anywhere, they're going to make decisions based upon genetics."

⁓

A remarkable confluence of circumstances predestined Indonesia to become a key player in the drive to save endangered animals. A combination of rich volcanic soil and tropical climes spawned one of the planet's most exotic and variegated menageries, then sprinkled it over more than seventeen thousand individual islands. Indonesia comprises less than 2 percent of the world's land mass, but it features more than 10 percent of all flowering plants, 12 percent of mammals, 16 percent of reptiles and amphibians, 17 percent of the world's birds, and a quarter of all fish species. Included among the animals were tigers, conveniently isolated upon three islands.

But man also was among the animals, and he flourished in the rich environment to the point where he eventually outcompeted the tigers on Bali and Java. Though brutally expensive in biological terms, those two extinctions now supply valuable opportunities for analysis, which can then be applied to a handy "third chance" of tigers on Sumatra.

In the early 1970s, concurrent with the decline of the Javan tiger, Ronald Tilson, a graduate student at the University of California at Davis, was completing a dissertation on gibbons and conducting his fieldwork in Indonesia. While there, he developed a fluency in the national language—Bahasa—which was to become all but essential in dealing effectively, efficiently, and cordially with anyone influential in the emerging nation's future. Against the backdrop of the imposed stability of the Suharto regime, the Indonesian stage was set for Tilson to conduct meaningful research.

Meanwhile, another stage was being set in Minnesota by Dr. Ulysses S. Seal. Almost a full generation older than Tilson, Seal had moved to the University of Minnesota from Georgia in the 1950s to conduct postdoctoral research. While he was there, a position opened up at the local Veterans Administration medical center that was perfectly suited to his expertise: They needed a biochemist to work in a reference lab studying cancer of the prostate. Seal took the job. "In biochemistry there's always an interest in comparative processes," he explains in his congenial drawl. "In other words, looking at different species as a tool for gaining insight into processes and mechanisms. When I got the VA position, I had the opportunity of running a lab to explore some of these ideas. . . . Developing tools and asking questions threw me into contact with wildlife biologists, and then with some local zoo people. We approached them about the possibility of getting samples from some of their species to explore some of the ideas we had." Thus commenced a cross-pollination that was to prove singularly significant to the evolution of tiger conservation.

A self-confessed professional omnivore, Seal expanded his involvement with zoos to the point where he eventually became widely recognized for his skills in reducing neonatal mortality among captive-bred animals, improving contraception among those not intended to be bred, advancing techniques for animal immobilization, and formalizing the system through which captive animals are individually identified and tracked. Therefore, when the state of Minnesota went looking for local advisers to help in the planning of a new state zoo in the 1970s, they naturally included Seal, whom they subsequently offered a position on the zoo's board of directors. Over roughly the same period, a worldwide association of wildlife-science authorities known as the International Union for the Conservation of Nature and Natural Resources (IUCN) launched an effort to see if zoos could be organized internationally, and their expertise applied to the conservation of animals in the wild. Seal's visibility earned him an invitation to one of IUCN's early conferences on the topic. "I listened to the discussion," he recounts, "and I basically suggested that a little working group ought to be formed because we needed to lay out some directions for it." His suggestion was employed, and the result was something that eventually came to be called the Captive Breeding Specialist Group—or CBSG—and Seal himself eventually was asked to be chairman of the group's board. Throughout all this he remained fully and solely employed by the VA medical center. "We didn't have anything," he says, outlining the budgets afforded him either by CBSG or the Minnesota Zoo. "Nobody. Nothing. All the traveling that was done I paid for out of my own pocket. And I used my other resources to help produce reports and so on." As a consequence, his Minnesota address naturally became the locus for all his CBSG correspondence.

In the meantime, Ron Tilson had completed his work in Indonesia and moved on to do postdoctoral research in Namibia. A few years of employment in Oklahoma followed, and then, in 1983, he was hired as a research director at the Minnesota Zoo. By that time Seal's research and his position with CBSG included not only work with tigers but also work with Indonesia. "Our working relationship started then," says Seal, referring to his partnership with Tilson, "but it has evolved, as all these programs have evolved, as CBSG has evolved, as the zoo's interest has evolved." That evolutionary process has included Seal's retirement from his career at the medical center in 1989, since which time he has devoted himself largely to CBSG. Tilson, simultaneously, has been elevated to Conservation Director at Minnesota Zoo and has devoted himself largely to tigers. In 1992 the two men traveled to the island of Sumatra, where they wove together all their common threads by hosting a series of workshops aimed at analyzing, and then integrating, the status of captive and wild tigers living there. Other workshops followed, and in 1995 Tilson returned with the team that was introduced at the beginning of this chapter to collect the samples to be tested by Steve O'Brien back in the States.

~~

CHAPTER 2

Fooling Mother Nature

W HILE THE TASK OF DETERMINING THE ANCESTRY of captive tigers commands preemptive focus among the captive-breeding crowd, it is not, in itself, the end goal. Once the superreductive quest for founder stock is satisfied, the product of all this sophisticated research will be, Ron Tilson and his colleagues vow, a host of reliable options for bolstering the populations of tigers *not* in captivity.

Here again, the isolation of the Sumatran tiger endows the animal with qualities particularly well suited to the analysis of endangered species. Clearly, tigers roaming through the jungles of Sumatra have not mated with any tigers from other surviving subspecies. The threat of a hybrid has been minimized to the greatest possible degree by simple geography. But that same geography has sharpened the other edge of the genetic sword, not only by limiting the amount of land available to the highly territorial tiger but also by compressing the competing human population into the available space (a factor applicable to all the other subspecies, it should be noted). The results of these conflicting dynamics are insular "micropopulations" of tigers, numbering, according to Tilson's calculations, no more than a few dozen animals each.* Hybrids on Sumatra may be unlikely, but inbreeding is unavoidable if indeed the populations are so small. Each successive generation offers fewer attractive candidates for founder stock, and a micropopulation left on its own, geneticists predict, will eventually homogenize itself through a process known as "inbreeding depression" to the point where its members will either give birth to sterile offspring or fall victim to an otherwise limited disease. (Such genetic uniformity in potatoes is what left the tubers vulnerable to a fungus that wiped out the crop in the middle of the last century and triggered the Irish famine.) Such small numbers also compound the impact of what scientists call "stochasticity," which means "chance" and includes everything from forest fires and floods to lopsided sex ratios and polarized age distributions. Even the healthiest of micropopulations will include only a handful of active breeders. "A population of twenty-five tigers is not sufficient to be safe for the future," Tilson submits. "Even if it's protected totally."

The conventional strategy to thwart such consequences was, and in some areas of the world remains, to link the micropopulations with corridors—literally to restore hallways of natural habitat between territories so the animals can mingle naturally and interbreed. However, the pressures of human populations upon already crowded tiger habitats show little sign of easing, let alone relinquishing land for some kind of animal highway. A host of sticky political and social obstacles must be overcome before corridors can be installed.

Coercive translocation of tigers from one micropopulation into another—trapping them and moving them—is even less promising due

---

*To avoid shining the spotlight too brightly on Sumatra and Ronald Tilson, it must be observed here that several groundbreaking studies have been conducted on tigers in many regions of the world over a continuing time span by numerous renowned researchers, including George Schaller, John Seidensticker, Charles McDougal, Mel and Fiona Sunquist, J. L. D. Smith, Alan Rabinowitz, associates of the Hornocker Wildlife Research Institute, et al. Several of these names will resurface later in this book, along with other innovators. Focusing here on similar work taking place in Sumatra is perhaps justified by its aggressive role in attempting to link the wild and captive populations.

to the animal's persnickety territorial customs. A disoriented transplant stands little hope of carving out a home for itself in an area already saturated with competitors. And even if the new animal were successful in displacing an established predecessor, the sum would be nothing more than another isolated micropopulation in need of a genetic transfusion. Additionally, such an invasion would be likely to disrupt stabilized breeding patterns for several cycles. And the evicted animals, who must go somewhere, would be prone to harass nearby human settlements. The disorder triggered by a translocation simply does not justify the genetic benefits an interloper might bring.

Since introducing far-flung, ornery adult tigers from one micropopulation into another is fraught with logistical and behavioral difficulty, research like that being conducted by Tilson's team aims, rather, to leave the animals where they are and collect only the parts of them required for a genetic transfer: their seeds. Artificial insemination (AI) and in vitro fertilization (IVF)—essentially the same procedures now employed by infertile humans around the world—may offer tigers the benefits of corridors and translocations without the problems associated with those two options. In AI, a female can receive sperm from a remote male and thereby enrich the genes of her offspring by half. In IVF, a "host" female could carry eggs from several other females, all of which could have been fertilized by sperm from different males; a litter of four cubs from such a mix would carry the genes of eight parents, none of them the birth mother. Additionally, through the technique of "genome resource banking," both time and distance can be spanned by freezing sperm, eggs, and even embryos for use at a later date or a different location. Such flexibility bolsters hopes among conservation biologists of managing *all* the tigers in a given subspecies, no matter where they are found, as a single "metapopulation."

A bit lower on the technology spectrum lies an option that might achieve the desired genetic enrichment with fewer intrusions into the natural process. Through a procedure known as cross-fostering, cubs born to one animal are swapped with those born to another. "Tigers don't rely on visual cues," explains Douglas Richardson, curator of mammals at the London Zoo and a recognized expert on captive-tiger husbandry. "They rely on olfactory cues. If it smells right, it *is* right." To achieve such aromatic approbation, cross-fostered cubs, Richardson explains, are dabbed with urine from the surrogate mother and left in place of her own offspring while she's away from the den. Once adopted, the changelings are raised to maturity without further human intervention.

The potential for these reproductive options calls out to the captive-breeding community like a siren. But there are significant, some say insurmountable, obstacles yet to be overcome. Cross-fostering requires tightly synchronized deliveries of cubs and split-second timing for the swap. But those complications are modest in comparison to the hurdles faced by AI and IVF, beginning with the collection of the gametes.

In strictly technological terms, the male tiger is the simpler of the two parents from which to gather material. A probe approximately the size and shape of an ear of corn is inserted into the anesthetized animal's rectum, and an electric current is passed through the nerves of his reproductive organs and accessory sex glands. A vial held at the tip of his penis catches semen ejected during the contractions induced by the charge. The process itself, known as electroejaculation, is simple and reliable enough, but the accompanying practical challenges are self-evident; knocking out a tiger so you can probe its bottom with an oversize electrode is not a simple or cheap thing to do, even in captivity.

But employing the female is more complicated by several orders of magnitude, even in AI, the simpler of the two procedures. "The first mistake we made," says Dave Wildt, "was assuming that all we had to do was collect the sperm from the male tiger, wash it a little bit, put it in the female, and produce babies. I can't tell you how many times we failed at that." The problem, he explains, involves the fact that female tigers are "induced ovulators," whose reproductive systems lie dormant until stimulated by the physical rigors of copulation. Even the peristaltic motion needed to carry sperm along the vaginal canal is triggered by mating, requiring, thereby, that the sperm (either frozen or fresh) from the male donor be inserted with a laparoscope directly into the uterus of the tigress. "Vaginal insemination is never going to work," Wildt observes. "And, to stimulate the females to ovulate, we have to give them hormones. We're still in the experimental stage with respect to working out the ovulation induction, the hormone dosage, and the timing of the two injections that we have to give. It's exquisitely complex." Nevertheless, in the event all these hurdles can be jumped, the actual fertilization of the egg can be left to Mother Nature in AI, along with the gestation and delivery processes.

Not so in IVF. While fresh or frozen sperm from the male can be handily introduced into the external fertilization container, eggs from the artificially superovulated female must be "harvested" from her ovaries with a laparoscope. Even that is easy in comparison to the final step. "The trick," says Wildt, "is getting the embryos back into the recipient." He then recommends that descriptions of the intricate endocrinological manipulations required to achieve such a restoration are better left to classrooms and laboratories.

As with any emerging technology, these reproductive wonders don't come cheap. And success remains elusive. Even the comparatively simple procedure of cross-fostering has succeeded only a handful of times, and only under ideal conditions. Frozen eggs and sperm are asleep in cryogenic vaults from Indonesia to Washington, D.C., but nobody knows the shelf life of such goods; none has been frozen long enough to conduct significant evaluations. "And we've only produced one tiger pregnancy through AI," Wildt concedes. "Only a single cub." IVF also has led to but a single tiger pregnancy, which produced three cubs.

Of much greater significance than a limited track record,

however, is the fact that all this reproductive experimentation has, to date, involved only captive tigers. The application of these procreative gymnastics to tigers in the wild remains little more than a hope, even among the captive-breeding contingent. People in the field can be downright scornful.

"I think captive breeding for the purposes of keeping genetic pools of tigers in *captivity* is fantastic," declares Valmik Thapar. "But to confront people who think they will tranquilize wild tigresses in estrus? Or artificially inseminate them?" He flings his hands up in wonder. "I want to see the day they do it." Thapar is the executive director of the Ranthambhore Foundation in India, a nonprofit group established in 1987 to benefit the national park from which it takes its name. Perhaps best known for the handsome tiger photo books that bear his name, Thapar also is widely respected for the sedulous observations he conducts of the daily behavior of the tigers who live in Ranthambhore Park. "I talked to a captive-breeding scientist in Sydney last year," he says, shaking his head. "He told me he would produce, through embryo transplants, a whole selection of Sumatran cubs, which he then would take to Sumatra, find a tigress in the wild who had the same cubs, or who had abandoned some, and *give* them to her." He pauses for effect. "I have studied three families of tigresses, and I am saying it is impossible."

Perhaps so, but steps are being taken to prepare. Among the technology transferred most immediately and directly into Indonesian hands during the 1995 visit from Tilson and his team was something called a Tiger Rescue Kit. Offered as a gift from the Australasian Regional Association of Zoological Parks and Aquaria, the kit was compact enough to fit into the back of a field vehicle while still featuring all the equipment necessary to perform exactly the same procedures on a wild tiger that the team had come to execute on captive animals—from immobilization through electroejaculation, even including dental work. No such capability had been available previously in

Indonesia, and the kit was graciously received on February 9 by none other than Ir.* Soemarsono, the incoming Director General of Forest Protection and Nature Conservation (an organization officially known as Perlindungan Hutan dan Pelestarian Alam, or PHPA) as one of his first official acts. The immediate application of the kit, and the source of its enthusiastic name, was only halfway wild. Thanks to strict domestic regulations in thirteen of the tiger's fourteen range countries, wild tigers can be legally removed from their habitats only under extraordinary circumstances. (Cambodia is the lagging regulator, and some of the others, it needs to be noted, are less than vigorous in enforcing their codes.) Typically, such a situation involves what is referred to as a "problem" tiger, so-called because of its propensity to eat either the livestock of neighboring human populations or the humans themselves. A variety of factors can lead a tiger to become a problem, including things like old age and injury, and provisions in the laws of most range countries readily allow for the removal of such animals by force—formally called an "extraction" if the animal is collected alive, a "take" if it is killed.

Sumatra has its share of problem tigers, and the Tiger Rescue Kit was hailed by both its giver and its recipient as a ready means to convert what otherwise might be takes into extractions. Wild-caught Sumatran tigers gathered in the past had suffered a variety of collection methodologies, ranging from villagers shooing them into huts while beating on pots and pans to the ministrations of so-called tiger *pawangs*, holy men believed to have magical powers over the beasts. The kit offered reliability with low risk, and the field-workers expected to employ the equipment—on hand for its presentation—readily expressed confidence that it would work.

Even if the kit were never put to any further use than extracting

---

*Ir. is a written title (Insinyur would be the spoken title) in Indonesia for someone with an advanced degree in engineering.

problem tigers from the wild, its value to the conservation of the Sumatran subspecies still could be viewed as immense by captive-breeding proponents. Here would come the source for both authenticated founder stock and voucher specimens. But secondary applications touted for the kit include the much more aggressive intention of immobilizing wild tigers destined to stay in the wild—Thapar's proclaimed fantasy. "I think we're to the point where we can start to seriously consider how to conserve the wild populations by doing these almost heroic acts," says Dave Wildt. "I see no reason why we could not generate large numbers of embryos by IVF in the field. For instance, if the female is radio-collared, find her, dart her with hormones, come back a couple of days later and give her the second hormone. Eighty hours later, go back and anesthetize her. Set up a tent right in the field. You've got the eggs, you've got the sperm, you create the embryos, you either transfer them into some of your generic females sitting back in North American zoos or European zoos or Australian zoos, or you bank 'em."

Heroic indeed, considering the evasiveness and temperament of the donors. Wildt's scenario leaves Thapar speechless with skepticism.

⤳

But what if we're too late? What if all these efforts at bolstering the populations of tigers still surviving in the wild fail? Is there any road back? Predictions regarding the demise of the wild tiger abound, some more aggressive than others (we shall investigate such forecasting soon), but nobody denies extinction as a clear possibility. Indeed, if each subspecies can be granted independent genetic status, three types of tiger are gone already. If it were deemed worthwhile to restore those three to their vacant habitats, could such a thing be done?

The subject of tiger reintroduction leads to arguments more volatile and divisive than any of those inspired by the subjects of AI and IVF. Felid behaviorists disagree radically on just how much of a tiger's conduct is based on instinct and how much on skill. The distinction is critical because a tiger raised in captivity will possess all the former but none of the latter. If tigers acquire the competitive edge they need to survive in the very unforgiving wild exclusively by watching their mothers in the wild, then the lapse of a single generation in captivity will forever exile future members of that line from its homeland. If, however, a tiger's prowess and finesse all are genetically "hard-wired," then the ingredients necessary to conjure the animal back from extinction can all be kept in a frozen vial.

Both poles have their proponents, and a range of theories hovers in between. However, even if reintroduction is not a sure thing, the degree to which it appears possible will influence critical decisions in ways both subtle and profound, either reinforcing or undermining conflicting conservation strategies. If tigers can be reintroduced, one argument goes, then why continue throwing good money after bad in a struggle to save what many believe is already a defeated species? Why not cut the losses now and regroup for the future? In an insidious refinement of that argument, the issue of subspeciation surges again, whipsawing one type of tiger against another: Since the South China tiger is clearly lost in the short run, why not just bank its gametes for use in a possible reintroduction in the future and redirect its current conservation funding to a subspecies with greater hope of sustained survival? The influence of such conundrums warrants early investigation of the technique, even amid hopes that it will never need to be used.

The reintroduction of captive-bred animals into the habitats of their extinct predecessors is not a new concept. California condors now soar through skies that sustained their absence for more than four years. Arabian oryx roam Saudi sands, surprising Bedouins who correctly remember hearing of the animal's extinction there. The howls of gray wolves announce their resurrection in Yellowstone National Park (technically, this was a relocation from the wilds of Canada, not a reintroduction of captive-bred stock). Other examples abound, including everything from crickets to sea mammals. But the technique is hardly perfected, either scientifically or politically. Those soaring condors keep snagging power lines, and ranchers next door to Yellowstone are livid at the thought of an extra predator from which they must shield their herds. In addition, each type of animal presents a unique behavioral profile. Condors are scavengers. Their food can be—is—laid out for them and closely monitored. Oryx are herbivores, whose food is both plentiful and stationary. Wolves are communal, assisting one another in the hunt and sharing in the spoils.

Tigers are none of the above. As largely solitary "superpredators," they are, in fact, among the most poorly suited candidates for reintroduction. For starters, each animal, depending on subspecies, requires from dozens to hundreds of square kilometers of independent territory. (This is a function of prey base. Abundant tropical climes can satisfy a tiger's needs in a matter of acres; Siberia must be widely combed for food.) In addition, they're big. An average adult male tiger must consume roughly 7 kilos (15 pounds) of meat per day, on average, to survive. A secondary complication of this aspect arises in the size and speed of the animals large enough to supply such bulk: Tigers must be superstealthy and superquick to succeed as superpredators. For every meal caught, ten to twenty get away. The difference between sustenance and starvation is deceptively small for what appears to be such a skilled hunter. Also, tigers are dangerous. An oryx might stray from its home into yours and eat the shrubs. A tiger might eat the kids. Combine these shortcomings with the ambiguity between instinct and skill discussed earlier and it's easy to see why doubts circle over the feasibility of tiger reintroduction.

"Not in the wild," swears Valmik Thapar. "Totally out. The captive tiger is a dog. You put it in the forest, a spotted deer will kill it. And our biggest problem in India is the man-tiger conflict in terms of livestock. Each of our tiger reserves is already plagued with cattle lifting. These are wild tigers. You put in a captive-bred animal, however much training you may have given it . . . and the chances of that tiger finally going back to man to kill are too high for this country or any park director to consider."

Advocates of the technique are equally adamant. "I get very annoyed with people who make sweeping statements that it's not possible to reintroduce tigers," states Sarah Christie. "For a start, one hand-reared tiger, which is not the ideal material to start with, has been reintroduced to India by Billy Singh." Here Christie is citing an instance of a purported tiger reintroduction that is often relied upon by boosters of the technique as proof that it can work. In the mid-1970s, Billy Arjan Singh, one of India's most well-known wildlife conservationists, brought a hand-reared tiger named Tara from England to a wildlife sanctuary in the north of India known as Tiger Haven, which he managed. As Singh tells it in his charming book *Eelie and the Big Cats* (Butler & Tanner Ltd., 1987), Tara thrived under his care, remaining so tame as she matured that she eventually struck up one of animalhood's most endearing relationships with Singh's dog Eelie. Gradually, the narration continues in this and other books by Singh, Tara drifted from his supervision back into the surrounding wild, eventually abandoning her captive past altogether. There is no reason to doubt Singh's rendition of the story, but neither is there any hard evidence to analyze. "Essentially what happened there is not any kind of scientific project," Christie admits. "We in fact do not know whether that tiger died or simply learned to live on her own." At best, therefore, the report is an encouraging anecdote. (To some, however, it is not encouraging at all: Tara was a hybrid.)

As a more compelling example, Christie cites a study conducted between 1989 and 1994 in India's Madhav National Park, where two tigers, a captive-bred male and a wild-caught female, were boarded in a 1.37-square-kilometer enclosure that featured all aspects of their natural habitat, including live prey. According to the study, the female not only retained her hunting skills, but also passed them on to cubs that she subsequently delivered. Evidence also surfaced that her mate at least made attempts to bring down wild prey.

"These are examples which I have now checked," sniffs Thapar. "They are completely false. The tigress did manage to kill a spotted deer, but she was caught in the wild. She was a cattle lifter, tranquilized and then brought into captivity. The male runs away from chickens."

Undaunted, Christie suggests an even more sophisticated follow-up in which several large enclosures would be built in a tiger-depleted reserve with a pair of captive tigers placed in each. "Leave them there," she says plainly. "You just don't go near them any more than you absolutely have to. The cubs will be born in there. They will not be used to the sights, smells, or sounds of humans. You feed live prey, and the adults will soon learn to bring it down. I mean, it's an instinct." To support that last point, she notes how readily domestic cats go feral, then cites a corollary sure to make pet owners everywhere nod sympathetically. "My domestic cat, which I got when she was six weeks old, did not learn to hunt from her mother, but she brings home mice all the time." Such evidence may sound dismissably quaint, but it is in fact worthy of respect; domestic cats are relied upon consistently by animal scientists around the world as a substitute for all the larger felids. By all accounts, they are a thoroughly reliable model. Even to casual observers, watching a tiger carefully for more than a minute or two will reveal uncanny similarities to a domestic cat. Every posture, expression, and movement is shared, dissimilar only in scale.

"When the cubs get to about eighteen months," Christie continues explaining her experiment, "which is about the time they'd be leaving home, you go in in force. You dart all the animals, knock them down, give all the cubs a complete veterinary checkup, make sure they're as healthy as possible. Put radio collars on them. Take the parents back to zoos. Breach the fences at a number of points and wait and see what happens. . . . If they left the enclosure area and moved off, you put the fence back up and do it again with a different pair of captive animals for different genes. If they hung around where they were, it would be more of a hassle because you'd have to build a different enclosure somewhere else. But you could eventually, over a period of fifteen years or so, reintroduce a fairly sound founder base."

Aside from a few key obstructions, all of which Christie readily acknowledges, the plan is almost tediously reasonable. It would settle the skill-versus-instinct dispute, the expenses for equipment and personnel are manageable, and there are captive cats available to participate. What is not available is a likely area in which to conduct the test. Tiger habitat, almost by definition, is dense with resident cats; when it ceases to be so, it is quickly conscripted by neighboring human populations, who are often responsible for effecting the vacancy in the first place. In such areas, Christie's experiment would run afoul of all the same consequences triggered by a mere translocation, which is effectively what it would become. Even Siberia, the place often pointed to by proponents of tiger reintroduction, is an unlikely venue. Despite scientific evidence to the contrary—some of which appears later in this book—realms of virgin habitat are widely believed to survive in the Russian Far East. Tales of such territory so excite tiger conservationists that plans for a reintroduction attempt just like the one Christie describes roil continuously.

But there is a curt antidote to all such musings. "It's a pipe dream," Christie concedes. "What's the point of any kind of reintroduction if you haven't eliminated the threat?"

⤳

CHAPTER 3

More Than Zero

D URING THE THREE YEARS between 1992 and 1995, Neil Franklin spent 440 days and nights in what biologists benignly refer to as "the field"—a term that conjures images of wheat swaying in a gentle summer breeze or cows lolling in a meadow.

The field in which Franklin spent his time was somewhat less pastoral. Among the resident life-forms he encountered while conducting research in the Kerinci Seblat national park in Sumatra were river leeches, foot-long albino centipedes with stingers on their tails, and spiders as large as his open hand. ("I thought it was a branch," he says of one such creature that landed on his head.) Additional challenges surfaced at the microbial level, including a foot fungus that peeled his skin off in layers and a bout of malaria that sent him down a river strapped to inner tubes in an emergency evacuation. "There were five of us at the beginning of the project," Franklin recalls in his very quiet, very English voice. "The others dropped out within the first few months."

His goal in enduring the hostilities of Kerinci Seblat was rather simple: He was there to count rhinoceros. The procedure is called a census—just as it is when applied to humans—and field biologists are painfully familiar with the task because it often forms the hub of their initial academic research. Franklin himself was a student at the time of his 440 days and nights in Kerinci Seblat, completing a Ph.D. in conservation biology to be taken from York University in the U.K. He'd come to Sumatra at the invitation of Philip Wells, an ex-accountant who turned to tallying animals rather than beans after reading the book *Into the Heart of Borneo* by Redmond O'Hanlon, in which the fate of the rhinoceros figures prominently. Wells and Franklin proposed a plan to the Indonesian government detailing their ambition to enter Kerinci Seblat, which was thought at the time to hold the world's largest population of wild Sumatran rhino.

"You have to apply for a sponsorship," Franklin explains of the complicated Indonesian proposal process. "That's the system, and that's the way it works with everything that happens here. You have a six-month vetting period as well. After that time, we finally got approval." A number of additional requirements had to be met before Franklin and Wells were allowed to set foot in the park. Indonesia is quite aware of its natural bounty, including its wildlife, and the government is picky about who gets near what. Some parks are readily accessible to tourists, but virgin territory is off-limits to all but the anointed. Capitalizing, after a fashion, on the draw that these research meccas exert on foreign scientists, Indonesian officials cleverly require all visiting teams to take on counterparts from among the domestic population. "You have to have somebody from a recognized institution, such as a university," Franklin explains. "We had three vets and one forestry scientist. The objective is to transfer ideas and technology, basically to work alongside and to publish together as well, so there's an output that is perceived to come from the home country." Dismissing suggestions that such prerequisites amount to little more than intrusive coattailing, Franklin goes out of his way to describe both the

Indonesian country and its citizens as uniformly capable, cooperative, and enthusiastic, despite whatever bureaucracy they may create.

The park into which Franklin eventually proceeded covers more than 1.5 million hectares in south-central Sumatra, stretching more than three hundred kilometers from end to end. Of the seven major protected areas in Sumatra, Kerinci Seblat is by far the largest, encompassing almost as much land as all the other six areas combined. "We've seen all areas of it," he reports. "We've conducted forty-two transect surveys, in just about every range. So we've really got good coverage of the whole place." Noting that he also paid visits to the villages surrounding the park, Franklin—who learned to speak fluent Bahasa in the process—concludes, "We feel we've got a good understanding of the situation."

While that understanding was developed primarily as he was censusing rhinos, Franklin also kept detailed records of all evidence he found of tigers. "Scratch marks," "pug marks" (paw prints), "feces," "remnants from a kill"—these and other descriptions march down pages of meticulously tabulated entries made by Franklin, all supplemented with precise citations of time, date, and carefully triangulated geographic coordinates. The one description that does not occur anywhere in Franklin's notes is "sighting." In 440 days and nights in the deepest reaches of one of the world's most abundant tiger habitats, a trained wildlife biologist conducting intricate analyses by means of sophisticated research techniques never once laid eyes on a tiger. "I've seen what I *thought* was the back end of one rushing off in the distance," Franklin says, shaking his head. "Couldn't be sure, though." If it weren't for the surfeit of secondary evidence Franklin found, his remarkable lack of a visual encounter could easily inspire the conclusion that there simply were no tigers. Clearly, however, the animals were in the area. Franklin heard them roar, sometimes within just yards of his camp. The only logical conclusion, therefore, is that they consistently eluded his direct observation.

With respect to the creature in question, such an assessment breaks no ground. Tigers are icons of cunning and stealth. To declare how furtive they can be merely states the obvious. And Franklin's track record is unremarkable in comparison to those of other field researchers. Aside from a few exceptional areas in India, such as Ranthambhore, tigers in the wild simply do not reveal themselves readily to humans. Also, particularly in Indonesia, their evasiveness is abetted by their habitat. Dense vegetation in all the protected areas of Sumatra covers mostly steep terrain. Flying over it in a helicopter would reveal nothing. "You can't even get a pair of binoculars out to scout around for them," Franklin notes, adding that he typically could not see more than five meters through the undergrowth. The significance of his being skunked, therefore, implicates not his skills of observation but rather the reliability of tiger censusing in general.

How many wild tigers are there in the world? Estimates are neither rare nor aggressively contested—they are relied upon heavily in this book. Who generates such figures? A dozen or so names surface repeatedly, most of them beyond distrust. How many of those people have seen with their own eyes even 10 percent of the tigers they claim to count? Not a one. The name commonly attributed to estimates of wild Sumatran tigers, for example, is Ronald Tilson, who has seen but a single wild tiger in his life, caught unexpectedly for an instant in the headlights of a car, in India.

"There is not a single authority who really knows how many tigers there are in any one country," Tilson confesses readily, and his counterpart counters readily agree. Instead, Tilson's totals rely on people like Neil Franklin and all the other research teams on the island of Sumatra dedicated exclusively to collecting tiger data—of which there are exactly none. "Nobody'd been working in Kerinci Seblat during the two and a half years we were there," Franklin says. The only other research teams he can identify anywhere in Indonesia are focusing on other animals. There was a promising spate of "photo-trapping"* in another Sumatran park between 1985 and 1990 by Mike Griffiths, who was then working with the World Wide Fund for Nature, but the fact remains: When it comes to counting tigers, the data on which the totals rely is based almost exclusively on secondary evidence, and only in the very best cases are qualified personnel collecting that evidence in the field. In certain cases, the evidence has been gleaned from such sources as archival newspaper reports that quote local individuals who claim to have encountered a tiger. Nobody, anywhere, is sitting on a hilltop making tick marks in a notebook as tigers walk past below.

So what? Voting patterns are forecast using only a fraction of a fraction of the electorate. Advertisers allocate billions of U.S. dollars in response to what they learn from no more than a few thousand Nielsen boxes placed atop TVs in North America. Statisticians supply never-ending streams of scientific justification for how a sample size of less than 1 percent is more than plenty. And wildlife biologists constantly rely on secondary evidence, some of it anecdotal, to count hordes of other animals, mostly with reliable results. Why should tigers not conform statistically?

They might. But small numbers magnify the proportional impact of miscalculations, and actions based on small numbers in critical situations tend to be convulsive, which can, in turn, lead to further miscalculations. The nuclear reactor at Chernobyl exploded during a low-power test. Numbers connected with wild-tiger populations are astoundingly small, even in their most enthusiastic iterations. Nobody puts the world total for all five surviving subspecies into five digits. Seven thousand is about as high as it gets. Sedated, every wild tiger now suspected to be living on the planet could be laid out on a couple of football fields. Between a half and two-thirds of those would be

---

*This process, in which a trip wire or an electronic sensor triggers an unmanned remote-control camera, was first used with tigers as early as 1927. It has only recently become popular with biologists, however, and is now widely heralded as an important tool in wildlife censusing.

Bengal tigers, from India and its neighboring countries. Another quarter would be Indochinese, from Cambodia, Laos, Malaysia, Myanmar, Thailand, and Vietnam. The remainder, fewer than a thousand animals, would break down into something like this: five hundred from Sumatra; two hundred and fifty from Siberia; three dozen or so from South China—barely enough to fill one end zone.

These are the numbers that alarm people interested in the survival of the wild tiger, and with good reason. Compared to the numbers tallied a century ago, the decline has been cataclysmic—instantaneous, in biochronological terms. At the turn of the last century, estimates put the worldwide population of tigers over one hundred thousand. So many were there, in fact, that the supply was considered not only inexhaustible but dangerous. The animal was ascribed "vermin status" in almost every range country, and bounties were paid for their carcasses—shot, snared, beaten, or poisoned—by governments eager to eradicate a pest that stood in the way of what every nation, at one time or another, calls progress. Trophy hunters, availed of increasingly accurate and powerful weapons and encouraged by local authorities, took down phalanxes of the beast, whose coats made such fine ornaments in the home and whose demise made such thrilling banter at the club. The siege continued for more than half a century before anybody even thought to look up. No one lamented the death of individual tigers. No one feared that such a ferocious, resourceful animal could possibly fail to survive as a species. In such an era, the words "conservation" and "biology" rarely came together in a sentence. China paid tiger bounties straight through the 1960s. In 1961 Prince Philip, husband of Queen Elizabeth II and forthcoming figurehead of the world's premier conservation concern, took part in a tiger hunt in India, bagging two of the animals. Sophia Loren owned a coat made of the skins from seven tigers. Right up to a single generation ago, killing tigers was hip.

As their numbers declined, their habitat naturally gave way to human development, which exerted secondary pressures equally as deadly as a gunshot, if somewhat more subtle. Encroaching human populations leveled forests and jungles, either accidentally by gathering firewood and building materials, or on purpose by creating farmland and pastures. The domesticated animals grazing on those pastures often outcompeted the wild fauna that formed the prey base for the local tigers, and sometimes the wild fauna themselves were killed by villagers for food. If a tiger retaliated by claiming members of the domestic herd or members of the human population, it was vigorously singled out and taken down either by locals wielding poisons and snares or by a hired gun. In every tiger range country, these practices persist to this day.

Somewhere around the beginning of World War II, the tigers on the island of Bali stopped hassling the native human population. Naturalists, curious about the phenomenon and suspicious of its cause, went looking for the animal and found none. Inflicted extinctions were nothing new by that time: The last dodo had died more than two centuries earlier and the last passenger pigeon more than two decades before, both with debatable consequences. The quantity of surviving tigers, some as nearby as the island of Java, preempted concerns that Bali's conveniently isolated evaporation might spread. With the intricacy and significance of subspeciation still obscure, the Bali tiger's disappearance was noted, filed, and forgotten.

Thirty years later when the Caspian tiger went away, times had changed. Environmentalism had surged through First World societies, riding a wave of concern buoyed in 1962 by the publication of Rachel Carson's eco-treatise, *Silent Spring*. Membership in the Sierra Club had soared into six digits from just four a few years earlier. Indira Gandhi was fostering environmental awareness among an increasingly educated and sizable middle class in India. And, perhaps most significantly, the analysis of animal endangerment had captured the attention of the global scientific community. People were paying attention.

They were forecasting, too. Based on what could be gleaned from the disappearance of the Bali and Caspian tigers, IUCN had issued warnings that voiced concern for every surviving subspecies of tiger except the Bengal in India, where, it was briefly believed, sufficient numbers survived to quell extinction fears—several thousand at least. Behavioral details were sketchy, as they probably always shall be with the elusive tiger, but groundbreaking fieldwork by researchers such as George Schaller (whose 1967 book, *The Deer and the Tiger: A Study of Wildlife in India,* set a standard that survives to this day) began uncovering the biological and social characteristics of tigers, many of which revealed the animal to be, as a species, potentially more delicate than was previously supposed. In particular, the tigers on Java looked immediately susceptible to all the same factors that had conspired against the Bali and Caspian varieties. When John Seidensticker and his Indonesian colleague Ir. Suyono conducted the first comprehensive field research on the island in the mid-1970s, they found a paucity of the animals and they accurately predicted its extinction within a decade.

Three down, five to go. Siberia remained chilled by the cold war. Nixon had just begun to court China. Aftershocks from Vietnam blocked much of Southeast Asia. The only wild tigers readily available for open research were roaming across the subcontinent of India and along the island of Sumatra. With Ron Tilson still thinking about gibbons, India was it.

Late in the 1960s, the Bombay Natural History Society challenged the complacency surrounding India's wild tigers by circulating among its members a questionnaire concerning the abundance of the animal. At roughly the same time, the director of the Delhi zoo, Kailash Sankhala, launched an independent study with a similar goal. Both efforts proceeded smoothly amid India's relative political stability, and both were endorsed by the country's environmentally savvy prime minister. The two inquiries gained momentum in 1969 when IUCN held its triennial general assembly in Delhi and agreed that a formal census of the Bengal tiger was in order. To jump-start the process, IUCN added the Bengal tiger to its official list of endangered animals, known as the Red Data books, based on early findings by Sankhala and the society.

Three years later, when the first nationwide inventory concluded in 1972, the final tally rolled in at exactly 1,827 individual tigers. Before anybody could stop to ask just how such astonishing precision could be achieved in counting an animal only slightly more common than Bigfoot, alarm bells went off. India was considered to be *the* tiger stronghold. Hearing that less than half the expected total number of animals could be accounted for galvanized the newly eco-sensitive global community and sent India itself, duly proud and protective of its rich natural heritage, into shock. By the time the smoke cleared a year after the census, Indira Gandhi had thrown vigorous support behind an effort that was to become the flagship of modern animal conservation.

Project Tiger is the most recognizable and enduring legacy of a simultaneous, comprehensive campaign known as Operation Tiger. Launched in the early '70s by British conservationist Guy Mountfort, who also was instrumental in founding the World Wildlife Fund—or WWF (an organization we shall learn more of soon)—Operation Tiger brought together nearly U.S. $2 million from around the world to be distributed by WWF on behalf of wild tigers in India, Nepal, Bangladesh, Indonesia, and Thailand. In India, Project Tiger, with Ms. Gandhi at its helm and U.S. $1 million of support promised by Operation Tiger, sailed forth. A Tiger Task Force was organized and empowered by the prime minister, who also took advantage of assistance offered by IUCN and other external sources. Primary habitats of the project's namesake were identified, consolidated, and eventually protected through legislation. "Buffer zones" were established around the edges of some areas, in which limited and wary intervention from nearby human populations could be tolerated while still allowing sufficient room for young tigers to roam on the fringes—so the theory went—while waiting for vacancies to open up inside. In a move perhaps more enthusiastic than fair, large numbers of villagers were "translocated" out of tiger territory. Finally, public awareness campaigns were launched both domestically and internationally. The word was out: The Bengal tiger was in trouble.

Certainly that was the case. Even if the census was wrong by half there was still due cause for concern. To this day no one disputes the pitch of the tiger's decline in this century, and although Project Tiger was headed for rough water, the people who launched it are more than entitled to the commendations they continue to receive for their decisiveness and perspicacity. However, the gusto with which the conversion from persecuting to protecting the tiger erupted left certain details overlooked and set an onerous trend. With tigers so seemingly countable, the world clamored for specific numbers—and got them. Each subspecies was tallied, the numbers were added, and the total was dreadful: Fewer than ten thousand wild tigers remained on the planet, one-tenth of what there had been just a few decades earlier. This was ample evidence for alarm.

But not for panic. To count the tigers for the 1972 Indian census, teams of wildlife managers employed a technique known as the pugmark method. In executing this procedure, a census taker lays a sheet of glass over the paw print of a tiger and traces the image so it can be kept as a record. Pertinent data are noted, including the condition of the ground on which the print was made and the so-called stride length of the animal—the distance between its prints. An estimate regarding the age of the print is calculated, and significant abnormalities, if any, are noted. At the end of a census relying upon this technique, tracings are compared. The basis for the precision of the numbers subsequently derived is that every single tiger can be reliably identified as an individual by its paw print. No other method was employed in 1972.

"It doesn't work," says Dr. Ullas Karanth. "The whole approach of trying to count every tiger in India is wrong. It simply cannot be done." Karanth spends half of each year researching the tigers in Nagarahole State Park in southern India on behalf of a New York–based operation called the Wildlife Conservation Society, or WCS—the same group with which such recognized wildlife personalities as George Schaller and Alan Rabinowitz are associated. Karanth is well known for his criticisms of both the pug-mark censusing method and Project Tiger (from which Nagarahole, one of the richest tiger habitats in all the world, is managed separately, Karanth notes). As early as 1987 he published the results of a test he conducted to settle skepticism he'd leveled at the pug-mark technique since the day it had been introduced. Using the tracings of thirty-three pug marks made on two different substrates by four captive tigers, Karanth asked six wildlife managers to estimate the total number of tigers represented and to link each animal with its pug marks. Of the six managers tested, none had less than four years of experience actively classifying tiger pug marks in census operations; one had over twelve. The lowest total number of tigers estimated to be represented by the four source animals was six; the highest was twenty-four. Not a single tiger was correctly matched to its pug marks.

Anybody associated even tangentially with tigers in the early 1970s could have supplied sufficient testimony that the animal's numbers were declining precipitously. Exact totals weren't necessary. But the 1972 census created an atmosphere of precision from which the tiger has yet to escape. Preemptive focus on specific numbers, from the size of a micropopulation through the number of a given subspecies, all the way up to the global sum, has dominated tiger conservation ever since and driven the decision-making process. When totals rise, efforts lag. When totals fall, panic reigns. Nowhere has this knee-jerk management style been more seemingly—and perhaps unfairly—evident than in Project Tiger.

A variety of tiger censuses have been performed in India since 1972, but their scope and schedule have been inconsistent. Authorities

point to a four-year timetable now in effect, and they struggle to rec-
oncile it with several plans used earlier. But not every park, or even
every state, participated simultaneously in every inventory. "There was
no system," admits Arin Ghosh, the former director of Project Tiger.
"No pattern." The one consistency in the counting, he confirms, was
the reliance on the pug-mark technique. Despite the historical murk-
iness of India's tiger censuses, two significant episodes stand out in
the Project Tiger time line.

Twelve years after the original census, another counting yielded
a total once again graced with exquisitely reassuring precision: Exactly
4,005 tigers were identified in 1984. In just over a decade, the number
had more than doubled. "Tiger numbers definitely had bounded
back," confirms Karanth. "The problem, of course, was that these
numbers, both the earlier one and the later one, were basically mean-
ingless. They had no scientific basis. So using them to proclaim success was very, very dangerous. It was going to lead to complacency."
And it did. Celebrations followed the '84 census, with the titles of
magazine articles asking questions like "What to Do When You Have
Succeeded?" and whole books documenting the apparent victory being published in response. The danger of the extinction of the Bengal
tiger was dismissed. "But the number of tigers was never scientific
material," argues Ghosh, "It has never been said officially in any
IUCN document, any international document, any central government of India's document, that Project Tiger was successful because
it raised the tiger from eighteen hundred tigers to over four thousand."
Karanth disagrees emphatically: "IUCN fed the complacency by re-
peating these numbers and giving them scientific credibility all around
the world, which they would have lacked otherwise. IUCN is to blame
for the complacency. I'm very clear on that."

Eight years later another census took place, but not so formally.
Tourists who had flocked to India's national parks to view the newly
omnipresent tigers began to complain of difficulty finding any. Park

managers, several of whom were capable of recognizing individual tigers on sight, followed up on the complaints and discovered widespread, unexplainable absences. Subsequent investigations by experts from WWF uncovered evidence of extensive poaching and smuggling, as well as proof that human populations near many of the habitats were egregiously disregarding protective legislation by collecting wood, poaching prey, and grazing domesticated animals inside restricted areas. Summary calculations put the national total of tigers well below the 4,005 mark. Magazine articles now proclaimed a "Second Tiger Crisis."

In twenty years, no less than U.S. $28 million had been spent in India funding Project Tiger. (Estimates rise into the hundreds of millions of U.S. dollars when things like the opportunity cost of not harvesting the trees in the protected areas are factored in.) No one considers that money wasted, but everyone agrees it did not solve the problem. Now, having survived one spike of optimism-induced complacency, India must decide what to do differently to avoid repeating history. One thing, clearly, will be to fight the focus on numbers. "A census is not a publicity tool," insists Ghosh. "It is not an indicator of success. But it is something like your face. It shows. It gets focused on. When Project Tiger was paraded as one of the major successes in the world . . . a hundred and one coordinates were taken into consideration to find out whether this particular project, over a period of time, did have a successful impact. Of all those, the number of tigers was the catchiest. So [the press] blew it up. We are really not interested in whether we have four thousand three hundred and thirty-two tigers or four thousand five hundred and seventy-seven. That's not the point. That's not what we are looking at."

Nevertheless, the pug-mark census technique and the precision it inspires survive to this day in India, with strong support from Ghosh. "Nobody's going to doubt that this is not a good method," he disclaims himself, "but two things are very important. One is the correct tracing of the pug marks, and second is the analysis of the pug marks based on the information that was collected. You need to put them through a set of experts who would really give the damn thing a very hard look. . . . Because of such scrutiny, I have no hesitation in saying that this particular [current] figure is possibly the rock-bottom figure. There is not one tiger less than at the point in time when we counted."

⤺

As Project Tiger waxed and waned, remarkable political developments in other regions of the world cleared the way for unprecedented access—not all of it good—to wild populations of other tiger subspecies. Russia relaxed. China marched toward normalization (stumbling once in Tiananmen Square). Even Vietnam started charming tourists. Amid the new openness, preliminary validations of tiger reports that have been seeping out of these regions for decades have confirmed long-term suspicions of low numbers. Also, an unhappy concomitant to the political relaxation surfaced in the equally open access it granted to many forms of tiger-hostile commerce, including everything from logging to cross-border poaching. "The border between the Soviet Union and China was absolutely closed under Communism," says Valentin Ilyashenko, Director of the Department of Biological Resources at the Ministry of Protection of Environment and Natural Resources in what is now the Russian Federation. "But now it's absolutely impossible to check everyone crossing the border." Acknowledging that some poaching for domestic customers took place even before the Soviet dissolution, he adds, "But there was no market from China." Consequently, with the disclosure of India's oversights, there was no good news anywhere to allay anxieties regarding numbers of tigers.

Fear is a powerful motivator. Amplified by supporting statistics, it can propel extraordinarily widespread campaigns toward goals that may be only vaguely defined. It can enlist copious resources, which it sometimes uses to manufacture its own fuel. What starts out as a valid concern ends up as an irrational phobia. In casting about for targets of blame for the tiger's crisis, the conservation community—an admittedly ambiguous appellation to be deconstructed shortly—has sometimes applied science equally as weird as that applied to tiger censusing. Predictions regarding the wild tiger's ultimate extinction often presume that the same forces that drove the population from a hundred thousand at the turn of the century to less than a tenth of that today will, without immediate and radical intervention, persist in a mathematically uniform manner to dispatch the animal by the end of the century. Some voices have written off the tiger already, refusing to allow for recovery or even persistence in the face of what are deemed to be insurmountable challenges. Other estimators give the wild tiger a qualified ten years, or five, or two.

Based on what? The tyranny of statistics? The tiger's decline may be undeniable in its velocity, but it is hardly precise either in cause or effect. Oppressive forces persist, surely, but they are different now, in sum, than they were just a few years ago, and the equation continues to change. At least one intervention—Project Tiger—has already been both immediate and radical, as well as deeply funded and powerfully backed, all to no avail. The life-form in question is so fantastically secretive it reveals significant new characteristics with each rare glimpse. Its census numbers, generated almost exclusively with secondary evidence, are so small they often fall into the realms of statistical insignificance—they *always* suffer from statistical weakness in terms of policy making. Out of context, raw numbers will support anyone's conjecture, which, through the process of data reliability inflation, will inevitably solidify into conviction, which will in turn enable further conjecture. The appetite for numbers is deadly in the face of such a sophisticated predicament. So long as the wild tiger remains governed by spasmodic, reactive approaches to its conservation, it is doomed to hover aimlessly somewhere above zero, with everyone suggesting a different optimum altitude. Should we be only half as worried about a wild population of forty South China tigers as we are about twenty of them?

To blur the world's focus on numerical precision, a variety of alternative approaches for gauging the overall status of the wild tiger have surfaced. (Note that we address only the diagnostic processes here, not the remedies, which shall be administered later.) "My critique of the whole business of counting tigers from tracks arose from the fact that what the results showed and what we know about the biology of the animals don't match," explains Ullas Karanth. "It's very clear that densities of tigers are very strongly linked to densities of prey. But when you look at the census data, this isn't reflected." To correct that problem, Karanth suggests evaluating the condition of any given tiger habitat through sampling rather than inventory. "At the most basic level, what a park manager really needs to know is how his tiger population is doing. Whether it's going up or going down. And he can keep track of that without knowing how many tigers are actually out there." Such monitoring, says Karanth, is quite simple. "Basic notebook-and-binocular science," he says with a shrug. Essentially, the data sampled in Karanth's discipline is secondary tiger evidence exactly like the kind Neil Franklin collected so meticulously in Sumatra. Feces, in particular, are valuable, Karanth notes, because they supply insights into the relationship between the tigers and their prey, which also can be monitored through sampling, just like their predators. "It's a quantitative index," Karanth observes, drawing a contrast with the pug-mark technique. "It's not subjective. Whether you do it, I do it, X does it, Y does it, you'll end up with the same kind of numbers . . . and these are all doable things, which reserve managers can easily learn and practice and monitor. You don't have to go beyond this to be a good tiger manager or to manage your tiger populations well."

Without rejecting Karanth's techniques, Ron Tilson (in the company of many others) has embraced a different process. "Population and habitat viability analysis is nothing new," he acknowledges, introducing a process familiar to most everyone involved in animal conservation by its four-letter acronym: PHVA. "You segment the parks into small sections and do it quadrant by quadrant. It's a more precise way of trying to come at a number than having somebody guess at one big one." Relying heavily on maps and sophisticated technology, the PHVA process yields what Tilson considers to be superior insight. "A second template that we lay over [after the grid] is the vegetation," he continues, "using satellite images. . . . Tigers don't live in montane forests. They don't live in lakes. They don't live in rice fields. They don't live where gold is being mined. All of these little pieces can be subtracted from the formula, and you have a better idea of how much space you've got. We can then use the VORTEX model, which is a simulated computer model that simply takes all the life-history characteristics [of the animal], feeds in how big the population is, feeds in the threats, and gives you an approximation of risk for those populations in terms of viability."

Karanth chokes on so much technology. "These attractive packages, these high-tech workshops, high-tech ideas, these population viability workshops, attract a tremendous amount of resources. . . . It's a misapplication of funds, in many ways." In particular, he warns against applying such resources outside the classroom or the laboratory, where, he readily acknowledges, such things as PHVAs and computer models have a place. "The danger is that these attractive packages are being presented before Third World tiger managers, who are not population ecologists, who do not understand the millions of caveats behind some of these formulations. . . . You need real data to make the model realistic. And as far as the tiger goes, and as far as its prey goes, as far as most of the other stuff that makes up tiger ecology goes, we simply don't have the kind of information to plug into these extremely sophisticated models. To show them to the Third World manager as ready-to-go projects that you can just apply and save the tiger is basically rubbish."

❤

CHAPTER 4

Whose Tigers
Are They Anyway?

W ILD: Living or growing in its original, natural state; not domesticated or cultivated. . . .

So says the dictionary. In an effort to determine how best that term can be applied to tigers, let us back toward it from its antonym.

A "captive" tiger sits in a cage. If the cage is small, the nature of the animal's captivity is clear: Bondage implies captivity. But as the dimensions of the cage expand—physically—the nature of the captivity contained within its boundaries quickly changes. Is a tiger in a cage the size of a football field equally as captive as one in a cage the size of a boxcar? How about a cage the size of a park? If all cages are equally captive of their contents, then the nature of captivity relies strictly on the concept of an imposed boundary—and our inquiry can stop right here: There are no wild tigers left; every area in which they now range "wild" is plainly demarcated by the surrounding human populations. The perimeters may lack metal bars, but the penalty to which a tiger will be subjected for transgressing the boundary will be just as stiff as for a tiger that slips through the gate of a zoo during feeding time. If it behaves itself, it will be subdued and replaced within boundaries. Otherwise, it'll be killed.

So, argumentum, let us admit that cages are not all equally captive. At the very least, a "spectrum" of captivity must be recognized, along which the amount of space afforded each animal carries influence. There is a handy midpoint in the spectrum, below which the space would be too small, at least by natural standards, and above which it would be larger than necessary. Tigers are territorial. Given an entire continent, they will, by choice, occupy only so much of it as is necessary to satisfy a few basic needs. Maintaining a territory is hard work, involving a sophisticated pattern of marking and patrolling. Abandoning the area spontaneously is not among a tiger's natural behaviors. Any enclosure as large as the total of the territories required naturally by the inhabitants, therefore, must be considered sufficient.

Once again, our inquiry leapfrogs to a conclusion: Tiger enclosures so large as the one just described exist only in the form of protected areas in the habitats where the animals originated. No circus, no zoo, no private menagerie, not even a commercial "wild" animal park comes close to supplying the kind of acreage the resident tigers would naturally select and maintain as individual territories. We can quickly rule out all these options in our search for wildness.

But even within the remaining mega-enclosures other aspects of wildness require identification. Surely the origin of the animals factors in. Tigers extracted from their native habitats are commonly characterized as "wild-caught," so they must have been, at some point, "wild," if in name only. When, exactly, do they convert to captivity? Reopening the dictionary for a moment, we see the words "original, natural state" within the definition of wild. Those terms now have added significance. Tigers originated, via random natural processes, in a variety of geographic locations. We find them there; we did not place them there. Left to themselves, they would contentedly stay there until some random natural process dictated further changes. When extracted, they lose the option of responding to random natural processes. They become, in effect, conscripts of humanity rather than of nature. (Note that the divine creator of your choice may be substituted for "nature" here without derailing the argument.)

In practical terms, this is a helpful guidepost in distinguishing between captivity and wildness, at least so far as conservation is concerned. Self-governance has long been the focus of philosophies that range from the political to the religious (sometimes one and the same) when applied to human beings. The right to individual free agency is touted as "self-evident" and "inalienable." Personal liberty is, essentially, a natural state, and all people are created equal.

What about all tigers? Such a question sounds ridiculous to some, but the so-called rights of animals are more in focus now than ever before, and the constituency that speaks on the self-defined behalf of animals, who cannot speak for themselves, is broad based, expanding, intricately organized, well funded, and passionate. It wields enormous political power in terms of conservation, even at the global level, and tigers are among the most prominent of its poster pets.

In opposition, there is an equally well-developed constituency that scoffs at what it identifies as pathetic sentimentality, snidely labeling its adversaries as "bunny huggers." This movement's progressive fringe argues that animals are incontestably subordinate to humans, and it is our right to decide their fate. Closer to the center comes the argument that the human animal is, at the very least, a participant in the biosphere, and the consequences of our actions, therefore, fall within the criteria for "natural processes." Why is it less acceptable for the human animal to outcompete the tiger than it is for any other animal to drive another species into extinction—a process that has happened thousands upon thousands of times already? If you were holding a loaded rifle and watching the last pregnant tiger stalk the last pregnant spotted owl, what would you do? Based on what rationale?

If indeed humans are entitled participants in the ecosphere, then there is no such thing as captivity; whatever dominance we demonstrate is merely a function of our capacity to outcompete other participants. If, however, we are inappropriately intrusive, then we are in fact the implementing agents of a captivity that we ourselves have defined. Either way, that argument is nothing more than a linguistic exercise. We *are* in the world, rightfully or not. We *are* outcompeting other life-forms, at an accelerating pace. Regardless of what force endowed us with this power—God, Mother Nature, blind chance, take your pick—we wield it, and we will continue to wield it until some equally superior force takes it away. Even to attempt not to invoke our authority at this point invokes it. Refusing to act is an act that often involves more effort than acting in the first place, and the consequences can be equally far-reaching. Discussing entitlements, therefore, is irresponsible. What we *should* do when it comes to tigers does not matter. The fact is that we *can* do. Our unique quality—the element that separates us truly from all our competitors—is not our superior ability to compete; it is our ability to choose whether or not to compete.

Evaluating the philosophical platforms of individual organizations is not the point here. Neither the members of animal-rights groups nor their opponents should feel either threatened or empowered by the arguments put forth on these pages. The point, rather, is to clearly recognize the motivating factors involved in the processes of making decisions in tiger conservation. If indeed the issue of animal rights is pertinent, fine. Let us recognize it and deal accordingly. If not, then we must make certain that critical decisions regarding the future of the tiger are not based upon it. Either way, a plan capable of preventing the process from being hijacked by forces working in either direction beneath the surface will emerge only under the scrutiny of such reductionism.

∽

Regardless of whether or not tigers are entitled to their freedom, it cannot be disputed that their freedom is a component of their wildness. In the case of tigers, the activities they pursue when free are identifiable and predictable. The salient consideration is simply whether or not they will be allowed—perhaps "enabled" is a better term—to follow such pursuits. The requirement for tiger wildness at work at this level, then, is freedom from intrusive manipulation. (Note that this component must be carefully considered in terms of the origin factor discussed earlier; regardless of how much freedom they enjoy, reintroduced tigers might be considered merely feral rather than truly wild.)

Amid such freedom, the basic needs that a tiger looks to satisfy within its natural territory are expressed in two recurring activities: finding sufficient food and making more tigers. Along with territory maintenance, these two simple manifestations of instinct comprise the natural agenda for tigers—an animal that many felid specialists refer to simply as "a land shark."

For the first activity, an adequate base of prey is required; for the second, a nearby selection of potential mates. Here again, the infiltration of the human race clouds all but a single vision of so-called preserves and sanctuaries as the surviving bastions of tiger wildness. Competition for prey resources, and sometimes for the prey itself, is endemic between tigers and their surrounding human neighbors, as discussed earlier. Even if there were plenty of food to go around, the insularity of micropopulationism may already have condemned every group of tigers but one to insufficient breeding options. Thus, by filtering science through logic, we have generated a basic definition of a wild tiger, which can be employed quite practically in evaluating not only the current situation, but also the most sensible path to achieving whatever goals are deemed appropriate: Somewhere beyond a tiger in a small cage lies the threshold of captivity; the exact point is of no consequence, and likely beyond definition, but the realms of tiger wildness clearly include, at the very least, sufficient space in a habitat of origin for each resident tiger to select, establish, and maintain—free from human molestation—a territory large enough to support the animal's need for food while still providing it with ready access to an ample number of potential mates who are unrelated enough to sustain genetic viability.

On the entire planet, there is but a single place where all these qualities of tigrine wildness are even hoped to persist. That place is known as Sundarbans, a netherworld of mangrove swamps and shifting deltas scattered between Bangladesh and India, where the river Ganges dissolves into the Bay of Bengal. Here the environment is adequately inhospitable to discourage all but the most intrepid of human infiltrators. The tides surge with force sufficient to redistribute anything that might pass for a shoreline and to intermittently submerge everything that falls in between. The land that does appear amid tides is soft and dense with the sharply pointed tips of tree roots that spike upward in search of oxygen. Crocodiles cruise the waterways, reluctantly sharing dominion with the poisonous snakes coiled nearby. Still, a few bold fishermen cast nets amid such competitors. Honey gatherers climb into the arboreal canopy to fight the comparatively docile swarms of bees for nectar. At low tide woodcutters walk gingerly below.

Tigers live there, too, and they display characteristics as strange as the world that surrounds them. For reasons not completely understood, the tigers of the Sundarbans have a taste for human flesh that exceeds the occasional opportunism manifested by injured, old, or confused tigers in other regions. Theories include an aggressiveness exacerbated by the saltiness of the drinking water or by the frustration of having to re-mark tide-washed territory constantly. There is also the possibility that human corpses that are washed downstream after "burial" in the Ganges provide a convenient and habit-forming source of snacks. Whatever the cause, the tigers of the Sundarbans are known, both colloquially and scientifically, as man-eaters.

They are also known as plentiful. Up to five hundred of them are estimated to roam among the mangroves in the single largest "documentable" contiguous wild population anywhere, a quantity sufficient to satisfy even the most pessimistic of genetic prognosticators. The formula is simple, many say: Of course there are more tigers there; there are fewer people. But as with every other estimate of tiger populations generated in this region of the world, the tigers in the Sundarbans are counted from beneath their feet. "The prey densities obviously are low there," points out Ullas Karanth. "And yet we see extraordinarily high tiger densities. This doesn't make biological sense. It makes me suspect that it is more a function of getting a lot of tracks in wet soil rather than there being more tigers." Even Sundarbans, then, may not offer the option of retaining an extant, complete situation of wildness.

However, there are dozens—possibly hundreds—of other situations in which the specific elements of wildness that have been lost might be restored. This is the "managed wildness" to which Sarah Christie referred in the first chapter. Just as in all its other usages, the term "management" here implies the coordinated application of specific agents and methodologies for the sake of effecting a desired result. When it comes to tigers, the concept has not always worked to the animal's advantage. Indeed, for the first half of this century, they were "managed" right up to the brink of extinction. Only when the desired result changed did the agents and methodologies of the management systems in force come into question. By that time there was no opportunity to save the animals in their original, natural state simply by terminating the old management systems. New ones had to be activated to counteract the old ones. Left to fate (siding briefly with geneticists), wild tigers everywhere except Sundarbans were doomed already by genetic limitations if by nothing else. (There was plenty else.) The coordinated application of everything from antipoaching patrols to land-use legislation sprang into effect. Both Project Tiger and its sire, Operation Tiger, were massive exercises in management of the closest things that were left to tiger wildness. Similar administrative influence has spread to the point where laws both local and international now affect the disposition of so-called wild tigers every-where. Looking toward the next step, genetic management may soon affect individual tigers in ways profoundly more intrusive.

The idea of a pristine, self-sustaining tiger wildness from which we can simply back away is, therefore, all but a fantasy, no matter whom you side with. At the very least there would have to be con-sensus—an aspect of management—among the people who would end up on the perimeter of any such area. Posting a ring of armed guards around the edge of Sundarbans or any other tiger habitat would take more management effort than Operation Tiger ever dreamed of mus-tering. Clearly, the human race is mired in the task of perpetuating tigers in the closest thing we have left to their original, natural state, which *everywhere* includes an assortment of human intrusions, ranging from maintaining fire-fighting trails to outright poaching. All the wild, in other words, is already under some form of human man-agement—including mismanagement—when it comes to tigers.

Whether we lament or celebrate this fact (even if we deny it), there is a simple way to sidestep the semantic conundrum that will hereafter arise unavoidably with every use of the word "wild." Field biologists long ago divided the term and conquered it by invoking two handy scientific phrases to express unequivocally the status of any given animal. If the creature is wandering through the habitat from which either it or its ancestors sprang, it is said to be in situ—Latin for "in position," meaning in its original place. If it is anywhere else, it is ex situ. These terms, while alien to the lay reader, are among the most casually employed jargon used by tiger conservationists every-where. They may sound suspiciously related to the factor of origin, but, in fact, they focus on the location rather than its occupants. Tigers in a fifty-thousand-acre park in California are incontestably ex situ, regardless of whether or not they are considered captive. Tigers rein-troduced to the habitats of their forebears are incontestably in situ, regardless of whether or not they are considered wild. But an animal *must be* in situ to be considered wild per the constraints of our earlier definitions. This refinement is subtle but powerful, especially when it comes to tigers. The animals breed readily ex situ. Their survival as a life-form does not depend upon the survival of their habitat. Only their wildness does—a clarification that resolves a number of the semantic dilemmas when it comes to conservation. What is actually being done with the animals is fodder for a different discussion; the discussion at hand concerns only *where* it is being done. If it's not being done in the animal's area of origin—or at least headed in that direction—it might be an effort at conservation, but it is indisputably not an effort at wildness. So, when the battle cry of "Save the tiger!" rings out, it must be answered with the simple, intermediating question of "In situ or ex?" Aside from "both" or "neither," each of which is achieved by the sum of its parts, there are only two possible responses: If the answer is ex situ, then the case is closed; we're already there. If the answer is in situ, the subsequent discussion must involve issues of management. There are no other options.

‿

Unless Sundarbans is deemed the only appropriate place to pursue the salvation of the wild tiger (unlikely, if for no other reason than it would preempt considerations for all but the Bengal subspecies), any management of tigers in situ must include the attempted restoration of lost elements of wildness among its provisions. The concept of management presumes the authority of the manager over the managed. It presumes, in other words, aspects of control. Our new vocabulary again gains added value here. Something that's wild is inherently free from external control; that which is wild is not controllable, nor is that which is controlled truly wild. But something that is in situ can most certainly be subjected to control.

In its most basic form, control is an expression of ownership. By definition, owners exercise discretionary authority over, and responsibility for, what they own—commonly referred to as their "possessions" or "property." The authority itself can be shared, as in co-ownership, or it can be held independently. It can also be transferred, either voluntarily or by force, and it most certainly can be contested. Laws go a long way toward making the authority associated with ownership recognizable and enforceable under different systems of government, but the definition remains essentially the same regardless of the vernacular: Something is owned, de facto, by whoever or whatever controls it.

Who owns tigers?

There are two requisite subsets to that question, the more problematic of which actually offers an easier place to start. Let us begin, therefore, with an investigation of who owns tigers in situ. (Ownership of captive cats follows in another chapter.)

According to ancient Roman laws, wildlife was considered "common" so long as it remained alive and free—it belonged to everyone and no one simultaneously, like the air and the ocean. Once killed, captured, or domesticated, however, it became the property of the collector. Elements of this standard, which is now referred to as the *res nullius* maxim, persist to this day throughout the world, ranging in form from unwritten attitudes to enforceable laws. The inherent liabilities of this standard are self-evident when it comes to endangered species. "You can imagine," observes Michael 't Sas-Rolfes, a South African environmental economist, "with an incentive system like that— stating that so long as the animal is out there, it's not worth anything to anybody, but as soon as you kill, capture, or domesticate it, you can capture the value—there is a strong incentive to take the wildlife. That has been the case over much of the world."

But even without the take temptation, the *res nullius* maxim is flawed in foundation. Using tigers as an example, we can clearly see how.

First option: Nobody owns them. Tigers are the creation of God or Mother Nature or blind chance and therefore beyond the ministrations of an uppity race of human beings who presume to . . . See the identical platform presented a few pages back in the context of competition. Such quibbling is great for the forensics team but worthless in practical terms. If nobody owns the tigers in situ, then nobody is responsible for them. Chaos ensues. The animals go away. This option is suitable only if the desired result is extinction. Despite such flaws, "Nobody!" is a common answer when the question of wild-tiger ownership arises—usually suggested with more energy than most.

Second option: Everybody owns them. See first option for likely outcome. Responsibility distributed with perfect evenness is nothing more than a bureaucratically glorified version of no responsibility. The only difference is that when the assured failure arrives, everybody starts pointing fingers instead of shrugging shoulders.

These two polarized expressions of the same effect do supply, however, valuable insights into one of modern ecology's most divisive quarrels. Up to this point, the term "conservation" has been used liberally in this book to describe the array of efforts aimed at forestalling the degradation or depletion of the world's natural resources—and it shall continue to be so used. But while the lay public may find the term adequate, the people whose efforts it seeks to describe are more discriminating. "Conservation" is now all but antonymous to "preservation." Both claim an identical goal—the salvation of the resource(s) in question—and their approaches sometimes share methodologies. But conservationists speak of saving resources *for* something (i.e., the human race) while preservationists speak of saving resources *from* something (i.e., the human race). Mere wordplay, it would seem, but the implications are sweeping. Early figureheads of these two disparate movements include naturalist and Sierra Club founder John Muir for preservationism, sportsman and U.S. president Teddy Roosevelt for conservationism. The controversies sparked by their philosophical polarity now hobble efforts at saving *anything* so tenaciously that the terminology demands interpretation. The kindled controversies, too, shall be investigated, but the declension at hand requires only this simple contrast: Conservation suggests everybody owns the tigers; preservation suggests nobody does.

A third option: Tigers are owned by the governments of the countries in which they live. Now we're getting somewhere.

When William the Conqueror successfully invaded England in 1066, he brought with him a new concept of wildlife ownership with which he displaced the active Roman traditions: The Crown owned the wildlife, and the Crown would decide what could and could not be done with it. This new philosophy works well so long as power remains concentrated in a single person, such as a ruling monarch, but it doesn't fly in a democracy. Hence, as the world matured after Hastings, the question of wildlife ownership surfaced again. Some countries relapsed into the *res nullius* maxim, as Mr. 't Sas-Rolfes has pointed out. Others experimented with new forms of ownership. Many have adopted a quasi combination of both democratic (Roman) and aristocratic (Saxon) control over wildlife. Regardless of the philosophy that drives a particular form of government, however, the net effect is control over—ownership of—a domain and its inhabitants. Citizens live and die by the laws of their land, not always justifiably so, and natural resources are put to whatever use the powers in charge deem fit. Tigers may well roam from one country into another, crossing borders for which they have no concern, but at any given moment they will all be found within the jurisdiction of one ruler or another, all of whom are most assuredly ready to claim title.

The relative values of governmental systems shall forever be disputed by theorists wondering what might be. In the meantime, pragmatists will proceed with the business of surviving under conditions as they are. You might wish your neighbor tended his yard differently, but that would be a foolish reason to rearrange your personal routine so as never to drive past his house again. On a global scale, countries now recognize one another and interact continuously despite political differences of the most profound scope and nature. Ambassadors from hostile nations live in one another's realms under special privileges of immunity and without fear of personal reprisal while temporarily overlooking practices that would invoke harsh penalties of law back home.

Were such diplomatic tolerances not afforded, civilization would be reduced to a cauldron of endless border disputes.

In Indonesia, domestic law clearly describes how the PHPA owns every tiger that walks upon Indonesian soil. Laws in twelve of the other thirteen countries where tigers roam in situ may be less discrete in language, but they are equally possessive in effect. Wild tigers are chattels. Diddle with them, and you run afoul of the laws of the land, for which there are specific domestic penalties—international ones too, perhaps, as we soon shall see. Amid their independence, all but one of the fourteen range countries have seen fit to install legislation more protective of their in situ striped chattels than exploitative. Despite the fact that certain countries are taking longer to come around than others, this beneficent uniformity is a happy, if spontaneous, triumph of twentieth-century tiger conservation. On this one issue, at least, brief political consensus has been achieved among the majority of the key players. Such symmetry is only so secure as the many not-so-stable governments involved, and a nation's wildlife conservation policies can be discombobulated with a single gunshot; witness Indira Gandhi. But in the mid-1990s there is—perhaps *was* by the time you read this page—unprecedented international political tiger harmony. How much more difficult the situation would be if one or more of the range states were still paying bounties for dead wild tigers.

Fusing this chapter with the last, then, we discern how the practical approach to tiger conservation now has less to do with asking "How many?" than it does with asking simply "Do we or don't we?" And the issue of wildness resurfaces: Do we or don't we *what?* Perpetuate the taxonomically independent life-form known as "tiger"? No problem there. Rabbits barely outbreed them. We must discard all perceptions that the life-form itself is endangered. The key question is this:

> Do we or don't we strive to allow some remnant of the tiger population to persist in the same situation its predecessors

encountered before human intervention put the survival of the species at risk?

When that question has been answered—and it is far from being answered definitively, though many voices proclaim it so—the solutions to countless secondary problems associated with tiger conservation will handily appear. Strategies will revolve from reactive to proactive. Focus will shift from products to resources. Appropriate numbers will dictate themselves.

A simple objective, but the task remains complex. Answering this key question requires several preliminary assessments and a number of semantic explorations, none of which yield information quickly or concisely. If they did, the tiger would not have a problem, nor this book any purpose.

∽

CHAPTER 5

What Color
Is Your Badge?

T HE SCHISM BETWEEN FIELD SCIENCE AND ZOO SCIENCE was addressed early in the first chapter of this book, and it will resurface repeatedly before the final page. The two approaches, as discussed, are unique, but they still are correctly considered to be related aspects of the single larger discipline of animal biology. Members of both teams readily acknowledge one another as associates within a common league. Differences, by and large, are technical rather than systematic.

In fact, from a slightly more distant vantage, field and zoo scientists merge seamlessly with other biologists into a single docile herd, particularly when viewed in contrast to the swarm of advocates, delegates, activists, devotees, dilettantes, lobbyists, agitators, crusaders, capitalizers, legislators, and zealots who populate the hinterland of conservation politics. No scientific degree is required—no degree of any kind—to participate vigorously, visibly, and potently in certain aspects of global wildlife management.

Not surprisingly, the vehicle through which many conservation efforts are enacted at the global level is the United Nations. Love it or hate it, the UN supplies an undeniably handy, far-reaching, and well-established forum for international political communication and, in certain instances, action. The global ecological environment is an aggregate of smaller ecosystems, none of which can be governed by national boundaries. Polluted rivers convey toxic waste from one country into another; diverted rivers rob downstream nations of their water. Dirty or depleted air wafts from continent to continent, untraceable to its source. Timber cut in one country is sold to a second, but affects erosion patterns in a third, which benefits neither from the purchase nor the sale. The UN is the natural political mechanism through which to handle such gangly natural predicaments, and the United Nations Environment Programme—UNEP—is the particular body within the UN chartered to address such issues. Though the UN and its minions often defy clear description, its environmental functions are reasonably well contained and they are essential to any analysis of the global dynamics of tiger conservation. Even to those not prone to international politics, the following explication should prove manageable.

Rumblings over the dangers of unbridled import and export of plants and animals threatened with extinction first surfaced at the seventh general assembly of IUCN in 1960. Three years later, at the next assembly, a resolution was passed that called for the establishment of a formal mechanism to regulate the international exchange of endangered wildlife. A draft proposal for that mechanism appeared a year later, but it languished for nearly a decade. In 1972 the UN, reacting to increased global awareness of things ecological, sponsored a gathering in Stockholm called the Conference on the Human Environment. (It is worthy of note that the lone overseas head of state in attendance was Indira Gandhi.) Wildlife conservation surfaced prominently among the concerns discussed at the conference, and a recommendation parallel to IUCN's nine-year-old resolution was adopted. Within a year, twenty-one countries had convened in Washington, D.C., to sign the resulting mechanism, christened the Convention on International Trade in Endangered Species of Wild Fauna and Flora—a mouthful handily acronymized into CITES, which is pronounced "SIGH-tees."

Precisely what CITES *is* remains a bit of a mystery. It is not just a piece of paper, though much paper is involved. It is not exactly a convention, though the word "Convention" appears first in its acronym and the people involved in CITES certainly do convene. The explanation offered most frequently in response to queries regarding the nature of CITES is that it is a "treaty" (a word that appears nowhere in the acronym), which countries can choose either to follow or not. Those who choose to follow become "signatories"—also known as "parties" or "members"—to the treaty through the execution of a formal document.

A better understanding of CITES, perhaps, can be found by focusing not on what it is, but rather on what it achieves. CITES now features more than 120 signatory nations, whose common objectives, vis-à-vis the language of the treaty, are to identify and correct violations of the treaty's guidelines on the international transportation of endangered plants, animals, and parts thereof (also known as "derivatives"). In essence, CITES signatory nations commit themselves to follow a strict set of regulations governing the importation and exportation of endangered species of plants and animals and their derivatives, all of which are listed in the appendices of the treaty. If the plant or animal being moved is not listed in the treaty, CITES regulations do not apply, even if the plant, animal, or derivative is being moved across an international border. If the movement is not across an international border, CITES again does not apply, even if the plant or animal being moved is listed in the treaty. Only countries that are members of the UN can become signatories to the treaty, and only countries who are signatories to the treaty can be held to CITES regulations.*

---

*Listing within the CITES appendices, it must be noted, is only one of many means through which a species can be designated as "endangered." In the U.S., for example, individual states have their own official lists of endangered species, as does the nation as a whole. Other lists, including the Red Data books of IUCN mentioned in chapter 3, rely more on

Participation in CITES is voluntary, so why do nations agree to subject themselves to these arcane trade restrictions? Recognition as a signatory to the treaty enhances a country's capacity to negotiate for other coveted commercial badges, such as Most Favored Nation trading status (MFN) and membership in the World Trade Organization. Conversely, failure to comply with CITES guidelines can diminish a country's eligibility for international aid or inhibit its viability in the global marketplace—even, as we shall see, to the point of sanctions. As the world turns increasingly "green," compliance with CITES has become increasingly eco-correct. Natural resources now are often seen as long-term assets to be conserved rather than exploited, and CITES, like the UN from which it sprang, supplies a ready-made political apparatus into which newly eco-aware nations can quickly fit themselves.

The way in which CITES operates—its nuts-and-bolts logistics —reveals still more about its nature and supplies a convenient means through which to introduce many of tiger conservation's most active participants. Dues from the party nations cover CITES operating expenses, which essentially involve supporting a permanent, full-time administrative "secretariat" of approximately a dozen professionals, a dozen staff members, and a secretary general, who manage CITES-related business from UNEP-supported offices in Geneva. In addition, a "standing committee" of representatives elected from CITES party nations in the world's six major geographic regions meets twice a year to review policies and procedures, after which it advises the secretariat accordingly.

Most of the real work of CITES, however, gets done once every other year when more than two thousand representatives assemble

---

taxonomic than geographic criteria, thereby transcending state, national, and even international boundaries. Coordination of these lists is attempted, but not always achieved. Overlap occurs, but is not always consistent. A species that does not appear on one or more lists may still be officially endangered, somewhere.

from around the globe under the auspices of the United Nations at a two-week-long event known as a CITES Conference of the Parties, or COP. Nine such COPs have convened since 1973, with the last being held in Fort Lauderdale, Florida, during the month of November 1994. Each COP is hosted by a different party nation, and COP-10 is scheduled to take place in Zimbabwe in 1997. Each party nation sends a delegation to the COP whose job it is to represent their home country's needs and desires with respect to the CITES guidelines. For example, if a particular species of plant or animal native to the delegation's country has diminished to dangerously small numbers since the previous conference, the delegates will likely seek to have that species added to the lists in the treaty's appendices. Once that happens, any other party nation caught importing or exporting the newly listed life-form or its derivatives will fall subject to CITES jurisdiction. This describes another of the primary activities executed by the delegates at each biannual conference: the citing of infractions and violations—who got caught doing what over the last two years and what's going to be done about it. In addition to these primary functions, there are numerous secondary activities to which the delegates must attend during the conference, along with a host of administrative chores.

To maintain order and momentum, the conferences are conducted largely under a form of parliamentary procedure. There are sessions, at which chairpersons sit before large groups (delegates, et al.), who must adhere to something like Robert's rules when it comes to being recognized and heard. An agenda is laid out in advance by the standing committee, and the items on it are tackled one by one. When snags occur, as they frequently do, focus groups break out to address the problems independently, after which they return and report. The action often slows to a painfully bureaucratic pace, and the language of the sessions sometimes lacks even a trace of wildlife vocabulary. (Merely distinguishing your native tongue amid the channels on the shortwave translation headsets can take time.) But emotions peak every now and again, especially when the subject on the floor involves a charismatic life-form like the tiger.

There is another dynamic at work at the COPs that tends to charge the proceedings. The delegates who come to represent the governments of their countries are by no means the only participants. They, and only they, possess the right to vote on matters effecting the nature and interpretation of the treaty, but just as there are powerful lobbyists cruising the halls of the U.S. Capitol, exerting their influence on persons endowed with voting authority, voteless representatives from a panoply of special-interest groups flock to every CITES COP to make sure their concerns are known. These are the "NGOs"— nongovernmental organizations—a three-letter acronym that ranks among the most valuable and effective tools available to anyone who wants to understand the machinations of global wildlife conservation.

In the preceding chapter we reviewed the relative values of identifying in situ tiger ownership, concluding with the practicality of recognizing that it is in fact the governments of the countries in which the tigers roam who ultimately control the animal's destiny. Having now examined CITES, we are familiar with what probably is the foremost (though not the only) political mechanism through which those governments are likely to address tiger conservation issues in an international context. The unifying factor is governmental power, the people in control.

In free-speech democracies such as the United States, John and Jane Q. Public have ample opportunity to participate in their governments, or at least to make sure their voices are heard. But there are no wild tigers in America. Many of the animals, in fact, are found in places like China, Vietnam, Cambodia. . . . Democracies they're not. How do John and Jane participate in the decision-making processes effected by these foreign countries concerning the destiny of the animals they care so much about? Primarily through NGOs.

Notice that the designation "NGO" does not describe what an

organization *is*. It describes only what it is not. The territory open to anyone who hopes to qualify for such a designation, therefore, is vast. You need only ensure that your organization is not comprised of governmental elements, and, voilà, you qualify to be—already are—an NGO. The significance of this freedom is important to keep in mind when segregating NGOs from their governmental counterparts. Care must be taken not to presume uniformity of purpose, method, or protocol between and among the adherents. Earth First! is an NGO, but so is the African Timber Organization. Greenpeace International is an NGO, but so is the Japan Whaling Association. (Note also that NGOs are formed to address every conceivable concern, not just those environmental.) It is this very breadth of inclusiveness, however, that endows the NGO option with its power. If you've got something to say, the designation of being an NGO offers you just enough credibility to say it in a forum where it just might be heard by an audience who just might be able to do something about it—like a CITES COP, for example.

Far from excluding or resenting nongovernmental participation, CITES welcomes NGOs to the conferences, invites them to many of the sessions, offers them a microphone at which to voice their concerns, and includes them in much of the focus-group activity. The only thing they cannot do is vote. Their status is clearly indicated by the color of a badge that they, along with every other attendee at the conference, must wear at all times. (Security is quite strict, in fact. This is, after all, a UN activity.) Permission to attend the conference must be granted in advance by the CITES secretariat, but the application process is simple and the requirements for qualification include little more than demonstrating you have a legitimate interest in things environmental. Thus the NGO window offers plenary access to one of the world's foremost political fraternities.

Unfortunately, that is also viewed as one of CITES's major weaknesses. NGOs, by and large, are highly visible. They have to be to attract the largely voluntary funding sources that make up much of their resource base—more on this later. Lacking, sometimes spurning, official means through which to make their voices heard, NGOs often opt for methods of communication more sensational than sensitive. Blockades, boycotts, advertising, and direct-mail campaigns round out an arsenal of techniques that include, at the lunatic fringe, such extremes as bomb throwing and property destruction. (Review, please, the admonition just stated regarding the hazards of lumping all NGOs together.) Among the interests officially represented at COP-9, for example, were such colorfully diverse pairs as the American Fur Industry and the Body Shop, the National Trappers Association and Friends of Animals, the Safari Club and the Defenders of Wildlife, the National Rifle Association and the Humane Society, and finally—poetically— Lyndon LaRouche and the Ringling Brothers and Barnum & Bailey Combined Shows, Inc.

Despite such bipolarity, there is a degree of homogeneous legitimacy at work in the hoard. NGOs are eager to access respected channels through which to expel their energy, and no channel is more accessible or more widely broadcast than CITES. A palpable sense of importance permeates the COPs. More than one hundred nations participate. The press attends. Powerful politicians show up, as do celebrated environmentalists and—yes—a contingent of respected scientists. This is unquestionably the big time. Most of the participants behave themselves. Radicalisms at COP-9 were limited to a dignified hunger striker from South Korea and a couple of press releases written in poor taste.

But CITES is the big time in only one arena: Trade. That limitation is one tine of a two-pronged criticism frequently leveled at CITES by members of the professional scientific community. Why, many field biologists ask, is there so much fuss over CITES when its jurisdiction can address only the transportation of certain things across international borders? What does CITES do "on the ground," they demand repeatedly, seeking quantifiable results in situ. To them, and even to many of their zoo-based counterparts, CITES often represents nothing more than an extra set of paperwork to be filled out before an animal or its blood, its tissue, or its gametes can be moved between facilities in different countries. NGOs active in CITES, of course, leap up to argue that stanching the indiscriminate exchange of endangered species and their derivatives cannot help but relieve pressure on those species in their native habitats, particularly from poachers.

Few disagree (some do, and we shall hear from them later), but worries persist regarding a potentially lopsided focus on aspects of conservation that have more to do with commerce than with science. CITES, many scientists jab with the second prong of their criticism, artificially amplifies the issue of trade by indiscriminately endowing colorful, vociferous NGOs with a highly visible forum at which to bang their drums. Hundreds of thousands of U.S. dollars are spent by NGOs every other year flying their representatives around the world and putting them up for two weeks at a time in expensive hotels so they can sit for hours on end in air-conditioned convention centers observing proceedings on which they cannot vote. In the meantime, as Ullas Karanth points out, more than a quarter of the guard posts at Nagarahole State Park in the south of India stand vacant for want of the U.S. $50 per month necessary to pay the people who would gladly fill them at that salary. No, it's not as simple as canceling the flights and the hotel reservations and sending the money to Nagarahole, but the proper application of limited resources to competing interests during critical time frames is a subject worthy of constant reevaluation.

There is a further criticism of CITES, one that grows from inside the organization itself and is leveled by participants both governmental and non. Merely writing words on paper won't modify anyone's behavior, no matter how august the authors may be, and especially when there's money to be made through the behavior in question. Only when the regulations outlined by CITES are *enforced* do they become effective, and the magnitude of resources necessary to effect that enforcement is staggering.

Since violations of the treaty occur at international borders, the

responsibility for identifying and seizing the outlawed material de-
volves largely onto customs officials. Anyone who has crossed an international border anywhere in the world can testify to the limited
likelihood of having your bags opened and inspected. Fly into Hong
Kong and you will immediately see that more than 90 percent of the
people who enter the colony via the airport are waved straight through
customs and into the next waiting taxicab without so much as a side-
long glance—tens of thousands of people every day. Add to that the
complication that any customs officer who does in fact detain a person
will, after dispatching the task of calculating and collecting import
duties, typically focus his or her attention on such high-profile contraband as weaponry and drugs, and it is easy to see how a handbag
made from the skin of an obscure snake listed in the appendices of
an international trade document only enforceable on certain countries
might just slip past even the most conscientious of inspectors. Furthermore, such incidental violations are not the bulk of the problem,
nor are the unwitting tourists who commit them the primary target of
CITES enforcement. It is, rather, the sophisticated and experienced
wildlife smuggler who will take the greatest advantage of this free-
flowing cross-border traffic, thwarting detection through every means
of camouflage and deception conceivable. Finally, take a moment
while in Hong Kong to gaze out over Victoria Harbor at the fleets of
ships bearing millions of tons of cargo into and out of that single port
every year, and you begin to grasp the dimensions of enforcing CITES
regulations. None of this is meant to criticize customs officials; there
simply is not manpower enough to inspect thoroughly the contents of
every package sent or carried across an international border, checking
for everything from gunpowder to animal hide, without choking off
trade completely.

A secondary but even more troubling aspect of CITES enforcement deficiency arises below the international level. What is the disposition of that snakeskin handbag once it slips through customs and
onto the city streets? Can it be seized from a shopkeeper or off the

arm of a customer who just bought it? What penalties can be levied against the owner of the bag if he or she was not the person who sent or carried it into the country? This is where CITES loses its grip. The trade is no longer international. Trade, in fact, may no longer be involved at all at this stage—merely possession. Yes, an international trade violation probably can be presumed to have been committed, especially if the snake that gave its skin for the handbag is not native to the country in which the bag is subsequently found. But the complexities of "grandfathering" back to that international violation make the already monumental task of enforcing CITES at the border seem simple by comparison. What if the bag was brought into the country before CITES was drafted in 1973 or before the country became a signatory to CITES in whatever year? Who is authorized to determine the age of such a bag? What if the bag was made from the skin of a snake subsequently born to two snakes smuggled across the border alive? . . . Before 1973? . . .

These questions and the never-ending string of secondary inquiries they spawn are beyond the scope of CITES. They are left, ipso facto, to be addressed by the domestic laws drafted and enforced uniquely in each of the more than 120 party nations. Snagging a violation at the border may be a hit-and-miss proposition, but at least the regulations are internationally uniform at that point. A single step beyond the customs counter demotes a violation of international significance into a domestic matter that may or may not involve illegality of any kind at that level. In a subsequent chapter we will see exactly how this secondary enforcement deficiency emasculates some of the most potent and aggressive campaigns undertaken by environmental NGOs on behalf of tigers.

⤸

While the NGO designation must not be used to bundle groups together indiscriminately, it remains an incomparably quick and precise utensil for separating certain politically significant aspects of organizational behavior. To wit, see if you can identify which of the following organizations are *not* NGOs. The Environmental Defense Fund; the Environmental Protection Agency; the U.S. Fish and Wildlife Service; the American Zoo and Aquarium Association; the U.S. Humane Society. If you don't know or can't tell, don't worry. NGOs, like other sensible organs of influence, often design their names specifically to sound commanding and officious. A simple question to any articulate representative of such a group, however, will quickly lift the haze: "Are you an NGO?" The answer will generally come quickly, since there is no reason for members of an NGO to be embarrassed or resentful of their lack of governmental affiliations—indeed, many consider it an advantage or a badge of honor. But the distinction is often so clear to insiders that they don't appreciate how surprised an outsider might be to learn of an organization's nongovernmental status. (The answer to the quiz, by the way, is numbers two and three: the EPA and the U.S. Fish and Wildlife Service are governmental organizations; the other three are NGOs.)

Why is it significant to be able to identify NGOs? Because it quickly answers a battery of questions concerning motivation, resources, limitations, capabilities, and accountability. It indicates in an instant who is and who is not primarily funded by a government, which, in the case of the United States, for example, means funded with citizen tax dollars. Determining an organization's NGO status may not reveal a comprehensive profile, but it lets you know immediately whether you're dealing with the mayor or the minister.

Unfortunately, when it comes to global conservation, that's about all it does, and not always with precision. The miasma of participants involved in CITES defies clear-cut segregation, sometimes to the point where the participants themselves face identity crises. Individuals often represent or endorse several NGOs, many of which have closely related objectives and funding sources, but some of which do not. Environmental NGOs tend to subdivide themselves while simultaneously linking with other like-minded organizations to form a sort of meta-

NGO. "Star" NGO personalities are courted to appear on panels and at press conferences in the company of persons with whom they may be in direct competition for donation dollars, or possibly even at odds with in terms of policy, approach, or basic conservation philosophy.

The confusion moves laterally as well as horizontally. At COP-9 in Florida, one prominent and influential (voting) delegate also represented one of conservation's most powerful and respected NGOs. His schizophrenic status allowed him—required him—to swap badges of different color at different times during the proceedings for the sake of fulfilling his bifurcated responsibilities. Then there's the niggling designation of IGO—*inter*governmental organization—which pops up intermittently to describe either a group whose membership includes, but is not limited to, governmental representatives, or whose functions are funded in part, but not necessarily in total, out of the coffers of more than one national government. The man with the different-colored badges at COP-9 was simultaneously listed on the roster of at least one IGO. (It's important to point out that this gentleman neither did anything wrong nor sought to be so versatile. His dilemma implicates not him but rather the complex nature of global conservation politics.)

In the face of such incest, it's not surprising to learn that the flow of money intended for conservation can sometimes be more difficult to trace than the source of acid rain. NGOs primarily generate funds through dues paid by members and through donations, both individual and corporate. Additional revenue also may be generated through the sale of products and publications. Greeting cards and calendars are particularly effective fund-raising tools for environmental NGOs, due to the photogenic appeal of the animals and landmarks many such organizations promote. NGOs are often incorporated, but some are not. Of those incorporated, some have tax-exempt status; others do not. Some NGOs pay their employees, some rely exclusively on volunteers, and some utilize a combination of both. Many NGOs get money or goods or services from other NGOs, and some also get money or goods or services from IGOs. The World Bank, an IGO (of sorts) whose structure outscrambles even the UN, is poised to issue more than U.S. $45 million through an auxiliary known as the GEF—Global Environmental Facility—to India for something called "eco-development." Whither comes that money? (Part of it may include your deposits at the local S & L.) Whence goes it? Such an audit could devour a career. The advisory committee of Indians negotiating the disposition of that cash includes government officials, both elected and appointed, and several prominent Indian NGO representatives, many of whom also participate on IGO advisory committees. "Thick as thieves" is how one committee member characterized the situation. Premier among the hot-button topics of those negotiations is who, exactly, will hold the purse strings for so much money, with half the committee convinced that if the other half gets its way, all India's wildlife is doomed. This is only one of several similar funding efforts currently under consideration by the World Bank, which is neither the only such funding operation in existence nor exclusively interested in funding environmentally relevant investments.

Does this hopelessly tangled web of power and capital mean the situation is hopeless? By no means. The worst that can be said of such confusion is that it is highly frustrating but only potentially dangerous. The very good news is that there is an extraordinary amount of interest in conservation out there, and it is backed by tremendous sums of money. Conspiracy theories aside, while the World Bank may be ominous in its scope, it is generally viewed as a benign if somewhat inept participant in a global effort to keep the planet from poisoning itself. There may be—certainly is—internecine strife among the players in conservation politics, but the end goals are undeniably homogenized. Nobody wants the plants and animals to go away.

∽

CHAPTER 6

Elementary,
My Dear Tiger

Having deconstructed the relevant aspects of science and politics, we now can erect a scaffolding on which to drape and compare profiles of the people, organizations, and governments seeking specifically to influence the future of the tiger. A few have been mentioned already on earlier pages, and one of those offers a sensible point of departure.

The International Union for the Conservation of Nature and Natural Resources, IUCN, came together amid the political debris of World War II. Famed British biologist Sir Julian Huxley was then the director general of UNESCO—the United Nations Educational, Scientific, and Cultural Organization—and under his guidance the union was officially formed with the help of the French government during proceedings conducted at the Château Fontainebleau just outside Paris in 1948. The organization was christened the International Union for the Protection of Nature, but it was renamed in 1956. It now tries to refer to itself as the World Conservation Union, but everybody—even employees of the group—clings to the widely recognized initials "IUCN." (Name changes are endemic to global conservation, in fact, further hobbling the already arduous task of navigating among the players.)

The political classification into which IUCN fits most readily, though not perfectly, is that of an IGO; it is a worldwide affiliation of governments, governmental agencies, and NGOs, funded largely, though not entirely, through membership dues. Much of IUCN's most significant work is conducted by volunteers, so the budget comprises mainly the administrative expenses of achieving the union's mission: "To influence, encourage and assist societies throughout the world to conserve the integrity and diversity of nature and to ensure that any use of natural resources is equitable and ecologically sustainable." (Keep your eye on that last word.) IUCN is recognized for its emphasis on research, and it has a reputation for thorough, unbiased, reliable analysis. Its rolls include the names of many of the world's most-respected and famous scientists, not only in the field, but also in zoos, at universities, and in laboratories.

Beneath the IUCN umbrella there are six ribs, each of which represents a "commission" specifically organized to address one particular aspect of conservation. Of the six, the Species Survival Commission, or SSC, addresses endangered plants and animals. The SSC rib comprises an array of "specialist groups," each of which has been chartered with the task of assembling a network of the best scientific minds available in a concentrated field. For the most part, these specialist groups separate along taxonomic lines, with each group focusing on a particular species of plant or animal. The Cat Specialist Group is the one that covers tigers, and the name of almost every person quoted thus far in this book has appeared at one time or another on the rolls of the Cat Specialist Group. (That alone should serve as ample evidence of the diversity of opinions and emotions roiling in this otherwise unified body, but there is much, much more.)

The chairman of the Cat Specialist Group is a gentleman named Peter Jackson, who is probably linked with tiger conservation more readily than any other person. The chairmanship of the Cat

Specialist Group, which Jackson accepted at the request of IUCN in 1983 and has retained on a volunteer basis since then, renders him the default spokesman for one of the world's most comprehensive collections of felid biologists. Under his chairmanship, the group has grown to more than 160 members, who represent more than forty countries around the globe. When researchers and journalists go looking for an authority to quote on the status of the tiger, or any other endangered species of cat, who better to reach than the person at the head of such a group? In addition to his role as chairman, Jackson serves as editor of the Cat Specialist Group's newsletter, *Cat News*, and he himself has written widely on the subject of big cats, specializing in tigers. There is hardly a tiger book now on the market that does not bear Jackson's name somewhere in its index, appendices, bibliography, acknowledgments, or a combination of the four. Scarcely a month goes by without a quote from Jackson popping up in one or more significant newspaper, magazine, talk show, or broadcast news report somewhere in the world. He is, in fact, a figurehead of tiger conservation.

Ironically, this quiet, proper Englishman who represents so much of tiger science is not himself a scientist. "I'm an ex-journalist," he explains without hesitation. "I got into cats by covering wildlife for Reuters." This vocational incongruity sometimes plagues Jackson with disrespect from the very scientists he is presumed to represent. By simple virtue of his visibility, Jackson both enjoys and suffers intense international focus on his personal views of the tiger's situation. As a consequence, he, more than anyone else, is responsible for promulgating the perception that the tiger is in immediate peril. "The tiger will be virtually extinct in the wild by 1999," he states, reprising an observation for which he has become internationally notable and notorious. Though few are willing to go on the record when expressing their reactions, felid specialists around the globe—members of the Cat Specialist Group, all—cringe when Jackson speaks those words, demanding evidence more reliable than a pug-mark census to support such claims and pleading for relief from the focus on statistics those claims inevitably reinforce.

"It's getting to the point where nobody really pays much attention, or people are questioning statements coming out of the Cat Specialist Group," asserts Dorene Bolze, the policy analyst for WCS (the scientifically oriented NGO with which Ullas Karanth works). "Tigers are going to be extinct in three years in India?" she demands. "That's a load of garbage.... All that stuff Peter Jackson circulates that's been reprinted now a million times? It's numbers out of a hat. It's nothing. It's garbage.... We don't know how many tigers there are. Period."

In another realm, however, Jackson's claims resonate harmoniously, often to the further consternation of already ruffled members of the Cat Specialist Group. The more liberal constituents in the NGO community readily latch on to Peter Jackson as an authority of rare prestige. His imprimatur brings an undeniable dose of respectability—he's the chairman of the IUCN/SSC Cat Specialist Group, after all—and the immediacy of the disaster he foresees for the tiger feeds the energy with which many NGOs prefer to sound their alarms. Before we step from beneath the IUCN umbrella to brave the hail of NGOs, however, let us take a moment to consider one other IUCN specialist group, whose name appeared on the first page of this book.

These days, CBSG stands for the Conservation Breeding Specialist Group, but until 1994 the C stood for "Captive" rather than "Conservation." The subtlety with which the alphabet offers up this politically correct substitution could hardly be more apropos of both the change it reflects and the dynamics behind the change. As we have already discussed, the word "captive" has forever suffered within the scientific community from its proximity to the word "zoo" and, by extension, the phrase ex situ. A captive animal simply is not perceived as wild. And when it comes to tigers, if it isn't wild we certainly don't need to worry about breeding the damn thing—we have too many captive ones already . . . or so the perception can go, especially among field scientists. Ah, but, without even needing to change its logo, the group of specialists focusing on the reproductive dynamics of the tiger (among a host of other animals) has handily transported its image across the situ gap, from ex to in. Challengers may argue that "captive" breeding has nothing to do with wild tigers, but who can fight the perception that "conservation" breeding most certainly does? Few PR maneuvers have been more effective, or more elegant.

CBSG is one of the few specialist groups in the IUCN's SSC that is not taxonomic in focus. This group concentrates on a process, not a species. All species breed, and it is this reproductive process that CBSG seeks to analyze and apply for the sake of species survival. The expertise of many of the specialists in this group, therefore, revolves not around a particular plant or animal, but rather around a cluster of scientific disciplines that includes reproductive physiology, genetics, animal behavior, and animal husbandry. If these disciplines sound familiar, that should come as no surprise; you've met a number of their prominent representatives in this book already. Yes, most of them have appeared at one time or another on the rolls of CBSG—as well as, in many cases, on the rolls of the Cat Specialist Group. When it comes to tigers, in fact, these are the two organizations that include among their now and former ranks (not always euphoniously, remember) the name of almost every scientist who has ever contributed to the salvation of the animal in any meaningful way.

The chairman of CBSG, as we learned in chapter 1, is Ulysses Seal. Like Peter Jackson, Seal volunteers his time to IUCN, and he, too, suffers a bit of vocational incongruity. He is a scientist—a highly respected one—but his original field does not include animal biology. He's a biochemist. He didn't get involved with endangered species until well after he'd established himself in medical research, and he has never drawn a salary in connection with his work with animals. Unlike Jackson, however, Seal is rarely criticized by the members of the group he chairs, most of whom go out of their way to laud the man in terms both professional and personal. Seal's opponents, rather, rise up from within either the field-research ranks of the Cat Specialist Group or from the NGO community. Seal and CBSG often are characterized as high-tech scientific dilettantes dabbling in fields beyond their ken and drawing focus away from what is happening "on the ground."

"Given the crisis in which the tiger finds itself," says Ullas Karanth, "I see very little relevance for the approach that CBSG is taking to tiger conservation. It has very little relevance to the field. . . . Park managers have an unpleasant task on the ground, facing irate villagers and keeping poachers out, and this is a much more attractive option—build captive facilities, build cryogenic banks, build high-tech stuff, and you will save the tiger. You don't have to really deal with the messy situation on the ground. . . . But even the whole idea of what a genetically viable population in the wild is can be scientifically attacked. There is no a priori assumption that inbreeding depression is the priority problem for tigers. The cheetah, after all, went through a genetic bottleneck ten thousand years ago and survived just fine without CBSG doing a PHVA on it."

With a smile and sad shake of his head, Seal responds, "Oh, dear old Ullas. He's disaffected from the world. He's worked harder at alienating himself from his own colleagues than any person that I've seen in a long time in India. It's just a pity." Reverting to the issue, he notes that "Ullas has never chosen to participate in or attend a PHVA workshop. We've invited him, but he hasn't chosen to do so. So he's speaking from a set of perceptions which are not based upon full experience. Many of these people, when they do participate in a workshop, come to appreciate that the approach of CBSG is not solely focused on either high tech or captive populations or gene banks. And his argument is specious on a logical basis. You don't have a control group for comparison or evaluation. You don't have a measure of the species that *have* gone extinct because of inbreeding depression. You've only looked at ones that have survived, and, therefore, 'If they can survive all can survive.' It's a specious generalization. Ullas is thinking in terms of his own lifetime, and that short-term view is not adequate if we're going to talk about survival of wild populations. He may not live to see some of his populations crash . . . but that doesn't mean the potential isn't there, and it doesn't mean the risk isn't there. The enormous weight of evidence says that it is."

Specifically with respect to tigers, Seal's defense of CBSG gets a credibility boost, of sorts, by virtue of the fact that Ron Tilson has assumed responsibility for CBSG's role in that animal's future. True, Tilson's original mammal of choice for research was the gibbon, not the tiger, but at least his scientific pedigree is zoological. Unlike Seal, Tilson rarely gets criticized for stepping beyond his scientific realm, particularly when it comes to the Sumatran subspecies of tiger. Tilson's heavier baggage comes in the form of his employer. He works for, and at, the Minnesota Zoo, deriving his income exclusively from that job. (Like Seal and Jackson, he gets no salary from IUCN.) When he travels—more than three hundred thousand kilometers a year—he meets and deals largely with people from other zoos or zoological associations. PHVAs, Tiger Rescue Kits, and clever organizational name changes aside, any effort CBSG makes at breeding tigers for the sake of in situ conservation will be launched by Tilson through an ex situ infrastructure of zoos, which, by definition, rely entirely on captive animals. For that reason, Ron Tilson, to many, is seen as the consummate "zoo guy."

Since the zoo/field schism in science has been dealt with, let us now focus on how Tilson's zoo-heavy involvement supplies an opportunity for political analysis. In North America, most zoos are members of something called the American Zoo and Aquarium Association (or AZA), a trade organization that derives its operating capital primarily from the dues its members pay. The AZA is a recognized, respected, and influential NGO. It has counterparts around the world, including, as an example, the EEP for which Sarah Christie of the London Zoo makes her Sumatran and Siberian tiger-breeding recommendations. For the most part, all zoo trade organizations are NGOs. It would, of course, be wonderfully convenient to be able to identify the zoos themselves as NGOs, and such a definition would be accurate if all zoos were private organizations deriving their income primarily from gate fees, as they do for the most part in North America. But many zoos around the world are heavily subsidized, as in India, where all but a handful are operated by the government. In yet another cruel victory of tiger conservation over clear navigability, the Minnesota Zoo is, in fact, an auxiliary of the state of Minnesota—which means Ron Tilson could legitimately be considered a government employee. Go figure.

In tandem with his ascendancy in CBSG, Tilson has also risen to lofty heights within the ranks of the AZA so far as tigers are concerned. Not unlike IUCN, the AZA sponsors groups of specialists interested in pursuing the long-term survival of individual species; the differences from IUCN's specialist groups arise primarily through the AZA's uniquely North American, uniquely zoo-oriented focus. Each of the AZA's specialist groups operates under what's called a Species Survival Plan, or SSP. Ron Tilson is the coordinator of the tiger SSP (Ulysses Seal was his immediate predecessor), and he wields, thereby, a degree of influence over the disposition of all the tigers held in AZA-member facilities. As with Sarah Christie in Europe, his authority is conditional, and his recommendations can be disputed and even ignored. But his position as the tiger SSP coordinator is the perfect complement to his role at CBSG, and by standing with one foot in each of those two organizations, he deftly straddles the border between a powerful domestic NGO and a global IGO.

However, the gaze of this would-be tiger colossus reaches farther still. In April 1986 he and Ulysses Seal adroitly accessed all the elements at their collective disposal to assemble a convocation of experts at what was rightly heralded as the first global symposium on tigers. The five-day event convened at the Minnesota Zoo, which cosponsored the symposium in conjunction with both CBSG and the Cat

Specialist Group. Representatives attended from around the globe, and while the crowd was predominantly zoo-based, there was also a healthy contingent of field researchers and even a smattering of governmental types. An assortment of sources, both governmental and non, contributed supporting funds to the symposium, including UNEP, the Smithsonian, the World Wildlife Fund, the U.S. Fish and Wildlife Service, and several private donors. The agenda focused on the presentation and analysis of tiger conservation strategies from around the world, with a goal of generating something dubbed a Global Tiger Survival Plan. After the symposium had adjourned, its proceedings and several papers submitted by persons who could not attend were published in a book grandly titled *Tigers of the World: The Biology, Biopolitics, Management, and Conservation of an Endangered Species* (Noyes, 1987). Though dense with scientific jargon, this tome includes the broadest mix of research conducted by the largest number of specialists, and it quickly became a standard reference work on tigers in every respectable felid research library in the world.

The last chapter of *Tigers of the World* presents a draft outline of the Global Tiger Survival Plan. Tilson and Seal incubated that plan for six years, and when it hatched in 1992 at a second caucus of far-flung tiger specialists, held at Edinburgh Zoo in Scotland, its name had changed to the Tiger Global Animal Survival Plan: "Tiger GASP" for short, and clever. Arin Ghosh of India's Project Tiger attended the two-day workshop, as did a host of representatives from zoos in Europe and the United States—not so big a group as the '86 symposium, but a respectable quorum nonetheless. As the workshop's title clearly indicates, the agenda addressed nothing less than the survival of the tiger throughout the world. By the time the workshop had adjourned, Ron Tilson emerged beneath nothing less than the title "Global Tiger Coordinator."

The title suits the bearer. Tilson is a resourceful, articulate, and capable individual who shrinks from neither responsibility nor criticism. He is robust and expressive, perhaps too much so for his own good, by some standards. When he travels through Indonesia, he chain-smokes clove cigarettes and is fond of wearing a red baseball cap emblazoned with a picture of a tiger leaping from beneath the word *pawang*—Bahasa for "charmer." On the inside of his left forearm he bears a crude tattoo of an ape, the remnant of an initiation ritual he endured long ago to gain the trust of the natives among whom he conducted his doctoral research. When Tilson settles on a goal, he remains focused, and there is little that can stop him from achieving it . . . including, on occasion, common courtesy and professional good sense. He is forever annoying his colleagues in the AZA, CBSG, and the Cat Specialist Group with sharp, sometimes smarmy commentary on their policies and methods while simultaneously spurning functions where he cannot set the agenda and direct the proceedings. His need for control, in fact, is immense. A misplaced room key sends him into a public fury. Members of the teams he takes overseas with him can be heard to grumble of being treated like children on a family outing.

Tilson makes no apology for his dominion, citing as a defense his responsibility to the people who fund his work and the scope of his achievements. Nevertheless, he suffers from a reputation for arrogance, and while his scope is undeniably broad, it is precariously shallow in places. He may be—is—the Great White Hope in Indonesia, adored and respected by government and indigenous NGO community alike for his vision of salvation for their tigers both in situ and ex, but his title as Global Tiger Coordinator draws smirks from inside India. He may be effectively moving northward from Sumatra to implement his vision through the whole of Southeast Asia, but zoos back in his homeland, as well as every circus on the planet, still thumb their noses at his breeding recommendations. With the possible exception of the Minnesota Zoo, Ron Tilson's authority over tigers is anything but absolute. Limitations notwithstanding, he remains a powerful, visible force in worldwide tiger conservation, and he will certainly persevere.

⌒

Having crossed the bridge between governments and NGOs, we can now proceed deeper into nongovernmental territory, where we shall find no shortage of foils for Ron Tilson and his ego.

First, however, a disclaimer, of sorts: The tiger's appeal makes it an irresistible icon for fund-raisers, some of whom derive more benefit from the animal than the animal does from them. Leaving purveyors of outright fraud to the police, there remains a universe of ad hoc organizations that claim to contribute, in large ways and in small, either to the conservation or to the well-being of tigers—far too many organizations to be analyzed comprehensively in any single volume, especially considering the nascency and short-lived existence of some. For that reason, only a sampler of the most enduring, effective, or visible NGOs who count tigers among their beneficiaries shall be presented here to stand for the whole. Representatives from several prominent tiger-boosting NGOs have spoken out already on these pages. Others will speak up later. Still others, such as the Global Tiger Patrol in England, prefer to pursue their respected work quietly. All such groups solicit money in one way or another, and it behooves any would-be benefactor to evaluate carefully the history, constitution, policies, methods, and objectives of any group to whom he or she plans to donate. It is not the intention of this book either to endorse or discredit the people or the organizations about to be named, merely to report on them for the sake of presenting useful analytical models. Thus shriven, let us proceed by reviving the name of an NGO that linked itself first and formidably with tiger conservation.

The World Wildlife Fund was launched in the early '60s primarily as a fund-raising mechanism for IUCN. In spite of the largely volunteer work of its members, IUCN needed money to finance its many far-flung undertakings, and a body dedicated to that purpose had become a clear necessity. Then, as now, scientists did better with a microscope than a tin cup. In 1961 E. M. Nicholson, a cofounder of IUCN, organized a committee in England to address the issue, accessing in the process the talents and connections of both Julian Huxley and Guy Mountfort. To attract capital as well as visibility, the committee offered the presidency of the board of trustees of the evolving organization to Prince Philip. His Highness declined, opting rather to head just the British chapter and suggesting his acquaintance Prince Bernhard of the Netherlands for the top spot. Bernhard accepted and served for fifteen years before being forced to resign in 1976 after a very public scandal involving charges of bribery in connection with the country's defense industry. Philip acceded to the international presidency, where he remained through September 1996.

WWF has been shrouded in secrecy from its earliest days, perhaps because competition for conservation money is fierce, perhaps because the fund has benefited from the largesse of such unsavory donors as Robert Vesco (on the lam in Cuba from U.S. fraud charges), Agha Hasan Abedi (founder of BCCI, Bank of Credit and Commerce International), and a person eventually linked with the charges that brought Prince Bernhard down. Whatever the reason, WWF suffers from a reputation for self-serving image management that does not complement the scientific objectivity of IUCN; the two organizations, in fact, officially parted ways in the mid-1980s, though their association remains close and liquid. The fund is also dogged by internal conflict, particularly from the U.S. chapter, which boasts more than one-fifth of the organization's total membership. (Sharing the proceeds from such a large and generous group with the international headquarters in Switzerland leads to resentment and recurring threats of independence.) Charges of "eco-imperialism" also hobble WWF, due as much to the lengthy presence of a colonial monarch at the helm as to an early tendency to install white managers in overseas Third World posts.

Despite these distractions, WWF still is recognized as a legitimate, commanding force in conservation. It is the single largest conservation NGO in the world, to which more than five million individual members around the globe contribute more than U.S. $200 million annually (and tax-deductibly), swelling a budget supplemented by grants from foundations, corporations, and tax-supported government agencies. WWF's international network of chapters features representatives in more than fifty countries and it funds conservation efforts in twice that many. To put it modestly, the original goal has been met.

In addition to its continuing ministrations under Operation Tiger, WWF pursues tiger conservation through a variety of projects and agencies, the most comprehensive of which, perhaps, is called TRAFFIC. An impeccably self-referential acronym, the letters stand for Trade Record Analysis of Flora and Fauna in Commerce. The group is arguably the most widespread, well-organized, effective, and respected NGO in all of conservation, though it is not without either critics or deficiencies. TRAFFIC is based in Cambridge, England, and has more than a dozen regional and national offices around the globe. Funding comes primarily from WWF, though IUCN is a large secondary supporter. Private donations also are accepted.

TRAFFIC is a monitoring organization whose employees—all paid—are described as "technicians" by Jorgen Thomsen, the former director of TRAFFIC International in the U.K. "We try to provide training opportunities for all staff," Thomsen explains, "not only in monitoring trade by using and interpreting data, but also in species identification." What these technicians officially monitor, per the name of their organization, are the commercial records that document trade involving plants and animals. The correlation to CITES is unmistakable here, and indeed TRAFFIC works in close cooperation both with the CITES secretariat in Geneva and with the domestic offices of Management Authority and Scientific Authority that each party nation must establish and maintain as a condition of alignment with CITES (the purposes of which, respectively, are to handle administrative matters and to monitor the status of domestic plants and animals listed in the CITES appendices). The statistics and reports generated by TRAFFIC are hungrily swept up by every CITES signatory and auxiliary, often constituting the primary evidence for charges of an infraction or a violation.

As an NGO, TRAFFIC enjoys access and flexibility that extend its reach both beyond and beneath the bailiwick of the United Nations. For starters, while CITES enforcement is stuck at the international border, TRAFFIC can operate domestically. National offices, often run by native staffs, can focus on the domestic laws in place and in force (not always the same thing) within a particular country, thereby supplying not only local analyses but also a means through which to correlate the results of that analysis with international objectives. Among governments, therefore, TRAFFIC is widely regarded as an analytical, administrative, monitoring service that helps countries—at its own expense, no less—align themselves with a treaty they have already publicly declared to want to follow anyway. Yes, infractions uncovered by TRAFFIC are embarrassing, but the point is to live up to the treaty, isn't it? Sure, at the official level. And TRAFFIC expends extraordinary effort poring over official customs files, shipping manifests, duty records, and the like, producing detailed reports that feature charts, graphs, and tables to demonstrate what they've found. An impressive example of just such a report was published in 1994 under the title *Killed for a Cure: A Review of the Worldwide Trade in Tiger Bone*.

Every piece of the tiger, from its whiskers to its feces, appears somewhere in the pharmacopoeia of traditional Chinese medicine (a discipline we shall explore in a later chapter): The nose is said to calm convulsions in children; the tail relieves various diseases of the skin; the flesh treats malaria; the brain cures acne; the fur drives away centipedes when burned. . . . It is, however, the bones of the tiger that are prized above all, particularly for their alleged potency in treating degenerative rheumatoid arthritis. For application, the bones are crushed and mixed with unguents to form a plaster that can be laid against the skin, or they are pulverized and made into pills to be taken orally, or they are soaked in liquor to ferment tiger-bone "wine." *Killed for a Cure* explains the global demand for tiger bone in all its forms, and the report represents the single most comprehensive analysis of the official trade statistics available, as of the date of its publication, to track the flow of tiger bone around the world. Overlaying geography with market dynamics, this fifty-two-page document systematically presents relevant trade statistics from each of the fourteen tiger range countries—establishing them as the sources of the product—then does the same for a host of "consumer" nations, comprising Belgium, Canada, Hong Kong, Japan, Macau, Singapore, South Korea, Taiwan, and the United States. The same sequence is then repeated for a country-by-country discussion of domestic legal controls over tiger-bone trade, followed by summary and recommendations. Not inappropriately (considering TRAFFIC's funding sources), Peter Jackson coauthored the report, working in conjunction with the director of TRAFFIC's Southeast Asia office, Judy Mills.

Consistent with TRAFFIC's erudite status among other NGOs, the language in *Killed for a Cure* is simple, reserved, and straightforward, despite the provocative title. Histrionic assessments and inflammatory conclusions are left to those who may choose to interpret the document thus. For their parts, Jackson and Mills rely on the data to speak for themselves, adding only the most reasonable of declarative observations. No one can accuse the authors of leaping to their conclusions. Indeed, the objectivity with which *Killed for a Cure* approaches its subject is so measured as to be self-effacing. "In summary," the report concedes no deeper than page 9, wrapping up a bulleted list of ten "significant limitations" of the data that follow, "many, if not most aspects of the global trade in Tiger [*sic*] bone and Tiger-bone derivatives remain undocumented." That admission, while commendable in terms of impartiality, leads straightaway to a question that implicates not only the report itself but also the very foundation of CITES: What is the point?

To fully appreciate the implications of that question, let us back up a step with an allegory. If you ran an import/export business in a country where no laws impacted your trade, what fear would you have of fully documenting and reporting every transaction you conducted? If, however, your country were suddenly to declare itself aligned with a UN treaty designed to prohibit the movement of your products across international borders, you now have a serious choice to make: Either you stop dealing with the products in question, or you stop keeping open records. The one thing you are *not* likely to do—not for very long, anyway—is continue recording and reporting what are now illegal transactions. You will either quit or move underground, and when an international organization, either governmental or non, comes looking to analyze all the official trade records available for the now-illegal products, the only records they're going to find, by definition, are those generated before the practice became illegal. At best, such an investigation will yield outdated patterns of questionable relevance. At worst, it will turn conscientious, law-abiding record keepers into suspects.

Precisely this paradox, in fact, played out with unhappy consequences for CITES, TRAFFIC, and the country of South Korea. Since South Korea did not actively seek to align itself with CITES until the middle of '93, the import and export of tiger bone remained legal there until CITES signatory status was granted in October of that year. Indeed, a unique category for tracking the flow of tiger bone into and out of the country had been maintained meticulously in customs records for more than two decades. As a condition of its alignment to CITES, South Korea initiated a one-year grace period during which domestic trade in tiger bone remained legal, followed by a further six-month domestic reprieve for products containing tiger bone as an ingredient. (Such dispensations are not without precedent among CITES signatory nations, all of which require time to install enforcement measures and convert their sometimes reluctant citizens to the new laws.) Hence, through March 1995 it remained perfectly legal to buy or sell anything with tiger bone listed among its contents on the streets of South Korea. In an effort to monitor both the effects and the effectiveness of the transitional period, the government established a process through which owners of tiger bone and its derivatives could voluntarily submit their stocks for official registration and tracking. Many complied, and as a consequence South Korea compiled an exquisitely detailed record of the nation's history in tiger-bone commerce, both before and after alignment with CITES.

Unfortunately, the diligence South Korea exercised in keeping such fastidious records supplied an irresistible target. "This country provides the most comprehensive documentation of Tiger-bone trade of any consumer nation," *Killed for a Cure* acknowledges, following with a handy table of statistics derived from those comprehensive documents. The figures are not incorrect, but their prominence in the report, hovering amid the absence of equally comprehensive data from other so-called consumer nations, shines a klieg light directly on South Korea. By the time that country's delegates arrived in Fort Lauderdale to attend COP-9 in 1994—where *Killed for a Cure* made its debut—they were fuming. They declined to be interviewed on the record for the duration of the conference, but they made no secret of their displeasure at seeing their homeland punished, in their view, for doing nothing more than striving conscientiously to align itself with CITES. Yes, the statistics presented in the report all were a matter of public record, and therefore fair game for precisely the type of analysis TRAFFIC conducts, but the timing, the context, and particularly the title of the document were considered indelicate at least, and potentially even hostile.

"South Korea is the only country in there that had decent records," Judy Mills admits, pointing to a copy of *Killed for a Cure*. "And that's because the trade was legal. . . . But this report was never meant to say, look, here's the scope of the trade. The purpose was to say that these are the measly data we have about a species that's getting ready to disappear from the face of the earth, and, my god, what are we going to do about it? That's why these caveats are [printed in the report]. That's my way of underscoring the crisis. It's what we don't know that is the most frightening conclusion of this report. But these data are the only thing that can really tell us even a piece of what is going on."

Good points, all. And it would be irresponsible to suggest that reports such as *Killed for a Cure* have no value despite (perhaps including) whatever ire they arouse. Public trade records supply a baseline, if nothing else, and they reveal established shipping routes. Employing them for condemnation never was the goal of either CITES or TRAFFIC, neither of which can be held responsible for the overenthusiastic interpretations of people who read their reports.

To overcome the inherent weakness of relying exclusively on trade record analysis, TRAFFIC employs a more exotic monitoring option to trail trade that moves underground—in a word, espionage. Discovering that a shipment of something now illegal has been made legally in the past may supply a lead, but catching someone with bona fide contraband in his or her possession supplies a perpetrator, an M.O., and evidence all in a stroke. The rules have been broken, end of story. Customs agents—the government's representatives—occasionally score such hits at international borders, but that is the only place they're going to make seizures under CITES jurisdiction. NGOs have longer arms and fewer tethers. If the government of Country X sends a person into Country Y to find out secretly if Country Y is living up to its agreements, that's called spying. Governments can't do that— not officially, anyway, since the results can't be used publicly without triggering all sorts of embarrassing diplomatic consequences. "We do not send undercover agents into other countries," asserts Carol Lee Carson, a senior biologist with extensive investigative experience in connection with the U.S. Office of CITES Management Authority (which, in the U.S., is administered by the Department of the Interior's Fish and Wildlife Service). "We do not have the authority to do that." But when a representative from a *non*governmental organization stands up at an international conference and waves a report that includes an incriminating statistic (or photograph or videotape) obtained by a private citizen or a visitor traveling legally under a valid passport, well, gee Country Y, what do you have to say about that? In part, this is why NGOs are welcomed to, even encouraged to participate in, governmental functions such as CITES. They can be the eyes and ears of policy makers who are effectively blindfolded and muffed by international protocols. This is the return half of the symbiosis generated by supplying NGOs with a microphone at international conferences: They get their forum; governments get their evidence. Nobody breaks any rules, officially.

Not everyone is thrilled with this arrangement. "That's one of the areas where other countries are very uncomfortable," Carson concedes. "NGOs use means that the U.S. government simply could not use and would not use, and which would not be acceptable in a court of law." Animosities fall partly along political lines, with democratic governments tending to be more responsive to covert NGO evidence than repressive governments, which tend to be resentful. There is also a cultural dynamic at work, particularly with the tiger. China, for example, is delighted to participate in the UN and duly proud to be a signatory to CITES, but their delegates bristle when undercover footage of a state-affiliated factory churning out tiger-bone plasters is shown in a continuous loop in front of an NGO booth at a Conference of the Parties. The validity of the evidence is discounted, they mutter, by the skulduggery employed in obtaining it. Such dishonorable techniques are unworthy of international politics, they suggest, and unseemly in the context of the UN. "Actions like that are not forthright," states Dr. Qing Jian Hua, a representative of mainland China at COP-9. "Technically, these NGOs are breaking Chinese law because they disguise themselves. We refer to such offenders as entrapment criminals, and we have officially summoned them to appear in court. We also have reason to believe they asked the manufacturers to falsify the production date so the product would appear to have violated laws in power at the time."

Indignities and counteraccusations notwithstanding, sensitive evidence supplied by NGOs finds purchase in terms of bad PR regardless of whether or not it changes the vote of a single delegate at any international conference. Clear political impact may even be secondary to the purposes of the exposing NGO, which often is more interested in launching a consumer boycott or simply raising public awareness. Chagrined government representatives are just a welcome windfall, in many cases.

To take full advantage of its reach, TRAFFIC often works in conjunction with other NGOs, especially when there is a common subject of reconnaissance. Resources are limited, and there is no logic in duplicating either the efforts or the risks required for surveillance. Depending upon the degree to which the trade in question is illegal, investigative techniques range from walking the streets and looking in shopwindows to posing as a buyer and negotiating with crime lords. Smaller investigative NGOs tend to develop specialties in particular methods, countries, or contraband, and opportunities to double-team their targets with assistance from TRAFFIC are rarely overlooked.

But shared credits sometimes connect TRAFFIC either directly or by association with organizations as far away from it in terms of protocol as it is from CITES, especially when it comes to tigers. The most charismatic of the megafauna attracts awfully charismatic saviors to its cause, and bedfellows in tiger conservation can become marvelously strange. TRAFFIC may be the Sherlock Holmes of international plant and animal trade, but the NGOs with whom its name sometimes is linked are more like Dirty Harrys.

⌐

"The Tiger Trust is the *only* conservation organization working exclusively on behalf of tigers," proclaims Michael P. Day, founder and driving force behind The Tiger Trust. "This is all I do, tiger conservation. It's just taken over my life." Regardless of the degree to which The Tiger Trust is indeed alone in its focus on tigers, Day has most certainly stolen the spotlight when it comes to working on behalf of the animal. His name is seared into the memories of scientists, journalists, members of most other NGOs, and heads of state around the globe.

A rather gallant former advertising executive from the U.K., Day turned to tiger conservation in 1990 following an encounter with a representative of the species. "We were trekking very, very deep inside the jungles of southern Thailand," he says, setting the scene. "At about five A.M. something was out in the camp. . . . We found these enormous footprints, with blades of grass just sort of licking back up. The tracker said, 'It's a tiger.'" Day and his fellow trekkers followed the animal to the mouth of a cave, "but the lead tracker threw his arms up when he realized the tracks were going in and not coming out. We ran back, and it was while on our way to breakfast that a feeling sort of bonded that we had walked into the mouth of the tiger cave. . . . Tigers came into my life. Touched something. A soul or a nerve somewhere. I felt maybe this was why I had gone to Thailand. I went there with a one-way ticket to look for something. That was the beginning of the story."

And what a story he has made of it. Like Saul to the gospel, Day abandoned himself to this new calling. He returned to England and launched The Tiger Trust, reviving his vocational skills to develop a style that favors very public revelations of evidence he obtains undercover and brutally provocative accusations against . . . oh, everybody, from park guards he says have gone bad to corporate representatives and public officials. "This subdivision of the Agricultural Ministry [of Thailand]," he printed in the winter 1994/95 edition of his newsletter,

Tiger News, "currently headed by Secretary of State Niphon Phrom-phan, who made his personal fortune trading logging concessions in the eighties, is a complete enigma to all but the most devious of those among us. Positions of authority at the RFD [Royal Forestry Department] are allegedly traded to the highest bidder. Why, one might well ask, would someone wish to pay $10,000 for a Head of Department's job with a salary of less than half that amount? The answer can only lie in the gutter of corruption and graft which has been apparently endemic to the RFD for as long as most people can remember." Thailand is one of Day's favorite anvils, and he ravenously attacks both the country's government and culture for what he claims is their support of tiger farming, a practice that sends the already grandiloquent Day into his most florid spasms of ridicule. "By advocating tiger farming for greed and profit," he writes, "Thailand clearly demonstrated its own selfish disregard (and complete lack of understanding) for wild tiger conservation. The country is a disgrace and could and should do more. Will the last tourist leaving old Siam please turn out the light?"

Little wonder that so much as a mention of Mr. Day's name can unleash torrents of venom from his critics, many of whom are targets of his accusations and will fire back—though off the record—with claims against him that would be as damaging, if they were made publicly, as his claims are against them. Day joins the battle enthusiastically, seeming to thrive on the fray. At turns he will praise and then denounce a once and potentially future ally or financial backer, leaving all to wonder at his next move. None other than Peter Jackson, coauthor of *Killed for a Cure* and foremost proclaimer of the impending demise of the wild tiger, is featured prominently as an "Honorary Adviser to The Tiger Trust" in the pages of *Tiger News*, complete with nice photo and glowing biography. But when Jackson declined to join the panel at a press conference that included Day at COP-9 in Fort Lauderdale, Day grabbed the elbow of every journalist he could find to announce vindictively, "If the world relies on TRAFFIC's statistics, the wild tiger is doomed." He then proceeded into the press conference to put forth the notion that since statistics for wild tigers are so highly unreliable (a perception for which he cannot be criticized), it might indeed be possible that the animal, as of the date of that press conference, only had *two* years left before virtual extinction. That announcement—the inaccuracy of which is evident with the release of this book—and the verve with which Day put it forth then and continues to put it forth in a kind of eternal, rolling-wave knell, is archetypical of the recklessness for which he is widely condemned.

Then there's his ego. As the publisher, editor, and head writer for *Tiger News*, Day fully exploits that organ of robust self-promotion by quoting himself and reviewing his own work adoringly in the third person. "Almost one year ago," reads a representative passage, "The Tiger Trust made the intrepid and unprecedented decision to travel to the Russian Far East in an attempt to see what could be done to arrest the severe decline in the wild of the critically endangered Siberian Tiger.... Undaunted by the formidable task ahead, The Tiger Trust team set about analyzing the extent and gravity of the situation." Not satisfied to vaunt himself in a mere newsletter, Day also has written a book, *Fight for the Tiger. One Man's Fight to Save the Wild Tiger from Extinction* (London: Headline, 1995). The tome has all the subtlety of a primal scream, and it is indeed a thrilling read. Were it fiction (some readers say that's exactly where it should be shelved), it might challenge the novels of Clancy and Crichton. Alas, it is meant to be believed, which means indulging the author's hopelessly, often hilariously, myopic perspective. In its more endearing manifestations, this flaw betrays itself with inflated cloak-and-daggerism, suggestions of divine guidance, and a forest of exclamation points; in ways more dangerous, it corrupts the narrative with whopping leaps of logic, an eclipsis of the scientific community, and shrieking Sinophobia.

But the same gumption that spices Day's prose and drives him to bathe every microphone offered to him in hyperbole makes him uniquely effective when it comes to delivering the goods. Some of the most damning photographs and video footage of transgressions against tiger-specific wildlife laws, both domestic and international, have been shot with Day's eye either literally or directorially behind the view-finder—including the reel showing Chinese-produced tiger-bone plas-ters cited earlier. The flair with which Day reveals such discoveries often outstrips the power of the fully documented proof, but these trophies glimmer nonetheless.

And his endeavors go beyond mere adventures in espionage. De-spite the glory with which he reviews his own work in the Russian Far East, the value of his efforts there is acknowledged—grudgingly —by even some of his most unsympathetic enemies. Operation Amba, an antipoaching patrol based in Vladivostok and organized under the auspices of the Environment Ministry of the former Soviet Union, has proved uniquely successful in reducing the number of illegal tiger takes in that region. By Day's account, the patrol owes its very exis-tence to him. The truth is that Operation Amba receives financial support from a number of NGOs, including the German chapter of WWF and a group based in Washington, D.C., known as the Global Security Network (the executive director of which, Steve Galster, would merit his own review here were it not for the comparatively conservative profile he maintains). In his less quarrelsome moments, Day is not ungenerous in acknowledging these cocontributors, but he prefers to upstage them and that ploy has worked. Most of his critics, when pressed, will cite Operation Amba as Day's one saving grace. Even the directors of the patrol itself acknowledge early financial support from The Tiger Trust—but only early support. They have pointedly rebuked Day for subsequently welshing on financial com-mitments he continues to allege.

That's the least of Day's worries. Far more ugly is the turmoil surrounding his utilization of funds garnered through a direct-advertising campaign in which concerned donors were offered the opportunity to "adopt" tigers in Thailand by contributing to the care and feeding of individual cubs that had been orphaned in the wild when their mothers were poached. There were indeed cubs, and they were indeed cared for. But the money trail is forked, and the people responsible for actually handling the animals cannot support Day any more vigorously than the directors of Operation Amba. "What is certain," says the text of an article that broke the scandal on January 31, 1996, in the *Times* of London, "is that none of the tigers named in the 'Sponsor a Tiger in Thailand' promotions . . . received any aid from the sponsorship. . . ." Day is quoted in that same article as defending himself by saying, "I can assure I am not the villain in all this. It was never our obligation to give money to tigers in Thailand. . . ." A plug for his commitment to Operation Amba follows, after which he concludes, "Our accounts are on public record. Everything is recorded." Lawsuits have been threatened in several directions. Resolution is pending. In the meantime, Mr. Day has turned his truck toward India, assuring us all that ". . . if nothing is done the Indian tiger will be extinct in five years."

Next most visible, but by no means lower, in the NGO lineup is a U.S. group probably known more for its work with marine mammals than with tigers. Earth Island Institute is the organization whose phone number appeared at the end of the film *Free Willy* and who subsequently applied the almost one million U.S. dollars earned on that hot line to benefit Keiko, the killer whale used in the making of the movie. The group is based in San Francisco and comprises a number of suborganizations, including one called the Endangered Species Project, or ESP.

One of the codirectors of ESP is a fellow named Sam LaBudde (pronounced luh-BUD-ee), who made a splash in the late 1980s when he posed as a cook on a Panamanian fishing boat and used a video camera to tape the inadvertent slaughter of dolphins trapped and dying in the vessel's tuna nets. The footage repulsed consumers of tuna to such a degree they readily supported boycotts of the meat and called

for revised legislation, which now compels tuna fishermen to use techniques and equipment that don't threaten dolphins. The little blue
"dolphin safe" seal that graces most cans of the meat is a direct result
of that campaign, and there is little question that fewer dolphins are
dying in tuna nets today than before. The long-term consequences of
that campaign are far-reaching and complex, however, and the debate
over its effectiveness rages still. Depending upon whom you listen to,
LaBudde can be credited with either the salvation or the eventual
extinction of dolphins. But that is a subject for a different book.

In the early '90s LaBudde enlarged his scope, via ESP, to include other animals and broader regions. The plight of the tiger had
long since become prominent, and it fell readily within his purview.
Relying once again on techniques that had served him well in the
past, he collaborated with Mike Day and others to take aim through
the lens of a video camera and collect secretly taped footage of transgressions involving trade in tigers and their derivatives. To a large
degree, his attentions focused on the island nation of Taiwan.

"Taiwan is *the*—capital letters—*the* world's premier market for
wildlife products from endangered species," LaBudde proclaimed as
early as 1992. "It's the terminus for many, if not most, of the tigers
poached throughout Asia." He was by no means alone in making those
accusations, and Taiwan, in fact, subsequently found itself at the eye
of conservation's most damaging political hurricane—an incident to
be looked at shortly. But LaBudde certainly singled himself out as the
most observable of Taiwan's critics by traveling to the island in 1992
and holding a series of press conferences in conjunction with a British
NGO known as the Environmental Investigation Agency. In front of
stunned members of the country's media, LaBudde unspooled videotape of flagrant violations of Taiwan's domestic wildlife trade laws,
including shots of live tigers—which do not occur naturally on the
island—pacing in cages at what LaBudde identified as a breeding
farm. Subsequent footage included evidence to indicate the animals
were being butchered for sale, a practice that had been both legal and

open in Taiwan until the late 1980s but that was incontestably forbidden by the time LaBudde said the videos had been shot. Claims of such lingering transgressions had been made already by numerous NGOs, but never with such moxie, such immediate evidence, or such specific objectives; LaBudde ended his press conferences by announcing his intentions to launch an international boycott of all goods manufactured in Taiwan, and he followed through by returning to the States and eventually placing full-page ads in newspapers around the country calling for just those measures.

Sam LaBudde is clever, well-read, and blindingly quick of thought. Where Mike Day is eloquent, LaBudde is direct. Where Day is dapper, LaBudde is rugged. Despite their differences in packaging and a few divergent philosophies, the two men are widely regarded as equals in energy, even though Day concentrates on tigers while LaBudde covers many animals. Day has been described as Sam LaBudde with an English accent, LaBudde as a cowboy version of Michael Day. In other words, LaBudde lacks patience, and his mental acuity gets the better of him frequently. The simplest of questions at a press conference evokes disdainful lecturettes from him when he's in a good mood, snide quips when he's not. He also suffers from an unfortunate habit of allowing himself to be profiled in *Atlantic Monthly* (July '89 and November '94) by Kenneth Brower, who is the son of David Brower, the celebrated and sometimes vilified "arch-druid" of environmentalism who founded Earth Island Institute. Regardless of how well written or researched Brower's articles may be, their motives and objectivity are hopelessly discounted by the relationship between the author and his subject. (In the interest of full disclosure: Mr. LaBudde also allowed himself to be profiled in the February '94 issue of *Penthouse* by none other than Cory J Meacham—an article LaBudde subsequently appraised very publicly at COP-9 in Fort Lauderdale as "a piece of shit.") However, not unlike with Mr. Day, LaBudde's image-management faux pas can be considered, in large part, nothing more than the fallout of operating at such high RPM. His snappish wit pleases his advocates as deeply as it disgusts his adversaries, and his impatience flings him almost recklessly into his work. As a result, the scope and depth of his investigations are unparalleled. In 1991 he received one of the six Goldman prizes presented each year to people whose commitment to the environment stands out. The prizes, bestowed by a private organization, carry both a cash award and prestige well beyond the boundaries of the NGO community. Then, three years later, the thirty-eight-year-old LaBudde was selected as one of fifty "promising young leaders" by *Time* magazine.

At COP-9 LaBudde debuted ESP's latest diggings in a report titled *Crime against Nature: Organized Crime and the Illegal Wildlife Trade*, a document that makes TRAFFIC's *Killed for a Cure* look downright bashful by comparison. Naming names and printing pictures of the alleged perpetrators, *Crime against Nature* strives to link mafiosi around the world—particularly drug lords—into a coordinated network of poachers and smugglers of endangered species, including tigers. Some of the evidence is compelling, some of it is tenuous, all of it is provocative and presented beneath an inflammatory glaze. "Unless the international community is ready to align its actions with its rhetoric about global priorities in the post–Cold War era," the introduction reads, "there may not be time to avert an impending ecological calamity. While the United Nations has increased its role in peacekeeping missions and nuclear disarmament, the UN Convention on International Trade in Endangered Species (CITES) has been left out of the new world order."

Crime against Nature found its audience, catching even the attention of certain members of the scientific community. But its thesis is only modestly supported by governmental sectors. "We don't seize or detect a large quantity of drugs in the shipments we've been involved with," says Frank Shoemaker, an assistant regional director with the U.S. Fish and Wildlife Service who formerly supervised investigations for the service's Division of Law Enforcement. "Occasionally it happens, but it's not something we routinely see." Not wanting to discount the idea completely, Shoemaker notes that Interpol—the international law enforcement cooperative—has formed a working group to investigate the link between organized crime and wildlife trade. "But it's more of a general statement," he concludes. "If they're smuggling drugs, there's a good chance they're smuggling wildlife or anything else that's normally smuggled." Changing tack, he inquires, "What's the definition of organized? Two people talk. That's organized."

Criticism from across the Atlantic is more pointed. "I'm not quite sure this is a real picture," says Valentin Ilyashenko of the Russian Federation's Ministry of Protection of Environment and Natural Resources (who also happens to be that government's deputy head of CITES Management Authority). His observation is literal, not metaphorical. He points to a photograph in *Crime against Nature* that indeed appears to have been doctored. Ilyashenko, himself listed as a source in the brochure, shrugs his lips and suggests, "Maybe it's some kind of combination."

⌐⌐

Having touched on Taiwan with plans to feel further, we now look briefly at a third NGO that also is well known for its undercover wildlife investigations in that country. Earthtrust is headquartered in Hawaii but has organized much of the surveillance conducted in Taiwan. Two Earthtrust associates, a husband-and-wife team, figure prominently into the histories of joint efforts coordinated on the island with other NGOs, including TRAFFIC, The Tiger Trust, and ESP. Distinctive among the qualifications of this pair are their dual heritage and polyglotism: The husband, Keith Highley, is Caucasian; his wife, Suzie, is Chinese; both speak fluent Mandarin.

After Sam LaBudde held his press conferences in 1992, perpetrators of wildlife crimes in Taiwan moved deeply underground, avoiding at all costs foreigners who looked or sounded even remotely like they might not appreciate the uses to which some Asian practices put the derivatives of certain animals. As a consequence, surveillance turned all but impossible for those who could not blend in. "The fact that these people who are trying to be eco-detectives are all white is just ludicrous," says Judy Mills. "I'm sorry. It's laughable. They're not going to get into the inner circles. They're not going to understand what's going on." Those observations are reinforced by Mills's subordinate, Dau-Jye Lu, who manages TRAFFIC's office in Taipei. "All the Chinese pharmacists in Taiwan are sensitive to foreigners and strangers now," he says. "It's almost impossible to conduct a survey."

To be sure, the Highleys are not the only conservationists capable of overcoming these cultural barriers. A woman named Rebecca Chen, for example, has become something of a legend for the undercover wildlife work she has conducted among citizens of Taiwan, her home country. Also, as with Lu, TRAFFIC's Taipei office has often employed staff of native extraction. Keith Highley and his wife simply serve as suitable representatives of a transition that has become a trend by necessity.

And their style includes more than just unique ancestry and language skills. Highley is peculiar among the eco-detective crowd for his civility. He is quiet, sensible, measured, and courteous. He seeks to defuse confrontation rather than foster it. "I'm tired of threatening," he observes. Perhaps so, but his commitment to his cause is no less sincere than LaBudde's or Day's. When pressed, he elevates the volume and speed of his arguments sufficiently to reveal roots of passion. But he labors to be cooperative, allowing himself to be interrupted more frequently than he interrupts. Such decorum would be nothing more than a charming personal attribute were it not for the access it affords him. Highley holds the singular honor of remaining persona grata in almost every arena of tiger conservation—including, no less, the scientific realms. In 1992 Highley participated in a Sumatran tiger PHVA organized and conducted in Indonesia by none other than AZA and CBSG. It may be common to see investigative NGOs list their names beside one another, just as it is common to see CBSG listed beside AZA, but to see Earthtrust listed among the participants at a PHVA is nothing short of a coup d'état. Sam LaBudde's request to participate would have been rejected; Mike Day's would have been set aflame. Highley's ability to straddle the gap not only among progressive NGOs but also between those NGOs and the scientific community (the credit belongs to him as much or more than to Earthtrust) is equally as powerful and significant as Ron Tilson's dual presence in an SSC and an SSP. Highley, however, has achieved his gains through finesse, not might, and his example is resonating globally.

CHAPTER 7

~

The Pot and
the Kettle

*J*UST AS INDEPENDENT SCIENTIFIC FORCES HAVE CONSPIRED to make Indonesia a uniquely important biological laboratory for the tiger, independent bureaucratic, cultural, and economic forces have collided on Taiwan to render it equally extraordinary in terms of gaining insight into the tiger's political dilemma. The following sketch—an aggressive attempt to compress decades of complicated Asian history into sentences—will offer little to sinologists, but it will at least introduce the political elements germane to the tiger.

The relationship between the Republic of China (aka Taiwan) and the *People's* Republic of China (the mainland) is one of the most curious political arrangements in modern history. When Mao took over the mainland in 1949, Chiang Kai-shek and his nationalist colleagues decamped—most say "fled"—to what then was China's province of Taiwan; a corollary would be to see the president of the United States reestablish his base of power in Hawaii after a violent uprising in Washington, D.C. From that time on, Chiang and his successors operated the island strictly under their nationalist rule, steadfastly proclaiming their intentions to "recover" the mainland, until they saw fit to lift martial law from the island in 1987 and allow a lively democracy to take hold. Beijing has insisted throughout that Taiwan remains a legitimate, if uncooperative, province of the mainland, and it also looks forward to "recovery," though under terms quite different from those of the nationalists.

Tensions were severe for decades following the Communist Revolution and led to a number of deadly skirmishes across the Taiwan Strait. During that time the United States and a host of other democratic countries uniformly supported Taiwan in a stand against communism. However, with the passage of time, the world realized the mainland wasn't going away, and it certainly wasn't getting any smaller in terms of land mass, population, or political gravity. A nation, especially an economy, of more than a billion people simply could not be ignored, particularly during an era of cold war with that other communist behemoth directly to China's west. On behalf of the U.S., first Richard Nixon then Jimmy Carter shifted formal loyalties from Taiwan to the mainland, closing an embassy in the former as a condition of opening one in the latter. There was, after all, but a single China, Beijing explained, so there would be but a single embassy.

The transfer was viewed by many as politically indiscreet, even in the U.S., but the tangible results were largely inconsequential so far as any impact on Taiwan could be detected. U.S. citizens still traveled freely to and from the island state, developing a long and mutually lucrative tradition of economic investment. Dollars, it seemed, were more popular than embassies. Indeed, commerce also flourished not only between the newly legitimized mainland China and its fresh allies, but even between the mainland and Taiwan itself despite the vigor with which the governments of both "countries" continued to denounce one another in the strictest diplomatic terminology. By the mid-1990s active trade between the two republics was estimated to exceed U.S. $1 billion per month, and even travel between island and mainland—for citizens as well as migratory foreigners—had become common.

But smoldering fires flared in 1995 when President Lee of

Taiwan received permission from the U.S. to attend his 1995 class reunion at Cornell University. From the day the U.S. embassy in Taiwan had been closed until the day Lee arrived to attend the reunion, no head of state from the island nation had so much as set foot on U.S. soil—a consequence of Beijing's enforcement of the one-China policy. (Lee himself had been confined ignominiously to the cabin of his airplane during a fuel stop in Hawaii en route to South America just a year before his trip to Cornell.) Beijing expressed its hot displeasure to Washington for such indiscreet hospitality by recalling its envoy and repelling America's incoming ambassador.

Were it not for the considerable military might poised in each republic toward the other, this détente between Taiwan and the mainland would amount to little more than a diplomatic snit. But there is indeed considerable might, and the snit turned grim when the mainland started lobbing missiles into the waters just a few miles off the coast of Taiwan shortly after Lee's visa to the U.S. came through. The maneuvers were dubbed "technical tests" by Beijing, and the warheads in the missiles were dummies, but nobody, anywhere, doubted what actually was being tested by the saber rattling. In particular the U.S. got the message and eventually sent the aircraft carrier *Nimitz* steaming protectively into the strait.

The mainland's glow had dimmed for many since the Tiananmen Square suppression of 1989 and a commensurate increase in political affection for Taiwan had taken its place. The island was quickly moving toward its first fully free election in March '96—the first instance in Asia's five-thousand-year history where Chinese people would select their own leader—which compelled the rest of the free world to offer at least fraternal support. Political wrangling in preparation for the election complicated the discord between the two republics exponentially and forced a global reevaluation of the choices made by Presidents Nixon and Carter. Finally, Beijing magnified its oppressive image just weeks after Lee's soiree at Cornell by arresting

Harry Wu, a U.S. citizen entering China under a valid U.S. passport and a valid mainland visa. Wu had embarrassed the mainland with secret videotapes of opprobrious prison-labor practices he'd made during earlier visits. Beijing charged him with espionage, an offense punishable by death. (Environmental NGOs considering further undercover work in mainland China will want to make a note of this.) Not since the Communist Revolution itself had tensions between China and the West been so strained.

Fortunately, good sense prevailed. Wu was tried, convicted, sentenced to a fifteen-year suspended jail term, and sent home to California. Taiwan went ahead with its election and installed Lee as the popular choice as well as the (formerly) political appointee. Beijing grounded its missiles, politely congratulated Lee on his victory, dispatched its envoy to Washington, and welcomed the U.S. ambassador coming the other way. Political harumphing resumed on both sides of the strait. Multilateral commerce continued unmolested. Long-term resolution to the discord between the Chinas awaits another day.

⌇

While the definition of "China" remains blurry, in fact it is clear diplomatically, and nowhere does diplomacy play bigger than at the United Nations. When Chiang Kai-shek relocated to Taiwan at the end of the Communist Revolution, he took with him his seat at the UN, which he and his nationalist successors occupied until 1971. In that year, the fallout of the redirection of interests from Taipei to Beijing included the loss of the UN seat to Beijing; one China, one embassy, one seat at the UN. Taiwan, petitioning as the "Republic of China," has continuously solicited representation in the UN since that time, but Beijing has made it continuously clear that they, and only they, shall sit behind any placard that says "China" when it comes time to negotiate at the global level. The punch line is this: Since all

CITES signatory nations must be members of the UN, Taiwan—the thirteenth most robust economy in all the world—is not eligible to become a signatory to CITES.

Were it not for two additional civic attributes of the island, that circumstance would be of little consequence to the wild tiger: Traditional Chinese medicine remains extensively popular in Taiwan, and per capita prosperity there is among the highest in the hemisphere— which enables the inhabitants to pursue the first attribute even if the ingredients are rare and expensive. These two attributes are shared by other states in the region, but only Taiwan among them is both a CITES outsider and not welcome to join. Into this dry powder introduce a few sparky foreign NGOs looking to expose the link between traditional Chinese medicine and the decline of the wild tiger, and you have all the fixings for a one-of-a-kind eco-political explosion, the fallout from which might cause mutations no one is capable of predicting. When Sam LaBudde rolled tape in Taipei, all the world turned to watch and shake its collective finger. Such transgressions must not be countenanced, everyone agreed. . . . Transgressions against what? Against CITES? Not only do CITES regulations not apply in Taiwan, they can't. Taiwan is not allowed to let them apply. To its ironic credit, the government of Taiwan took steps unilaterally to regulate domestic commerce in endangered species, and in 1989 it passed a comprehensive package of wildlife-trade legislation modeled closely on the guidelines set forth in CITES. It is those domestic laws, and only those laws, that are clearly violated in every frame of LaBudde's video.

A pause for perspective. As pointed out earlier, environmental NGOs are often less interested in political protocol than in results. They are concerned by the consumption they observe, regardless of what laws do or do not regulate it, and they will bring to bear on the consumers whatever forces are available through whatever actions are necessary. The fact that CITES does not officially apply to Taiwan is of secondary significance to many NGOs. As far as they are concerned, it *should* apply, and something like its moral equivalent already does. If domestic laws are the heaviest hammer available to be swung, fine. Any weapon in a war. But even Sam LaBudde moved quickly beyond the domestic bailiwick of Taiwan's violations by calling for an international boycott. And while NGO surveillance has focused on numerous other tiger-consuming nations in Asia, the combined influences of demand, money, and relative freedom from regulation produced a per capita vortex for tiger derivatives on Taiwan that even the government of that republic itself came to acknowledge, as we are about to see. Unfortunately, that vortex also swept in the rest of the world's attention, including that of the CITES secretariat and of the U.S. Department of the Interior.

Working partly out of an environmental momentum generated during the 1992 presidential campaign and partly at the behest of adamant NGOs, the Clinton administration pursued the implementation of a recondite piece of U.S. maritime law known as the Pelly Amendment, through which wildlife-trade sanctions can be enacted against any country that is deemed by the U.S. to be undermining an international conservation agreement. Early in the first Clinton term, U.S. Secretary of the Interior Bruce Babbitt initiated the implementation of the Pelly Amendment against five national entities based primarily on NGO-derived evidence of wildlife-trade practices egregiously out of line with the granddaddy of all international conservation agreements: CITES. The five implicatees were Southern Yemen, Hong Kong, mainland China, South Korea, and Taiwan. The first three were already parties to CITES, the fourth was being ushered in, the last was not eligible.

The initiation of the Pelly Amendment was only an informal first step—an alert, of sorts—followed by a grace period of several months during which the five implicatees were given opportunities to avoid the second step of formal Pelly certification by demonstrating their willingness to align themselves more precisely with CITES. At the end of the grace period, all five were reevaluated. Only mainland

China and Taiwan were subsequently certified; the other three passed muster. A second grace period ensued, followed by secondary reevaluations in early 1994. In the summer of that year, for the first time in history, trade sanctions authorized via the Pelly Amendment were enacted by the signature of the president of the United States.

But only against Taiwan. When the ninth Conference of the Parties to CITES convened in Fort Lauderdale later that year, the following unique scenario commenced: Bruce Babbitt, delivering the keynote address to the assembled delegates, NGO representatives, and press, explained how "in the history of CITES, this was the first time that trade sanctions have been imposed by a member state." Specifying the connection between the decline of the wild tiger and traditional Chinese medicine, Babbitt continued in his CITES-rich vernacular to observe, "These sanctions, taken unilaterally by a member nation [the U.S.] but within the context of CITES support, are the kinds of enforcement actions that I believe are necessary for all of us to consider for the long-range success of our efforts." Taiwan was left discreetly unnamed in Babbitt's speech, but a mention of "the responsible officials in Taipei" averted any ambiguity regarding who had been sanctioned.

In Taipei is exactly where those officials remained, conveniently unwelcome at the very ceremony where Babbitt had cited them. A press corps from Taiwan was present in force, however, and when Babbitt stepped from the podium he was swarmed by its members.

"Can you tell us the status and the progress of the further review that you said would take place by the end of the year?" one reporter asked, referring to a promised postimplementation assessment of Taiwan by the U.S.

"We will be consulting with the CITES secretariat about the appropriate form of review," Babbitt responded. "We have, in the past, found it to be very effective to have reviews carried out in cooperation with the CITES secretariat. So we will consult with the secretary general."

"Then it wasn't a unilateral decision?" came the next question, challenging Babbitt with words from the address he had just completed.

"Yes," the secretary defended his position.

"But now you have to consult with CITES?"

"It is not required, but I think it is very important."

"Taiwan is not a party to CITES."

"I understand."

"So how will you conduct that kind of consultation?"

There was a pause, after which the secretary responded, "We have done it in the past, and we will continue to do it in the future."

He answered one other unrelated question before leaving the hall.

⤚

No one argues that Taiwan might have been innocent of the transgressions for which the Pelly sanctions were invoked, not even the citizens of Taiwan who attended COP-9 as NGO representatives—the only credentials through which they could gain access other than a press pass. Environmental awareness is growing rapidly in Asia, particularly among the younger generations, and more than a few inhabitants of the region welcome the scrutiny that leads to stricter ecological standards. "I'd like to talk more with other NGOs outside of Taiwan," says Dr. Hsiao-Wei Yuan, spokeswoman for SWAN International, Taiwan's foremost environmental NGO. After noting that some of the techniques employed thus far in Taiwan by outside NGOs might be more effective if tempered a bit ("I can feel people's anger," she cautions), Yuan states, "I'd like to see what we can do, work together, to monitor our government and push them to do a better job in wildlife conservation. There's been a lot of progress, but I still think they have a lot of room for improvement."

In the complex case of Taiwan, however, this support does not extend to the Pelly Amendment. Whatever gains accrued to the U.S.

and CITES through the sanctions were diluted by, perhaps even lost to, political fallout. "I think it's really unfair," says Yuan, changing tack to verbalize the sentiments of her muzzled nation. "That's the one thing I feel kind of angry about. Conservation is related too much to politics. That's the part I really hate."

While the absolution of Hong Kong, Southern Yemen, and South Korea could be overlooked by Taiwan, amnesty from Pelly for mainland China smacked of favor. How, possibly, Taiwan wanted to know, could a country of more than a billion people reverse itself so completely in a matter of months as to diametrically outperform a population only one one-hundredth its size and operating under precisely the same cultural dicta? Per capita income discrepancies notwithstanding, Taiwan could barely contain its amazement that the mainland had not, at the very least, been treated equally. "If they want to have punishment," says Yuan, referring to the U.S. government, "then both mainland China and Taiwan. I think we were equally bad."

Not so, says Brooks Yeager, Deputy Assistant Secretary for Policy in the U.S. Department of the Interior (under which jurisdiction the Pelly Amendment falls). "At the time of the decision, the government of the People's Republic of China had made some fairly strenuous efforts to clamp down on the trade," he observes. "And it was an intention on their part to continue to do so. We weren't similarly convinced that strenuous efforts had been made by the officials in Taipei." Marshall Jones, former chief of the U.S. office of CITES Management Authority, supplies details: "A lot of people went to jail [in mainland China] as a result of decisions made in early '93 to crack down on the trade. They also consolidated their stockpiles. Stockpiles that had been dispersed in factories and in shops, as many as they could get their hands on, were moved into eight provincial centers. They've got an accounting. I've personally been to two of these and have seen the stocks, where they are under lock and key. In Taiwan, all the rhino horn and tiger bone, especially rhino horn, is in private ownership. Dispersed. They can't even find it. They had a registration process that theoretically was the way to control it, except when we dug into it we found out there was absolutely no punishment in the law, no provision to punish anyone who hadn't registered."

Such clarity between these two Chinese situations would be impressive if it were durable. Within just a few months of Jones's personal inspection of the mainland's stockpiles (and following COP-9), however, tiger-bone wine was once again readily available in mainland China. It was openly for sale at the duty-free counter of the international terminal of Beijing's airport, and numerous travelers were observed casually carrying the contraband onto their flights—at the other end of which customs officials were as likely as not to miss the transgression. Those passengers deplaning in Vladivostok needed look no farther than the open-air market on the airport steps to find tiger-bone plasters, imported from mainland China, for sale.

In Taiwan, actions taken by the government seem to validate Jones's assessment. Just days before COP-9 convened, the Council of Agriculture in Taipei responded to the Pelly sanctions by issuing a set of amendments to its 1989 wildlife-trade legislation, stipulating specific prison terms and monetary fines for violators. "I saw the text of the amendments in draft," Brooks Yeager said at the conference, "and I think that they are a significant step." His enthusiasm, however, went no further. "The mere fact of having passed a set of amendments is not, on the face of it, evidence that enormous progress has been made." Despite such circumspection, the amendments apparently hit their mark. On June 30, 1995, President Clinton announced the revocation of the Pelly Amendment sanctions against Taiwan, and on September 11 of the following year Taiwan was decertified altogether.

Regardless of whatever legislative brinkmanship prevailed in Taiwan's battle to convince Washington of its commitment to control domestic wildlife trade, the Pelly Amendment itself must be kept in perspective. For all the attention they drew as tools of punishment within the context of CITES, the sanctions that were implemented against Taiwan amounted to little more than a drop in an economic ocean. The scope of both the Pelly Amendment and CITES is limited to the arena of wildlife, so only the trade of wildlife can be sanctioned thereunder. Computers, TVs, toys, and so forth, do not qualify, and such goods continued to flow without delay across the Pacific before, during, and after the Pelly sanctioning process. Only animals and their derivatives were stopped, mustering a total cost to Taiwan of just over U.S. $20 million annually—hardly enough to threaten the country's status as the United States' sixth-largest trading partner, a ranking achieved through some U.S. $40 billion in bilateral commerce each year. Many industries in both countries, in fact, remained unaware that sanctions of any such kind ever were launched, so meager was the impact of Pelly. In spite of their diminutive price tag, however, the sanctions carried a blistering diplomatic sting, particularly in contrast to the almost simultaneous renewal by the U.S. of MFN trading status with the mainland, and a concurrent relaxation of the seventeen-year-old trade embargo against a revivified Vietnam. The only logical explanation for singling Taiwan out with such a slap, many posited (in many nations), was the island's convenient lack of membership in the UN.

Within the global eco-political community, the Pelly slap has been touted as a knockdown punch, especially by the deliverer. But the umph behind the impact came largely from NGO evidence, and even the NGOs are now wondering at the magnitude of their victory. "Taiwan has been a scapegoat," says TRAFFIC's Judy Mills. "Everyone focused in on Taiwan because TRAFFIC International went in there [first] and did a study that showed Taiwan was consuming a lot of rhino horn and tiger bone. But all that did was take focus off of other countries. . . . Japan, for instance, is sitting back and just breathing easy because Taiwan is taking all the heat. This is a global problem. This is a problem that exists wherever there are people devoted to the use of ancient traditional Chinese medicines, and those people are everywhere."

Indeed, to say simply that traditional Chinese medicine is administered widely throughout Asia grossly understates its availability. More than twelve thousand traditional pharmacists are registered to do business on the island of Taiwan alone, and the practice is so uniform that a pharmacist's shop in Taipei is indistinguishable from one in Beijing, Saigon, Seoul, Bangkok, Tokyo, Hong Kong, or even those in the Chinatowns of San Francisco, London, Montreal, Brussels, New York. . . . Faith among Asians remains strong, including devotees in the world's most progressive countries. Pregnant women of strict Asian heritage, for example, seek out traditional pharmacists as part of an overall obstetrics program that is otherwise indistinguishable from those of their modern Western neighbors. The appetite for prescriptions that might include components from endangered animals is massive, persistent, and decentralized. Illustrating that fact, Mills offers a comment that folds the political conundrum of Taiwan, CITES, and the Pelly Amendment back on itself yet again. "I believe that possibly the greatest consumer of endangered species as medicines in the world is North America, and probably the United States."

Who? Did she say the U.S.? Is Mills suggesting that the mirror be turned back on the world's foremost accuser?

She is, and she is not alone. More significantly, an analysis of her accusation reveals international policy inequities so curious that they preempt the question of whether or not she and her coaccusers are even right. Logistically, all the elements necessary to support her claims are present: There is clearly a market for traditional Chinese medicinals in North America. "We have some of the largest, wealthiest Asian populations in the world," observes Mills, a U.S. citizen. Indeed, more than seven million Asians live in the U.S., with a median annual income per family of over U.S. $40,000. And the U.S. is a string bag when it comes to guarding its borders. A national perimeter of over thirteen thousand kilometers (not including Alaska and Hawaii) presents ample opportunity for anyone so inclined to come or go freely via land, air, or sea. Such illicit traffic is readily demonstrated not only by the freeway speed of drug dealings into and out of the country, but also by the inability of dedicated border patrols to stanch the flow of illegal immigrants literally flocking through checkpoints south of San Diego. Even at its formal ports of entry, the U.S. is no better staffed to handle physical inspection of incoming goods than any other developed country. "We only have 220 agents and eighty wildlife inspectors in the U.S.," observes Frank Shoemaker. "And that includes Alaska and Hawaii." Divide that shortage by the volume of incoming material, and Victoria Harbor starts to look manageable. "Just in the port of Newark, New Jersey," Shoemaker points out, "if we tried to open every container coming into the U.S. and do 100 percent inspection, we'd have trade backed up forever. We simply do not have the personpower, nor ever did we have it, to sufficiently inspect everything that comes in."

Motive and opportunity for traffic in Chinese medicinals, then, are clearly present in the United States. But those two factors alone do not a crime perpetrate. Evidence must be found to support Mills's charges. In light of the logistical complications Mr. Shoemaker has so discouragingly delineated, however, it is no surprise to learn that the evidence he and his colleagues have been able to seize in executing their interdictive authority at the international borders is all but worthless in terms of analyzing the national situation. "If it's detected it's seized," he says with a shrug. "We're not seeing a trend." So where is the proof to support an accusation that the U.S. is a major consumer, perhaps *the* major consumer, of traditional Chinese medicines containing derivatives of endangered animals? It's in precisely the same place where it's found in all the other consuming nations: on the shelves of traditional Chinese pharmacists. From the Golden Gate to the 59th Street bridge and in dozens, if not hundreds, of cities in between, Chinese pharmacists are catering to the traditional tastes of what is perhaps the most prosperous customer base their product enjoys in all the world. How do we know? The same way we know about similar products in other countries: through the NGOs. "We've gone to Asian markets in San Francisco, Honolulu, Los Angeles, New York . . . and it's there," confirms Andrea Gaski, director of research for TRAFFIC USA. The States, it seems, have a bit of domestic house-keeping to take care of. . . .

Oh, but it is not nearly that simple. North America's newly dis-covered prominence among tiger-consuming nations has revealed an unpleasant little detail of U.S. domestic wildlife law that threatens to undermine every eco-centric aspersion—let alone every sanction—the country dares to cast. "It's not contraband in the U.S.," says Shoemaker. Another double take. *Not* contraband? Meaning, perhaps, that it's perfectly legal to possess, display, and even sell or buy pieces and parts of endangered animals—*tigers?*—on the streets of the United States? "Right," Shoemaker drones, reaching for a current copy of the U.S. Code of Federal Regulations. "Contraband, for example," he illustrates while flipping to section 17 of title 50, "is an illegal drug. The law prevents you from possessing an illegal drug." He spins the heavy binder and invites inspection of the regulations that implement the U.S. Endangered Species Act. "But you *can* possess a whole tiger." Were that not the case, he observes, every circus and zoo in the coun-try would be in violation of the law. Yes, certain permits are required, but we shall see in a moment how even that process fails to regulate Asian medicinals. There is no federal law that preemptively restricts the possession or exchange of the parts or products of endangered species in the United States of America. "Possession is not a violation," Shoemaker repeats. "And you can sell it in intrastate commerce." Asked, then, just what the hell something like a tiger-bone plaster *is*, vis-à-vis U.S. domestic federal law, Shoemaker shrugs and says, "It's a product whose importation is prohibited."

That's a key word, importation. As in every other CITES sig-natory nation, all the animals and derivatives listed in the CITES appendices fall subject to strict control at the international borders of the U.S. Tiger-bone plasters can be seized at the port of Newark, New Jersey, because at that point, but only at that point, the Endangered Species Act empowers the attending enforcement personnel to seize that item under the subscripted jurisdiction of CITES. "This is why it's extremely important for our agency to make the detection at the time of import," Shoemaker says. Part of the problem, he explains, involves what many U.S. citizens consider to be their country's most valuable legal attribute. "We don't have the authority to go into every Asian section of town and say, 'I want to inventory everything you have in your store,'" Shoemaker notes. "Under what legal authority? The U.S. Constitution protects you from unreasonable searches and seizures." Since the material in question is not contraband, such a search would not be reasonable.

Andrea Gaski offers a refinement on this point. "Under the Constitution, as I understand it, the federal government doesn't have the power to restrict the sale and possession of something unless it has been proven to be either detrimental or not safe for the general population." No such proof exists for the animal matter within Asian medicinals (yet), so there is no public-safety basis—likely to supply the most immediate prohibition—on which to proceed. "If we can't even ban the sale of automatic weapons in the U.S.," Gaski observes, "how can we ban the sale of tiger bone?"

At the risk of a paralyzing glance at the Medusa of parafederal legislation, we must note that there are, theoretically, secondary legal measures through which to pursue the seizure of endangered species and their derivatives inside the U.S. Each state, for example, can legislate individually regarding what can and cannot move across its borders and countertops; California features just such laws, prohibiting the tiger by name. Aspects of this lower-level legislation also can fortify portions of the federal code. "If an animal was taken or imported or exported in violation of other state, federal, or foreign laws," notes Carol Lee Carson, "that would be covered by the Lacey Act." To avoid reaching for another binder of federal code, she summarizes: If anything connected with the death or movement of the animal in question, and/or of its derivatives, violated any law *anywhere*, that animal or derivative can be seized under a provision of U.S. law called the Lacey Act regardless of where the item is found.

Well, here is the magic wand, it would seem. Killing tigers is about as illegal as it gets in all but one of the animal's range countries, isn't it? (Yes.) Even more directly, didn't we just hear that the Endangered Species Act makes the importation of tiger stuff illegal at all U.S. international borders? (We did.) And since America is not a range territory for the tiger, can we not presume that everything in the U.S. made from a tiger must have come across one of the country's international borders at some point? (Sure—to preserve the mood, let us forget temporarily the existence of zoos, circuses, and Las Vegas.) All right, then. By extension, the Lacey Act *always* applies. Does it not?

Carson kills the fantasy. "No. You've got to prove when it was imported." Reminding us that CITES itself is barely two decades old, she adds, "It had to be imported after 1973."

The chronological aspect of this observation is troublesome enough, but the word Carson stresses is *prove*. "The legal trail has to be proved in a way that is upholdable in a court of law," she elaborates. "To find a shipment [of medicinals] in a store and be able to trace back, that likelihood is very, very minute." Here, once again, is the demon of enforcement. Who cares what the ink on the paper in the binders says? If you can't make it stick, the animals go away. "And there are so many subtleties and so many details in the law," Carson notes, shaking her head. "Then, each October, it's updated."

Andrea Gaski commiserates on the subject of proof, then circles back to wipe out any lingering hope of a chronological remedy. "The onus is on the government to prove [the medicinals] were illegally taken or illegally imported or illegally transported across state lines, and it's almost impossible to do that with these products because there's no way to determine age." Very little at all, in fact, can be determined about Asian medicinals when it comes to tiger derivatives, although it's not for lack of trying. We shall investigate such efforts shortly.

So what good are these laws? Has anything, ever, been seized inside the U.S. international borders under the authority of either the Lacey Act or the Endangered Species Act? Certainly, and it would be reckless to overlook the benefits that accrue to exotic wildlife, both domestic and foreign, through U.S. legislation. "Oh, we've done it," Carson attests. "We had a very large case in Pennsylvania where we traced back an individual's history of smuggling in endangered species. That case produced some of the largest fines I've ever gotten, and the longest jail time—over two years. He was definitely paying for his crimes." The difference, she explains, is the nature of the product. The Pennsylvania case involved hunting trophies—skins, horns, heads, and the like—big, noticeable chunks of animal that tend to make lasting impressions on owners, traders, park rangers, and customs agents. Small, processed, uniform packets of ageless, formless, anonymous substances do not. In what many will consider a cruel irony, the traceability of big-game trophies is fortified in the U.S. through the issuance of permits to the hunters. "When we issue a permit for something listed in CITES," says Carson, "it has to be determined that it is not being imported for commercial purposes." In other words, the owner/importer cannot immediately turn around and sell the trophy. If he does, there will be clear, traceable evidence of the violation, per the terms of the permit. The only legitimate reason for possession or importation of a big-game trophy in the eyes of the Fish and Wildlife Service, therefore, is so the hunter can keep what he has personally killed.

In a still sharper splinter of irony, this licensing idiosyncrasy points up an aspect of U.S. domestic law that is, in fact, stronger than that of many other CITES party nations. The legality of killing an animal is determined by the laws in force in the country where the take occurs and when it occurs. Killing an elephant for sport in Kenya, for example, is illegal (currently). But if the pachyderm strolls across the border into Tanzania—as many do—it can be shot quite legally—as many are—so long as the hunter doing the shooting has a valid license issued by the government of Tanzania. If that hunter lives in Tanzania, he can take the carcass home and do whatever he likes with it. But if he's from a foreign country, he's going to need to have all his CITES paperwork in order before crossing the border of any party nation—including Tanzania. As he leaves that country, one of the CITES criterion he will need to have satisfied includes, by extension, the approbation of the Tanzanian CITES Scientific Authority that the death of the elephant he shot has in no way endangered—is a so-called "nondetriment" to—the long-term survivability of the species. (Without this approbation, the license to shoot the elephant would not have been issued to a foreigner in the first place, lest Tanzania risk its status as a CITES signatory.) If the hunter is a U.S. citizen heading back to the States, he will have to present to U.S. customs a permit issued by the Fish and Wildlife Service before the inspectors will allow him to import his trophy. But before that permit can be issued, according to provisions in the U.S. Endangered Species Act, the Fish and Wildlife Service will need to be satisfied that the death of the elephant in fact enhanced the long-term survivability of the species. "Our domestic legislation is the stricter of the two," Carson notes. Then, begging her own question, she asks, "How can hunting trophies be considered enhancement?" We shall soon see just how, including how some people think it might be applied to tigers as well as to elephants.

Despite whatever enforcement successes the U.S. can claim when it comes to big-game trophies, Asian medicinals made from the derivatives of endangered animals remain unseizable in that country due to their lack of traceability under eccentricities of domestic law. (Japan is another First World CITES signatory with lax domestic legislation, it is worth noting. But Japan doesn't squawk about similar deficiencies elsewhere.) The following strange reality, therefore, survives: When Sam LaBudde or Michael Day or Keith Highley walk the streets of Taipei or Beijing or Seoul or even London, focusing their hidden video cameras on shelves filled with tiger-bone products or coaxing reluctant shopkeepers to reveal hidden stockpiles of the bones, they can legitimately ring alarm bells. Laws are being broken. The goods can be seized. But when LaBudde or Day or Highley refocus their cameras on exactly the same products available on shelves in the United States, there is no bell to ring. No law is being broken—at least not in any way that's even close to being provable in court. Among the countries identified by TRAFFIC as tiger-bone-consuming nations, the United States stands legally impotent.

CHAPTER 8

⟳

A Bone
Is a Bone
Is a Bone

WHILE THE USE OF ANIMALS AS MEDICINE has a long and respected heritage among Asians, Western minds are quick to reject the practice as mumbo jumbo. Many aspects of traditional Chinese medicine ("TCM" hereafter) are rooted in belief systems as old as the culture from which they spring, and equally hermetic to outsiders. The precepts of an ancient Asian canon known as *jinbu*, for example, dictate that humans can enhance specific physical attributes by eating the appropriate organs of animals endowed with the desired trait. Consuming the eyes of a nocturnal beast improves night vision, *jinbu* avows. Drinking a soup in which the penis of a particularly fecund animal has been cooked fosters robust sexuality. . . .

Voodoo, we of occidental descent huff, and legitimately so. But *jinbu* is no more a valid representation of all TCM than a renaissance barber is of a modern surgeon; the practices may have converged historically, but their present forms reveal more distinctions than similarities. Aspects of *jinbu* persist to the present day, as do aspects of barbering. Only recently, in terms of Asia's protracted history, have medicine, religion, and philosophy diverged in the East, and alien

123

disciplines have been reinforced by earlier centuries of commingled practice between TCM pharmacists and shamans. As in so many perspectives—from language and physiognomy through fashion and cuisine—East and West have vastly separate origins for their medical traditions. Comparisons falter accordingly. The Chinese themselves, whose native language identifies their land as the "central" country, separate methodologies of medicine (*yau*) along geographic lines: *syi-yau* is literally "Western" medicine, encompassing all modern techniques; TCM is *jungyau*, or "central" medicine.

Despite such clear-cut linguistic distinction, these twain in fact do meet, and the equalities can be as startling as the differences. Aside from the hundreds of animal parts called for in TCM prescriptions, the vegetable and mineral kingdoms also are accessed. In those realms, the two medical hemispheres are all but parallel. What Westerner will deny the restorative properties to be found in the so-called milk of magnesia? Aspirin, the most avidly consumed medication in the developed world, is a derivative of willow bark. In a further vegetable comparison (one sure to make oncologists everywhere bow Eastward in sympathy), Taxol—the drug suspected of holding more potential against ovarian cancer than any other—is derived from the bark of the yew tree, a severely endangered form of flora.

Even among animal sources, the Western creed leans perilously toward the East. Insulin, injected millions of times a day to save the lives of people afflicted with diabetes, was originally harvested from the pancreases of slaughtered pigs. (It now is readily synthesized.) The gangly octopus receives serious scientific scrutiny for its ability to produce a chemical that fights high blood pressure. Bile from the gallbladder of a bear has so many uses in Western medicine that its synthesized component, ursodeoxycholic acid, can be found in hundreds of citations on the Internet's Medline database—an especially apropos example, this, since the market for bear gallbladder is the third member of an informal triumvirate of most-serious offenders against endangered animals in TCM, along with the markets for rhino horn and tiger bone.

Then there are the examples of wholesale cross-cultural adoption. Acupuncture, disdained by the Western medical community until the mid-1970s, when Chinese physicians demonstrated irrefutably how the procedure could control pain during surgery, now offers a perfectly respectable alternative for people around the world seeking help with everything from stress management to substance addiction. Some of the world's most famous hospitals offer the procedure, and some of the world's largest insurance companies will cover its cost. Less formally, a surge of casual interest in things ancient and Eastern has swelled steadily in the West for several decades, culminating in the so-called New Age movement. This diametrically misnamed contingent readily embraces elements from older ages, including medical modalities. The phenomenal popularity of Deepak Chopra's books on alternative therapies (*Perfect Health, Quantum Healing,* and *Ageless Body, Timeless Mind,* among others), in which the author, an M.D., discusses the five-thousand-year-old Indian system of Ayurveda, demonstrates the eagerness with which contemporary sufferers will look backward as well as forward for relief. The sharpest irony between the medical legacies of the Orient and the Occident, however, arises through the compelling and thoroughly legitimate argument now employed aggressively by conservationists to urge protection of the world's rain forests: Who knows what miracles of medicine may lurk among the creatures in the treetops? Lost forever, lest we save their habitat.

At this point many would argue that a critical difference between old and new lies in the modernness of scientific technique. Organic sources of chemicals may be similar, the argument goes, but Western medicine applies sophisticated research methodologies to eliminate all but the most repeatable of results. Supremely delicate modern equipment yields data at the molecular level, providing insight that simply was not available to anyone who lived before this century, or even this decade. You can't validate an ancient theory just by pointing out a technicality or two that it happens to share with modern science. . . .

All right, then. Let's go the other direction. The cultural credibility barrier drops further still when the most modern of analyses are applied to the most ancient of medical practices. In laboratories as sophisticated as any in North America or Europe, Dr. Paul Pui-Hay But of the Chinese Medicinal Material Research Centre at the Chinese University of Hong Kong does just that. "The methods I refer to are those used in the courtroom of O. J. Simpson," he says, introducing his work in the most contemporary of vernaculars. "Genomic fingerprinting." The analogy may be dramatic, but it is valid. Dr. But himself is often summoned into courtrooms to testify regarding odds that rise into the millions-to-one category based on DNA analysis of TCM components. "In terms of describing an herb to the jury, or the defense lawyer, or the prosecutor, we can tell them morphologically the herb looks like this, anatomically like this, chemically like this, and, at the molecular level, the DNA patterns look like this. We then conclude what it is, so there will be no defense against it."

The focus of But's work actually centers more on efficacy than identification, but both emphases found new application a few years back when the link between TCM and endangered animals became clear. Not only did the identification of particular substances take on new urgency in terms of prosecuting the smugglers and dealers of animal contraband, a parallel interest in the efficacy of TCM arose; if the stuff could be broken down so thoroughly by modern science, the interested parties reasoned, surely its bioactive influence also could be thus explored. When just such a query arose from South Africa concerning the efficacy of rhinoceros horn, and when bipartisan financial support from sources as diverse as WWF Hong Kong and the Tung Fong Hung Medicine Company Limited arose to fund such research, Paul But initiated the study.

The earliest surviving reference to the use of rhinoceros horn as an antipyretic—a fever-reducing agent—appeared in the *Divine Plowman's Herbal* in the second century B.C. (Contrary to popular misconception, rhinoceros horn never has been prescribed in Chinese medicine as an aphrodisiac.) More than two thousand years later, we know why the reference was made, and why it survives. "In dealing with a patient with persistent high fever," Paul But wrote when the results of his study were published in the *Journal of Ethnopharmacology* in 1990, "the judgment of the dealers and herbalists, albeit necessarily law-abiding, becomes very much a moral one. It is, therefore, most crucial to check the validity of the reputed actions of rhinoceros horn. . . ." And, according to his results: "The aqueous extract of rhinoceros horn consistently demonstrated a significant antipyretic effect 30 min [*sic*] after treatment." In laymen's terms: Rhinoceros horn reduces body temperature. Lo and behold, everybody be damned. The stuff works.

No one knew exactly how to react at first. Was this good news or bad? And for whom? Certainly TCM was validated by But's findings, but the pressure to stop using rhino horn clearly wasn't going to ease as a result. If anything, it would probably increase due to the heightened awareness spawned by the study—a reaction that in fact played out as presaged. Conservationists were relieved, sort of, to know that rhinos had not been sacrificing their horns needlessly for millennia, but the mumbo-jumbo argument was clearly about to take another hit. "Efficacy is a nonstarter," Judy Mills concludes, not hiding her frustration (and speaking from the very offices where WWF Hong Kong issued its funding to support But's study, offices where TRAFFIC East Asia once shared space). "The users [of TCM] are convinced on the basis of the test of time, and a lot of them don't give a fuck about what shows up in some Western laboratory."

But's methods, materials, techniques, and reputation were beyond reproach, but critics of his rhino-horn study complained that the tests had been performed on rats, not humans. Besides, they grumbled, a Tylenol could achieve the same effect as a dose of rhino horn without endangering a species of pachyderm. Dr. But—a Ph.D., not an M.D.—employs both grievances to further demonstrate how widely separated the two medical traditions are. "The whole approach of Chinese medicine is different from the current use of Western medicine," he begins. "At the very start [of TCM] two thousand or more years ago, the method used to approach the human body was as if it were a black box." Invoking the image of a Christmas present, he explains, "You shake it, look at it, feel how heavy it is, and try to guess what's inside.... [In TCM] it was necessary to develop sensitive detection methods, such as feeling the pulse, looking at the tongue, the smell of the body, and the temperature. This method may sound unscientific, but think of it two thousand years ago. When you come at the body like a black box, you have to look for anything, no matter how small it is. And you will detect subclinical symptoms regarded as mumbo jumbo by Western medicine."

The gulf between the medical orthodoxies is wedged further open, But elaborates, by differences in application. Unlike the modern Western standard of seeking a cure only when afflicted (even then many modern modalities focus on symptoms rather than causes), practitioners of TCM undertake comprehensive, long-term treatments aimed at harmonizing various forces continuously at work in the body. In the West you get sick from infections; in the East you get sick from imbalances. "Think of a seesaw," But suggests. "If it's tilted to one side, you can remove weight, and the seesaw will return to that balanced state. But there's another approach," he submits, shifting hemispheres. "You can also add weight to the other end [of the seesaw]. When you think of the body as a whole, there are different approaches."

In light of such fundamental differences, But suggests that the comparison between rhinoceros horn and Tylenol is misguided. "It's not that simple," he says, noting that rhino horn never has been prescribed casually. TCM divides the body into different "layers" of affliction, he explains, and only a fever identified at the deepest layer—

the so-called blood level—calls for rhino horn. Applying the remedy to fevers at shallower levels would in fact injure the patient, he emphasizes. "Life-and-death situations only. Things like encephalitis B, ...where the fever is so serious the patient would have delirium." Summarizing the obvious risks attendant to such situations, and adding that M.D.s from the medical school with which the Research Centre shares a campus are involved in every aspect of his research, But brushes aside criticism of his reliance on rats instead of human subjects. "No sensible M.D. would jeopardize his practice by organizing such a study."

However, one study But and his colleagues are eager to pursue involves researching the efficacy of tiger bone. WWF Hong Kong offered to fund this study, too, tendering money supplied by ESSO U.K. (yes, the British petroleum agglomerate, whose masters, minions, and money all shall resurface later to succor their logo). Everything was in place, with one exception: the substance to be tested. Paul But had no tiger bone. A simple problem to resolve, it would seem. For his rhino-horn tests But had accessed contraband seized by Hong Kong law enforcement officials during smuggling busts; after the necessary legal proceedings, such evidence was customarily turned over to the Research Centre. Tiger bone is an equally popular commodity among import outlaws, and kilos of the stuff, in a variety of forms, also has been taken into custody.

Or has it? The difficulties involved in confirming the derivation of a bone purported to have come from a tiger are so intricate, and they hatch such fantastically complicated implications, they turn the goal of determining the medicinal efficacy of tiger bone into a mildly interesting afterthought by comparison. Pursuing such confirmation stretches the very boundaries of contemporary science, taxing, in the process, the sharpest minds and the most elaborate machinery available to be put to the task. Even then, the possible consequences look to be either mutually exclusive or collectively self-defeating—or both—leading, even in the most satisfactory outcomes, to a legal

Penelope's web that unravels as quickly from the bottom as it can be woven at the top.

⸎

A rhinoceros horn, whole, has certain morphological character-istics that render it readily identifiable to anyone even moderately familiar with the species of animal from which it was taken. Fakes are attempted, but few are convincing; most would fail to fool even a tourist. The provenance of a horn, therefore, can be verified almost without question.

Not so a tiger bone. Were the entire skeleton of a tiger laid out on an examining table beside the skeleton of a lion, few people on the planet would be skilled enough to distinguish between the two. Not Ron Tilson, not Sarah Christie, not Paul But, not Sam LaBudde, Ullas Karanth, Peter Jackson, Ulysses Seal, Mike Day, Jorgen Thom-sen, Judy Mills. . . . "Even TCM pharmacists cannot identify tiger bone," says TRAFFIC Taiwan's Dau-Jye Lu. A handful of felid phys-iologists, accompanied, perhaps, by a paleobiologist or two, could make the call, and only then by picking up and closely examining a few particular bones known to manifest subtle morphological char-acteristics. The skull of a lion is purported to rock a certain way if placed jaw-down on a flat surface, for example. The top few vertebrae of each cat also are said to be distinct.

That's as easy as it gets. Failing such clinical circumstances, the process of identifying tiger bones plummets toward impossibility. By simply removing the skulls and the top few vertebrae from the tiger-lion skeleton comparison you could challenge even the world's most capable experts. Disassemble the remaining skeletons and jumble them together in a bag, and the challenge becomes a mystery. To be cruel, you could toss in a few bones from a leopard or a cheetah.

From there it gets really tricky. With only one exception beyond the skull and the top vertebrae, the separated bones of a tiger cannot be individually distinguished even from bones outside the animal's phylum. Many bear bones look like tiger bones, as do many cow bones, dog bones, pig bones, horse bones, sheep bones—none of those last five deriving from endangered animals, you will notice. The exception is the humerus, or upper front leg bone, which features a perforation known as the "phoenix eye" in most large cats. At least the horn of a rhino is clearly distinct from the horn of a bull.

But we have yet to reach even beyond the intrinsic forms of these objects. What happens when natural morphology is altered so that horns and bones no longer look like horns and bones—when they are, say, ground into powders? This is where tiger bone takes its compositional leave of other animal products favored by smugglers of TCM, and where it leaves science shrugging its collective shoulders.

Rhinoceros horn is essentially fused hair. It is made of keratins—proteins—that comprise specific combinations of amino acids, each of which retains its integrity down to the molecular level. No matter how fine the powder you make by grinding up a rhino horn, laboratory analysis still can yield a unique profile of the substance, thereby allowing for reliable identification. A bear's gallbladder is an organic tissue as well. Each cell contains bear DNA. Again, the lab can trace the source of a piece as small as can be cut or ground (even though bear gallbladders are rarely reduced to less than their original anatomy before use—something like a small drumstick of chicken) Ivory would present more of a problem if it were pulverized, since it, too, is essentially a bone—a tooth. But ivory tends to retain its value only so long as it remains in pieces large enough to be decorative, at which dimensions it retains reliably identifiable morphological characteristics.

But at the levels currently analyzable in the most sophisticated laboratories now dedicated to the cause, a bone, when powdered, is a bone is a bone is a bone. It is calcium. A basic element. Indivisible, and indistinct.

"We are having extreme difficulty," confirms Kenneth Goddard, director of the National Fish and Wildlife Forensic Laboratory in

Ashland, Oregon. "We have several million dollars [U.S.] of instrumentation and some of the best forensic scientists and general scientists I can find in the country. Plus, we are working with every scientist we can get our hands on from the outside world to resolve these problems."

While similar to Paul But's laboratory in terms of the technology employed, Goddard's lab, through the efforts of more than thirty scientists and administrators working in a U.S. $4.5 million facility, is uniquely focused on crime. "The mission statement," Goddard explains, "is to provide forensic support to wildlife law-enforcement officers at the state, federal, and international levels." Essentially, the lab is tasked with analyzing evidence submitted by the fifty state fish and game agencies, plus anything gathered by the 220 federal Fish and Wildlife agents scattered throughout the U.S., plus whatever is submitted by the eighty wildlife inspectors at the ports of entry. "In our spare time," Goddard jokes, "we're supposed to be a crime lab for the hundred and twenty-five signatories of CITES."

Despite the excessive workload, the Ashland lab is revolutionizing the application of criminal law to wildlife products. "What we do as a laboratory," explains Goddard, echoing his counterpart in Hong Kong, "is come up with new species-defining characteristics that allow us to go up onto the stand, raise our right hand, and testify in court that this piece, part, or product came from a certain species or subspecies, and from nothing else in the world." It's the "nothing else in the world" that makes work like Goddard's essential. "If a conservation officer seized a whole elephant," he posits, "attached an evidence tag to its tail, and dragged it into the courtroom, you wouldn't need a four-point-five-million-dollar crime lab. We feel you could get the average jury of twelve to agree that it's an elephant. And they would agree because of certain morphological, external characteristics. Trunk, tusk, ears, big rear end. But we don't get whole [animals] in as evidence."

Furthermore, as with the conflicted implications of Dr. But's results, not all the insights Goddard and his team are able to supply are clearly helpful or even encouraging. "Tiger bone is a problem," Goddard reiterates. Noting that TCM manufacturing processes completely destroy proteins, he explains, "If we had the marrow, we'd have a chance to use DNA. But if we have the bone, then what we are probably looking at is calcium. Things that are non–species specific." It is a secondary observation from Goddard, however, that proves most troubling. "Of all the tiger-bone products we have looked at," he says slowly, "we have yet to find any calcium."

Let us pause for a moment to consider—guided by Goddard—the many things this might mean. The Ashland lab can detect the presence of proteins, such as those in rhino horn, at one-half of 1 percent in composition—one part per two hundred. "We take known rhino horn and make the preparations to that level to make sure we can find it," Goddard explains. "But we can detect calcium at far lower levels," he notes, speaking in parts per million. "If it's there, we're going to see it." And yet they do not see it in any of the products marked as containing tiger bone that are submitted by any of the hundreds of agents around the world who turn first to Ashland for analysis of the evidence they seize. Tigers are being poached; evidence for that is overwhelming. Products claiming to contain the bones of tigers are reaching market shelves in numerous countries, and a suitably random number of them are being intercepted along the way and sent to Ashland for analysis, where they all have been found to contain no bone whatsoever. The question is begged: Where are the tiger bones going?

"If I were doing this, and I had no scruples, and I liked money a lot," Goddard begins an astonishing analogy, "I would, at whatever price necessary, buy up the bones of tigers and then pay poachers to kill the rest." In short, Goddard would become a tiger-bone speculator. That suggestion may sound like a far-fetched plot turn in a spy novel (Goddard, in fact, successfully writes and publishes crime-based fiction as a hobby), but evidence of exactly such wildlife commodification is readily available for other endangered species. Massive stockpiles of rhino horn have been discovered, along with anecdotal reports from poachers claiming to have been instructed to kill rhinos in the wild whether they have usable horns or not. "If the animals become extinct," Goddard observes, "those stockpiles become infinitely valuable."

TRAFFIC's Judy Mills supports Goddard's innuendo. "We know there are people stockpiling rhino horn for that very reason," she states. "They're banking on extinction." Regarding the development of a similar practice for tiger bone, Mills backs off only a step. "I don't doubt it may be happening. I met a gentleman in Sapporo, Japan, who is breeding a pure strain of Hokkaido brown bear taken from the wild because he is banking on its extinction. He talks with pride about how he will have the one and only last pure strain of Hokkaido brown bear. . . . His investment pays off big time. He's able to say, 'I can sell you gallbladders from a pure strain of Hokkaido brown bear.' "

To an ailing individual who believes, accurately or not, that gallbladders from purebred Hokkaido brown bears are necessary to cure his or her ills, the gentleman in Sapporo will be the closest thing to a living deity—literally holding in his hands the perceived keys to life and happiness. If he's benevolent and generous, all will be well. If he decides to take advantage of monopoly market forces, however, he will have the power to extract awesome fees for his merchandise. The price of not meeting his price will be misery, perhaps death. What supplicant will hold back for the sake of his or her health, or the health of his or her spouse, parent, or child? This is what separates TCM from other markets when it comes to endangered species. It's not an issue of fashion or luxury. It's a quality-of-life issue at the most fundamental level: avoidance of physical suffering and early death. If you pass up the leopard-skin coat and buy a Gore-Tex parka instead, or if you wear a plastic bracelet instead of an ivory one, your ego might suffer a bit, but you'll recover. If you pass up a cure, you might die.

That contrast handily invokes a discussion of appropriate substitutes for animal derivatives in TCM. Fashion offers alternatives; how about medicine? This revives the significance of Paul But's research. Once the bioactive elements in tiger bone, if any, are isolated and identified, the possibility of a synthetic substitute—or even an organic one, from a less-endangered source—will drift within reach. That will lead to alternatives, surely, but the availability of such substitutes must not be considered the isolated solution to the predicament.

For starters, the terminology of TCM itself is very loosely defined. "Dragon horn" and "Phoenix membrane" appear among the ingredients listed in contemporary TCM prescriptions, along with numerous other elements of equally whimsical origin. Even the most devoted patron of TCM realizes that substances used under such aliases do not in fact derive from their namesakes. (Actual sources of "dragon" and "phoenix" include everything from living plants to fossilized animal bones.) Collective terms are used simply to identify groups of ingredients that act uniformly on the individual "layers" of the body—described earlier by Paul But. Swapping one specific ingredient within the collective family for another has never been any more unusual to patients of TCM than it would be for you to treat your aches and pains with a Bayer aspirin instead of a Tylenol instead of an Advil instead of... whatever is closest at hand. In just the same way that you have the option of accessing one substance over another based on preference, availability, convenience, or price, TCM users also select from among alternates. And "general tiger bone," in the TCM pharmacopoeia, *legitimately* can mean bear bone, dog bone, pig bone, deer bone... another curve for Ken Goddard and his staff at the Ashland forensics lab. The only concession to specificity is the differentiation between "general" tiger bone and "true" tiger bone, with even the latter referring to what can come from a tiger, a lion, or a leopard. These genuine articles, of course, have always been more expensive than their domesticated substitutes, and only a portion of the clientele—then, as now—had the luxury of affording the top of the line. Deception, surely, in the absence of strict regulation and/or dependable analysis of origin, has been employed to get the higher price for the cheaper substitute, or even for an outright fake, but medical shysters everywhere do that. By and large the goods employed over the centuries in TCM have been procured and sold as advertised (in the vernacular apropos), with substitutions playing a significant and thoroughly acceptable role. The practice of TCM, otherwise—based solely on the influences of economics, reliability, biology, experimentation, and so forth—simply would not have survived.

To avoid letting even a sliver of the substitutes argument fall through the cracks, let us pursue that debate to its absolute conclusion. Complete scientific precision notwithstanding, the medicinal application of the products used in TCM will *forever* compel its consumers to turn away from substitutes and back toward originals just as surely as it now convinces grocery-store shoppers in America to purchase expensive brand-name pharmaceuticals instead of cheaper generic substitutes, regardless of incontestable scientific proof that the two products are identical both in chemical composition and remedial effect. No matter how speedily Dr. But proceeds with his analyses, the match between a tiger's bones and *any* substitute will never be closer than the match between Tylenol and off-the-shelf acetaminophen—a proximity that still fails to draw many "sensible" consumers of "sensible" medicine away from the former and toward the latter despite significant economic incentive. When it comes to matters of health, many people simply refuse to take anything close to what they consider (again, accurately or not) to be a chance.

"There's all this talk about substitutions," Judy Mills summarizes. "But there are many [TCM] doctors who tell me, 'There is no substitution for tiger bone. There are things that can be used for rheumatism, but they're not as good as tiger bone, and there never will be anything as good as tiger bone.'"

Though substitutes may not be the answer to the endangerment of the wild tiger, they remain, in the opinion of many, worthy of pursuit. Aren't all options welcome in a crisis, regardless of how little relief they may offer? . . . But if genuine tiger bone indeed is found, through the rigors of modern science, to be effective in treating ills, the market for its application will quickly spread beyond just Asia. What sick person will spurn this new therapy? With the "true" sources of the derivative both protected and diminishing, substitutes will be essential rather than merely welcome. This self-propelling side effect of TCM efficacy and substitution research reinforces arguments put forth by many conservationists that dabbling with the question of whether or not the stuff actually works or can be synthesized is recklessly time-consuming and potentially counterproductive in the face of a quickly declining wild tiger population already below the ten thousand mark. Mere talk of searching for substitutes endorses suspicions of efficacy, the argument goes, and therefore promotes continuing utilization. Many insist the practice simply must stop, at least for the time being, regardless of whether or not it is either effective or replaceable. Paul But himself is sympathetic to the position. "We have to stop for a while," he agrees, ". . . and wait till [the population of wild tigers] becomes larger." Acknowledging that tiger bone, unlike rhino horn, typically is not involved in treating life-threatening afflictions, he still cautions, "I don't know if [TCM users] are willing to stop or not. But I do agree that there is such a need to curb or correct or alleviate the situation. That's my personal viewpoint."

Unfortunately, the issue of willingness among TCM users to modify their practices often gets mired in cultural backwaters. Tiger conservationists have an unhappy history of launching anti-TCM campaigns from platforms based disdainfully on the mumbo-jumbo perception, which inevitably, if unintentionally, drags the debate into a sociomoral arena. How can anybody be so stupid, the message often comes across (not always in subtle terms), as to gluttonously hunt the world's most beautiful carnivore into extinction for the sake of what amounts to little more than *sorcery?* The distorted delivery goes further askew when the message comes, as it repeatedly has, from an organization based in a country that is not a home range for the wild tiger, does not have domestic laws against TCM trade as strict as those in place in other nations (perhaps even the country under attack, as we have seen), features a human population that is primarily affluent and/ or Caucasian and/or Judeo-Christian, does not have recorded ancient histories or traditions of its own, or possesses *several* of the forerunning characteristics. Beneath such baggage, the striped, four-legged, intended beneficiary of the campaign cannot help but suffocate.

An unfortunately apropos example of just such a misfire occurred only weeks after CITES COP-9 adjourned in Florida. Earlier in the year, Ogilvy & Mather, one of the world's largest and most respected advertising agencies, had approached the Wildlife Conservation Society in New York regarding the possibility of arranging space in publications throughout Asia for public-service advertisements aimed at raising awareness concerning the link between TCM and the endangerment of the tiger. O & M, a company with ties to conservation that trace back to a former directorship under the same Guy Mountfort who launched Operation Tiger, not only offered to donate time to help design the ads, but also agreed to negotiate pro bono placement of them. Input from WCS was sought largely because the organization is famous for its stable of eminent tiger researchers: George Schaller, Alan Rabinowitz, Ullas Karanth, et al.

Who could resist such an offer? Public awareness, especially among *that* public, is one of the foremost deficiencies lamented by conservationists. What better, quicker, broader way to boost awareness than through direct mass-media advertising, and who better to organize it than a team pairing WCS with O & M? All of it *free*, no less. The deal seemed perfect in every aspect (indeed, everyone involved proceeded with objective, sensible, conscientious intentions), and WCS agreed enthusiastically to participate in the effort by assigning representatives to the ad-design committee and by allowing the WCS logo to be featured with the artwork. The ads began running in December 1994, carried in such widely circulated publications as *Asia, Inc.* and the Asian editions of *Time* magazine. Covering an entire two-page spread, the copy of one of the ads opens on the left-hand page with the statement, "Eating the parts of a tiger is said to give you its legendary sexual prowess." A small picture of a recumbent tiger follows, beneath which appear the words, "You too can make love for a full fifteen seconds."

Sex sells, but sex also leads this ad into murky water before it even reaches its second page. Human sexuality has a curious, isolated, abstract prominence in Asian cultures (e.g., the sex shows of Bangkok, the explicit *manga* "comic books" of Japan, and the frequent intersection of *jinbu* with aphrodisia), but to address the subject directly in a public forum is considered vulgar and shameful, especially by the Chinese. It is exactly the kind of thing they expect of Westerners, whom they often stereotype as crude, extroverted, and salacious. Evoking the image of the reader of the ad actually engaged in sexual intercourse—"You too can make love..."—reveals an intrusively insensitive lack of appreciation for Eastern mores.

It gets worse. The facing page of the ad carries twenty-five lines or so of smaller copy, all saturated with snide language, reproductive innuendo, and sexual double entendre. "The act of tiger copulation usually lasts a rather limp 15 seconds," the ad winks. "...The real Casanovas can maybe plug away for a minute or so. Every month or two.... Unless something is done, the tiger will have come, and gone, more quickly than any of us imagine [*sic*]."

Pretty spicy stuff, even for some jaded occidental eyes. Advertisements referring to "come" in a sexual context rarely appear on the pages of mainstream publications such as *Time*. A similar ad, discussing how tiger penis soup is often faked, was equally salacious. Representatives from WCS insist that Asian consultants reviewed the ads before they went to print, but no one on the original nine-person committee assembled by O & M and WCS to design the material was of Asian descent. In a further irony of misdirection, the ads ran only in English for almost a year before being translated into any of the range-state languages.

The general impudence of these ads might be forgiven as the overambitious attempts by an industry not known for subtlety to snag the attention of busy readers. (Indeed, the New York Art Directors Festival eventually awarded a gold medal to the campaign for "Best Public Service Print Advertising on environmental issues.") But a much more onerous problem surfaces on the second page of the ad just quoted: Contained in that copy, and reinforced by other verbiage in the ad, is the unambiguous insinuation that even the most potent tigers copulate for only "a minute or so. Every month or two." That is patently incorrect. Male and female tigers couple for only seconds at a time during coitus, that much is true. But throughout the expanse of a mating interlude, the pair will unite over and over and over again every fifteen minutes or so for hours, often days, at a time, with the male achieving his feline equivalent of an erection repeatedly while he delivers serial ejaculations. Not a bad trade for limited endurance per copulation, many human males might argue. Thus, even the scientific rationale presented in the ad is questionable.

Among Asians who read the ads many were nonplussed, though not particularly surprised when they discovered the (Western) source. Louder declamations arose from within the very community expected to embrace the campaign. Conservationists from TRAFFIC to AZA to SWAN, particularly those familiar with Asian culture, choked when they saw the ads, disappointed by what they repeatedly identified as "a wasted opportunity." Advertising space does not come cheaply, nor do the services of image-shaping leviathans such as Ogilvy & Mather. To have misfired with such precious and potentially effective resources to reach such a well-defined audience—worse: to have insulted them and fudged the facts while doing so—was embarrassing. If anything, some critics lamented, the intended audience now had another reason to *spurn* Western concerns for the tiger in favor of TCM. No one blamed WCS for participating, but the majority of conservationists were left shaking their heads in frustration.

The most vocal condemnation of all, however, rushed at WCS

from its counterparts within the scientific community. Felid biologists everywhere were outraged at having been conscripted into the ads via statements embedded in the copy such as "...even the most naive zoologist can testify..." and "...scientists are as one in concurring..." In fact, scientists were almost as one in concurring that the most naive zoologist could testify that the information presented in at least one of the WCS advertisements is conspicuously *misleading*. Biologists from inside WCS itself winced when they saw the ads.

The incident as a whole demonstrates a phenomenon introduced earlier in this book through the term "eco-imperialism": the suppression of one culture by another for the sake of the environment. A weighty concept, and one, on the whole, observed more in theory than demonstration. Much has been made of the tendency among rich, white nations to influence and even control the disposition of natural resources in developing countries at the expense of indigenous cultures. There is no question the pattern exists, and Raymond Bonner went a long way toward documenting it in his book *At the Hand of Man* (Knopf, 1993). But one nation's "imperialism" is another's "liberation" or "relief" or "assistance." And charges of trampling human customs underfoot in the stampede to save nonhuman biota often are leveled by outside observers with private agendas rather than by the people actually "oppressed."

In fighting such charges, Ron Tilson and Ulysses Seal proudly discuss their policy of working only inside countries that have issued formal invitations to them, and they eagerly supply the documented proof. "I am happy to confirm that the Royal Forest Department would like to invite CBSG to conduct three workshops..." opens a letter to Ulysses Seal dated 26 December 1994, and signed by then deputy director general of the RFD of Thailand, Watana Kaeokamnerd. A similar missive sent to Ron Tilson on January 18, 1995, from then director of the Chinese Association of Zoological Gardens, Sheng Shuling, entreats, "You and experts you suggested are welcome to offer your advice and to help us with our work concerned. . . . Please tell us how many people will come and who they are. With such information, we will send invitation letters to them." Ir. Soemarsono, director general of Indonesia's PHPA, responded as follows when questioned directly regarding eco-intrusions by foreigners such as Tilson: "We invite all experts on the Sumatran tiger, and also on other species classified as endangered. . . . We are very grateful and very appreciative of all who are involved in this activity of conserving the Sumatran tiger." (To finish out this frame of the Tilson/Seal window, it needs to be noted that Russia seems satisfied for the time being with scientific connections already established there and about to be presented here. India, too, remains recalcitrant in summoning CBSG, though Seal hints at inroads.)

Certainly a case can be made that indigenous governments themselves often lack the insights and appreciations necessary to preserve the very cultures they control, sometimes readily exchanging traditions or land or clean water for foreign investment. And some of the governments so anxious to lay out a welcome mat for Tilson and CBSG have deplorable track records in terms of preserving either their cultures or their environmental heritages. Indeed, by achieving such lofty political altitude—signatures on their invitations often fall just an office or two short of the head of state—Tilson and Seal risk associating themselves with politicos more odious than fragrant in the international leadership bouquet. And at such levels, the dialogue veers away from eco-anything toward politics in general, which everyone, conservationist or not, must handle in terms of basic international administration anyway.

⤙

In addition to the genial sentiments he expressed for Tilson and CBSG, Ir. Soemarsono observed, "I do hope this cooperation will continue, because I think the [Sumatran tiger] does not belong to Indonesia. It is global."

Here we have a curious hybrid of the philosophy and politics

that were so carefully segregated in earlier chapters. Soemarsono, per
the laws of Indonesia (also presented earlier), embodies the de facto
ownership of every tiger, wild or captive, that walks upon Indonesian
soil. He controls them—"owns" them—in the terms previously defined. Yet he recognizes, at least for the sake of the microphone, that
his responsibility transcends the borders of his country. His decisions
affect more than just the people to whom he answers, and while he
is hardly likely to favor foreign preferences over domestic ones, he
retains a global perspective. His observation sounds suspiciously like
the claim that "everybody" owns the Sumatran tiger, but he and his
country are very clear on who calls the shots when it comes to their
cats. Foreigners, like Tilson and Seal, are welcome, respected, and
may even be significantly influential, but they do not own the tigers.
And it's clear that if they screw things up they'll be invited to step
aside. Indonesia's ability to balance local control with global responsi
bility—an equilibrium commonly expressed as "stewardship"—demonstrates the degree of sophistication in leadership that will be necessary
in all the tiger range states if the five remaining subspecies are to
survive in the wild.

Fortunately, there is evidence that Indonesia is not alone in its
percipience, either among its governmental counterparts or the NGO
fellowship. "We are a global community," agrees TRAFFIC's Judy
Mills. "We share resources. OK? Yes, we originated from many different cultures around the world, but right now we're sharing this spher-
ical ecosystem. All of us. And therefore it is incumbent upon all of us
of various cultures to make sacrifices to preserve biodiversity and the
health of our habitat, the habitat we share with other beings. This
transcends culture. It's as simple as that."

Despite such perspicacity, cultural friction like the kind fostered
by the WCS advertisement continues to hobble efforts to benefit the
tiger. At the risk of increasing the heat, the cause behind the discord
needs to be magnified yet one step further.

To its credit, kind of, the O & M/WCS design team latched on to what are unquestionably the most compelling aspects of the tiger-versus-TCM debate. ("In terms of getting attention," one NGO observer quipped, "it's a big success. They got both sex and violence into the single ad.") The TCM "prescription" specifically referenced in the advertisement is one of the most infamous concoctions available in the entire pharmacopoeia: tiger penis soup. Here, in one bowl, you get the quirky, necro-erotic, homo-cannibalistic animism of *jinbu* all served up in a single dish. What could possibly be more perverse? To the Western palate, nothing. Placing a penis—especially a dead one—in your mouth, particularly if you're a guy, violates occidental taboos set by everyone from Rush Limbaugh to Martha Stewart. But Asians, in yet another manifestation of how sex and sexuality inhabit utterly non-Western realms of their psyches, have been nibbling on animal phalli for generations. Snakes, deer, seals, tigers, crocodiles. . . . Name the creature, they've eaten its privates. Who *now* is crude, extroverted, and salacious? And, in an equally important question, who now is doing the stereotyping?

Efforts to elevate one culture's morality over another inevitably lead nowhere, but tiger penis soup still provides an irresistibly charged image around which to build a campaign. WCS is hardly alone in accessing it. Sam LaBudde, as just one example, beat them to it by more than a year when he placed full-page ads in the *New York Times* and the *Los Angeles Times* in late 1993, stating: "A bowl of Tiger Penis soup sells for $320 in Taiwan. Only while supplies last. . . . Save the tiger. Boycott Taiwan." A picture of a dish of soup hovers in the center of the ad, into the liquid of which the image of a tiger's face has been superimposed. In the wake of promotion such as that, it's not difficult to understand why literature published around the world by NGOs, governments, scientists, and individuals interested in heightening awareness regarding the endangerment of the tiger quickly adopted the example of tiger penis soup as a leading connection between the animal and TCM.

It is tempting to condemn the hype surrounding tiger penis soup as the misguided focus of sensationalistic Western sensibilities on a titillating but obscure remnant of the shamanistic origins of TCM, but to do so would be wrong. Tiger penis soup has in fact enjoyed significant popularity among Asian consumers, right into this decade. The reasons are twofold and related. First, with a flair fully deserving of the scornful tone used by WCS and ESP in their advertisements, many hawkers of TCM remedies don't hesitate to boost the claims of benefits from certain therapies into the ionosphere. Bald? They'll give you hair. Fat? They'll make you thin. Limp? They'll pump you up. Charlatans and quacks will of course say anything to make a sale, and such claims are neither new to Asia nor unique there; Americans need look no further than the back pages of any number of popular magazines to find equally reliable cures for baldness, fatness, and limpness. Caveat emptor.

Perhaps the most infamous Asian locus for this chicanery occurs each evening in Taiwan's capital city of Taipei as hucksters line a bawdy boulevard known as Snake Alley. With the slap of a cane and a megaphonic bark, these self-styled apothecaries beckon the crowds of curious onlookers, some of whom, the hucksters know, will inevitably be willing to purchase and consume concoctions containing derivatives of animals from every phylum, including snake oil squeezed straight from serpents slaughtered right before the queasy customer's eyes. Premier among the benefits assured to accrue from stomaching such potions is increased sexual stamina, and VCRs unspool provocative testimonials to past successes.

Snake Alley is something of a carnival, buoyed by its own flamboyant reputation, but innumerable similar bazaars are scattered throughout Asia, catering to unsophisticated tastes. (Not a few of the paying customers, it needs to be reported, are Caucasians.) These days, of course, elixirs made from endangered species have been secreted away, but tiger penis soup remains available to those who dig a little. Before legislation made it illegal and public opinion made it unfashionable, the brew was among the most popular of the potions hawked.

Its compound lure of power and sex, not surprisingly, is equally as irresistible to advertisers in Asia as it is to those in New York City. Some of the broth is real, but much of is either "substituted" per the same provisions afforded general tiger bone, or it is faked outright. The average penis of a tiger is actually quite small — shorter than many a man's — and therefore disappointingly incongruent with its potent reputation. Overcoming scarcity and insufficiency all at once, resourceful artisans fashion ersatz tiger genitalia from those of other animals. Cattle, deer, and seals all are better hung than tigers, and they are more plentiful. They do, however, lack the trademark feline feature of a barbed genital tip. That deficiency can be overcome by incising the spurious organ carefully as it dries after being removed from its host. Unless the buyer of the resulting counterfeit is an expert in felid physiology, he will not be likely to detect the ruse. (Indeed, faked tiger penises often fool undercover investigators and end up pictured as the real thing in NGO literature, thereby inadvertently increasing the likelihood of future misidentification.)

Again, commentators from afar are likely to consider the envy displayed by connoisseurs of tiger penis soup to be both puerile and perverse. But the roots of what has indisputably grown into mutated foliage are deeply anchored and persistently watered. Back in Hong Kong, an energetic young man named David Choy is the executive director of the Tung Tak Tong Chinese Medicine Manufacturing Company Limited. In addition to the role he fills with that company, he is also the honorary life president of one of the oldest, largest, and most respected TCM trade associations operating anywhere in Asia, the Hong Kong & Kowloon Chinese Medicine Merchants Association Limited. Each year several hundred members of that association convene in Hong Kong to recognize achievements performed over the past twelve months and to discuss concerns that have simultaneously arisen. The atmosphere at such gatherings is redolent of the culture and territory in which they take place, but aside from the language being spoken and the eager clap of mah-jongg tiles during every break, the business conducted is indistinguishable from that pursued at any convention of modern medical professionals anywhere. Attendees wear expensive but tastefully subdued suits. Name cards are cordially exchanged. Cellular phones and pagers sound relentlessly. Guest dignitaries — Ph.D.s all — present recondite theories. Elaborate meals are served. Toasts are made. Awards presented. . . . A bunch of Snake Alley hucksters this is not.

"We are absolutely willing to work with modern scientists and doctors of Western medicine," says David Choy. "And we will live by what their research shows. We are ready and willing to sit down and discuss this, so long as it takes place in an atmosphere of mutual understanding." Choy is so thoroughly contemporary and Westernized he seems, at first, an unlikely spokesman for TCM. Educated in America, fluent in English, Mandarin, and Cantonese (his native tongue), he comes across for all the world like a PR confection hired especially to deflect nosy foreigners who might not be properly respectful of the trade group he represents. But he is in fact linked quite traditionally to his traditional profession, having inherited his title at Tung Tak Tong Limited from his father. Furthermore, he not only advocates the medical tradition for which he speaks, he practices it personally. TCM is part of his daily regimen.

"We are not trying to kill tigers," he declares, taking a break from his formal responsibilities during the 1995 convention. "We're trying to save human lives. The laws, the way they stand now, are good for tigers but not for people." Choy knows the law, and he knows the score. Nothing about the conflict between tigers and TCM comes as news to him, and he is conversant on every aspect. "Everybody here is willing to have the rules for the use and trade of tiger derivatives handled by the government — the highest possible authority. Everybody," he repeats, sweeping his arm at a crowd that includes, in addition to the predominantly domestic membership, TCM practitioners from mainland China, Taiwan, the U.S., and elsewhere. (Also among the guests is a representative from the Chinese Medicinal Material

Research Centre at the Chinese University of Hong Kong, a colleague of Paul But's, whom Choy makes a point of introducing.) "That way," he continues, "we'll have something consistent and concrete to follow instead of what we have now, which is essentially control imposed on us by foreigners."

But just as Choy's savoir faire is about to clinch the deal, he dispenses an abrupt reminder of the rift between his affiliation and those of his critics. "Tiger penis soup is definitely a part of TCM," he confirms with a shrug of his lips. "It's for when you have a problem with your dick." Without flinching, he refines his observation only so far as to lament the overenthusiastic promotion of the remedy by charlatans such as those in Snake Alley and to point out, "It's the whole formula in the soup that's the key. The *mix* of ingredients." Asked, one more time, just to make sure, if he is referring precisely to the fermentation that agitates Western conservationists so—a bowl of soup in which a penis cut from a *Panthera tigris* has been steeped—he enthusiastically reiterates, "Sure. Absolutely."

The irresistible follow-on: Has he ever tried it?

Wry smile. "No. I don't need to. I use TCM regularly."

Even the most urbane adherents, it seems, are convinced that derivatives from tigers are valuable in treating discomfiture in humans, including all the derivatives and discomfitures that make polite company squirm a bit. This shakes the ground beneath the hope that younger Asian generations will be more receptive to the mumbo-jumbo argument than were their parents and ancestors. David Choy was thirty-eight when he made the statements just quoted.

Perception is reality to the perceiver. A firm grasp of reality—any reality—makes life more comfortable for us by offering reliable, repeatable consequences to uniform actions. Changing our perceptions, therefore, is not a simple thing to do. We don't like having doubts cast upon our formerly stable realities, and we typically de-

mand powerful, newly reliable evidence before we can justify making
a change in our belief system.

Scientific data has become, for many, the most powerful and
reliable evidence available, so potent that some of us will sacrifice
even our most tried perceptions in the face of contradictory scientific
evidence. That is why, despite its undeniable deficiencies and risks,
work like Paul But's must proceed. So long as the scientific jury remains out regarding the efficacy of animal derivatives, the desperation
associated with disease will continue to lead to radical demands far
beyond even the historical, cultural, and geographical boundaries of
TCM. An AIDS patient in America recently agreed to have marrow
from the bones of a baboon injected into his body in hopes that the
animal's natural but unexplained resistance to the disease might somehow infuse him with defenses against it. No one associated with the
experiment, including the doctors who performed it and even the
patient himself, was confident of success. But the ravages of that disease have so confounded conventional medicine and exasperated the
sufferers that *nothing* is beyond hope. (The baboon-marrow experiment was subsequently deemed ineffective, after which, as though
rehearsing a script taken from these very pages, a conflict ensued between the AIDS patient and activists concerned with the rights and
welfare of the baboon.) Also, lest we cast our mumbo-jumbo smirk
too narrowly upon the Chinese, the ancient Ayurvedic tradition of
India so vibrantly resurrected by Deepak Chopra and his followers
includes, among its original texts, prescriptions that call for tiger fat.
Suppose tigers are found to manifest a resistance to AIDS or Alzhei-
mer's disease or cancer. Who then will seek to harvest — perhaps
stockpile — tiger derivatives? With what motive? At what price?

The snag upon which we left the discussion of Paul But's work
dangling involved the integrity of tiger-bone evidence taken into custody by wildlife law-enforcement authorities. Not unlike the geneticists
and forensic scientists who must confirm the lineage of their specimens before employing them to establish baselines, Paul But cannot

risk presuming that a bone identified to him as coming from a tiger indeed derives from that species just because a smuggler or a TCM pharmacist or a customs officer or *anybody* says it does. If it's not the skull or the top few vertebrae, no one, anywhere, can proclaim its source with anything close to the certainty required to launch an efficacy study, especially a study with such far-reaching implications. If it's not the humerus bone, it can't even be certified as feline. If it's powder, it cannot be linked incontestably to the animal kingdom. The only way to verify beyond a doubt that a voucher specimen of bone comes from a tiger is to lift it directly from the carcass of the cat. Killing a tiger just to do that would be hard to justify, but what about a tiger that dies from other causes? A tiger in a zoo, for instance. What becomes of its bones?

Just as one snag comes free another develops. There are no tigers, captive or wild, in Hong Kong. Not even in zoos. If there were, it would be a relatively simple matter to arrange for the transfer of bona fide tiger remains to Paul But's laboratories. The carcasses of zoo tigers in other countries are routinely supplied to museums, research institutions, and educational facilities instead of being interred or incinerated, which are the typical means of disposal. However, as we have learned, since the species is endangered, transporting its remains across international borders is sticky business. Short of "smuggling" a bone into Hong Kong for research purposes (which would merely result in an equally questionable provenance, once all was said and done), the logistics involved in passing a bone from the body of a tiger into the hands of Paul But, verifying officially at every step that the material en route has not been either swapped or tampered with, are complicated, expensive, and time-consuming. There is no shortage of important research competing for Paul But's time, most of which is free from such impediments, so he cannot be blamed for moving on. Money for the research is available, but that sum can be (and has been) safely and legitimately set aside, awaiting its raison d'être. Parties acutely interested in the results of the research are scattered hither and yon, insufficiently organized, wealthy, knowledgeable, or free to research and process all the transactions necessary to facilitate the transportation of the bone. For more than a year, consequently, But's tiger-bone research languished for lack of ingredients.

However, early in 1995 Sarah Christie of the London Zoo learned of the predicament and stepped in to resolve it. Her responsibilities as the coordinator of the captive breeding programs for the EEP's Sumatran and Siberian tigers afforded her precise familiarity with the whereabouts and status of tigers throughout Europe, and ESSO U.K., sponsor of Paul But's pending research, had long supported her work at the London Zoo. Further justification for whatever effort Christie expended in brokering the exchange derived from the fact that England, at the time Christie initiated her efforts, still had two years of direct governmental authority over Hong Kong; at least a portion of the paperwork was bound to be simplified in Christie's hands, even if the tiger to be donated did not come straight from or through the U.K. Shortly after she put her ear to the ground, a likely candidate surfaced from among the zoos for which she coordinates tiger breeding. She alerted But, contacted the proper authorities, and effected a transfer. But's research with the product commenced as this book went to press.*

Back in Ashland, Oregon, work has proceeded unhindered. Without direct concern for the efficacy of the products they scrutinize, Ken Goddard and his team are comparatively free of the issue of whether or not the calcium they seek actually comes from a tiger. . . . Comparatively free, but not completely. The fact that the lab has yet to find any calcium whatsoever is the windfall that relinquishes them from obligations to ask questions about the source of the nonexistent substance—an advantage that persists only so long as they continue to "fail" in their quest to find calcium.

---

*Results from other research into the medical efficacy of tiger bone have been published elsewhere, but their origins are dubious and their methodologies heterodox.

Such failure, however, breeds its own brand of success. In a curiously convenient criminal irony, every single smuggler who attempts to import into the United States TCM products that list among their contents derivatives from endangered animals is culpable of a federal crime simply by virtue of the attempt. Once confiscated (at the point of entry), if the products were indeed shown to contain what they claim to contain, the perpetrator would go away thanks to CITES and the Endangered Species Act. When the goods are shown to lack one or more of the ingredients listed, the prosecution can proceed under the provisions of the federal Fair Packaging and Labeling Act, which outlaws the use of any label on any consumer commodity that purports to contain an ingredient when in fact it does not. The limited likelihood of intercepting the contraband at the point of entry remains a problem, but at least the merchandise will indisputably *be* "contraband" under one legal definition or the other . . . so long as it is seized at that point, so long as it states that it contains tiger bone, and so long as it contains no calcium. An additional dose of legal solace is found, by some, in the fact this same section of U.S. packaging law provides for the prosecution of anyone selling TCM *anywhere* if the merchandise does not contain everything it says it does, regardless of where, when, or how it entered the States. Unfortunately either a sufficiently constitutional cause or an empowering state law is required to seize such products from off store shelves, and the unhappy satire, of course, is that if calcium were then subsequently found in the products — regardless of where or under what authority they were seized — the case would drift back into the foggy realms of enforcing the Endangered Species Act or the Lacey Act.

It is the seeming success of actually discovering the calcium, therefore, that would burden Ashland with the currently impossible task of proving that it came from a tiger, and — as Goddard has noted — "from nothing else in the world." When no calcium is found, the lab has fulfilled its crime-fighting charter. That aspect of a tiger-bone case comes officially to a close. The lingering uncertainty regarding the true destination of the bones taken from poached tigers remains unresolved. Such investigations are not among the duties listed in Goddard's job description. "The issue," summarizes Frank Shoemaker of the Fish and Wildlife Service Law Enforcement Division, "is that if the article is in fact run through a chemical analysis that shows it does not contain any bone, then we don't have a case of someone importing tiger bone. You may have false declarations, you may have false advertising, you may have human and health concerns that are involved. Look at what other chemicals are in that material. But if it's not tiger bone then we [Fish and Wildlife] have no case."

Shoemaker's observation regarding health concerns points up another secondary victory enjoyed by the team in Ashland. Although they have yet to discover any calcium in the TCM products they've analyzed, they have discovered significant amounts of arsenic and mercury, among a host of other human toxins. This opens the door for prosecution by the U.S. Food and Drug Administration under the provisions of legislation known as the Federal Food, Drug, and Cosmetic Act. In the previous chapter, Andrea Gaski pointed out how unlikely it is that anyone will be able to prove the dangers of consuming tiger bone. But similar dangers associated with arsenic and mercury are less ambiguous, and news of the discovery of toxins in TCM has been ardently broadcast by conservationists eager to supply users with reasons to quit. Reaction among Asians has been mixed. Some argue that toxins are introduced as a means of triggering the body's natural defenses, like a vaccine. Less diplomatic devotees proclaim the Ashland findings are nothing more than a scare tactic. The origin of the toxins within the medicinals is not precisely clear, though Dr. Edgard Espinoza, the lab's deputy director, suspects they are inadvertently introduced through minerals such as cinnabaris, pyritum, and smithsonitum, which are then either improperly blended or unevenly distributed.

The simplest way to gather together all these variegated aspects of crime connected to the commercial use of endangered species, many conservationists submit, is for each country to install simple domestic legislation at the federal level that makes the importation or possession of anything even *claiming* to contain derivatives of endangered species an offense. All the knotty subdivisions, handoffs, and secondary investigations required to prosecute such crimes then would go away. Hong Kong and the U.K. already have just such laws in place, and there is evidence to suggest their effectiveness. Legitimate concerns have arisen that smugglers and salesmen will simply start labeling their products differently, thus driving what is now a detectable trade underground, but those concerns are balanced by what advocates of the laws suggest are the values of eliminating what amounts to a public endorsement of endangered animals as good medicine by leaving such products on the shelves while trying to determine whether or not they actually contain the offending material. The medicines threaten the continued existence of the animals regardless of whether or not they actually contain any of those animals' derivatives, the position sensibly states, so let's make the laws reflect our pursuit of the de facto effect we desire — protecting tigers — rather than the incidental logistical detail of whether or not there is any calcium in the mix. Goddard and his team could then be left to pursue their science on cases for which their skills were intended and on which their testimonies will apply. The installation of such laws, of course, would have to overcome the issues of efficacy, humanism, and several others about to be introduced, but from a strictly legal standpoint such laws make simple sense.

⸰

If the trove of some would-be tiger-bone speculator were discovered, what would be his most likely defense? If he's clever, or given to intrigue, and if he's found in a country where casual possession of such stocks are not permitted, he might produce forged registration documents. Or he might attempt to wrangle clemency with hard-to-dispute claims regarding the pre-CITES age of the bones. But such shenanigans, in fact, are quite unnecessary. "They aren't *really* tiger bones," he would more likely say. "They're cow bones, or pig bones, or dog bones, or . . ." Skulls and humeri would, of course, conveniently be missing. Even if the goods were clearly labeled "tiger bone," remember that the term is just a general designation. It often legitimately includes the bones of other animals in TCM. How is such an adversary fought?

With any luck, he'll also be stockpiling pelts or ivory or rhino horn, or some other confirmable contraband, for which he won't be able to access such handy dodges. But nobody, yet, can determine precisely the origin of those bones . . . including, we realize in a flash of hopefulness, the stockpiler himself and even the customers of TCM. *Everyone's* deceived, we imagine. Perhaps there is no more of a market for bones of tigers than there is for dragon horn or phoenix membrane. Eureka, maybe.

Two problems abide. First, we know tigers are being poached, and the evidence and testimony associated with those cases continuously demonstrate an irrefutable link between the animals and TCM. The bones are going *somewhere*, and in between the "producer" and the customer—be that a stockpiler or a user—the product is of known origin regardless of where, along the market chain, it loses its inviolable identifiability. This leads to the second, significantly more troubling, potentiality. "I would want to make damn sure I get the real stuff," says Goddard, putting himself momentarily in the place of a sick person who believes tiger bone will cure him. "So I want somebody who is absolutely trustworthy. And if you're talking about my daughter [being sick], I'm going to see the bone ground up. I may go out there and shoot the tiger."

Ah. Paul But cannot afford to mistake a cow bone for a tiger bone based on professional concern, but a sick parent will be even more passionately motivated toward certainty. Just as the global scientific community has gone to extraordinary trouble and expense to get Paul But a 100 percent–guaranteed sample, average citizens will surely be willing to sell everything they have, flout any law, take any risk, move heaven and earth to save or succor their loved ones. Someone of incontrovertible devotion must lift from the tiger with his or her own hands the bones to be used in Paul But's experiments. Accomplices of equal or possibly even greater trustworthiness and devotion will be sought out by customers who believe those bones have personal medical value. There is good reason to believe such pacts already exist.

"I have had people say to me," recounts Judy Mills, "that they will go to America and travel to see the bear killed before their eyes so they can see the gallbladder plucked from the bear's belly because they want the real thing. . . . And I have talked to people who have paid thousands of dollars for a live bear in Korea because they thought it would save a loved one's life." Talk is cheap, but there is hard evidence to support what Mills has heard. In 1995 a man named William Jintaek Lee was convicted of bringing wealthy foreigners into the United States to participate in illegal bear hunts in northern California. Asked if she feels these ursine examples bode badly for the tiger, Mills answers without hesitation. "There is an exact corollary." Ken Goddard has heard similar testimonials, which he combines with the results of his laboratory research to forge this summary: "The overwhelming sense we have is that the vast majority of the [tiger-bone] market is either fraudulent or it's presented in such a dilute manner that effectively you are getting nothing. However, a small portion of the market—the wealthy, influential people—are getting the real thing."

Even if the portion of the market that gets the real thing is infinitesimally small, the math is bleak. If just one-tenth of one-tenth of 1 percent of just the country of China, for example, were capable of arranging a tiger "hit," that's 120,000 tigers—ten times the number alive today, including all those in captivity. "The simple reality is we can't meet the demand," Goddard observes. The gap, he reiterates, is being filled through fraud, although "there is the possibility that [tiger bone] is there, but in *extremely* dilute amount. One tiger bone might be ground up and mixed into a vat with ten thousand, a hundred thousand, a million pills. That's conceivable." With a quick review of how sensitive his equipment is, however, he discounts that scenario and offers additional reason for doubt: "If you have a tiger bone worth thousands of dollars in your hands, are you really going to grind it up into a fine powder and mix it into a hundred thousand or a million pills? Or are you going to make those pills fake—nobody can tell the difference anyway—and sell that bone whole to somebody with more discriminating taste and the money to buy it?"

Goddard apologizes frequently for what he calls his "cynical" remarks, but his pessimism is based firmly on the evidence he finds. A still deeper guilt nags at him for another unavoidable hazard of his job. "Every time we testify in court, we teach, at the very least, one bad guy how not to be caught again. If he's got any brains whatsoever, he's at least taking notes." Indeed, the growing savvy among not only the perpetrators of this tiger-bone fraud but also among the customers who seek to avoid such fraud is fostered primarily by formal efforts to analyze the trade overall—including, regrettably, the one printed here. "I almost hesitate to [grant interviews]," Goddard confesses. "The logical thing for a smuggler to do once he's read this is to go out and look for some cow bones and toss them in." The consequence of such an enhancement, of course, would be to introduce just enough bone into the products to erase the hairline advantage Ashland now enjoys over the research conducted by Paul But. With calcium among their contents, confiscated TCM tiger-bone products will no longer supply clear-cut evidence for false advertising charges, yet they will simultaneously remain insufficiently specific to serve as evidence of smuggling derivatives of endangered species. The concept of a vi-olation of any kind, in fact, will disappear: The products will fall quite legitimately within the boundaries of "general" tiger bone, as defined by TCM.

⤳

Until the bones of tigers can be infallibly identified in whatever form they take, the pursuit of tiger-bone TCM traffickers — indeed, the pursuit of *any* tiger-bone trafficker who is as little as a single step away from the carcass that gave up the bones — offers nothing to the conservation of the animal. Due to its enormity, and considering the likelihood that we are years or decades away from infallible identification of tiger bone, a statement like that carries with it requirements for qualification and refinements, as follows:

The funding and manpower associated with efforts to establish an infallible identification mechanism for tiger bone should proceed, but only so long as they do not compete with other tiger conservation efforts. Tiger-bone traffickers who are more than one step away from the carcass of a tiger eventually will almost certainly have to be pursued if the wild species is to survive, but efforts to thwart traffickers who literally are within one step — that is, the poachers — are particularly important and effective, as we shall see in a later chapter. Both efforts are important, but the latter predominates.

Finally, we must remember that the *trafficking* of TCM is but a single aspect of the phenomenon that is open to intervention. Trafficking is nothing more than the intervening span between supply and demand — the conveyor belt, so to speak, that carries products from their sources to their consumers. In the case of tiger bone, that span is not yet sufficiently susceptible to control from the outside to offer meaningful interruption of the flow. But the poles at either end of the equation also are subject to influence. This chapter has covered the nature of one of those poles — the demand for TCM — in addition to the examination of trafficking just presented.

What about supply?

CHAPTER 9

Yes, You Can't

I N CHAPTER 4 WE DISCUSSED the ownership of tigers that live in situ, concluding with the arguable observation that said animals are owned — controlled — by the governments in power over the lands on which the cats roam. Those cats, in that chapter, were identified as the more "problematic" of the two situ subsets of tigers, a designation that is technically correct but potentially misleading.

The ownership of ex situ tigers is less problematic only because the apparent identity of the owner is more quickly and individually ascertainable than such a thing as an amorphous, collective national government. Ex situ tigers whose owners aren't close at hand, readily identifiable, and eagerly attentive tend to get screamed at and shot. The ownership of an ex situ tiger, therefore, may at first seem unworthy of further discussion; the cat belongs to its owner, doesn't it? The owner can do whatever he likes with the animal, can't he?

Or *can* he? The ownership of ex situ tigers in fact seethes within a philosophical cauldron all its own. What, exactly, can an owner of a captive tiger do with the animal? Can he make it jump through a hoop? Can he make it jump through a *flaming* hoop? Can he set the animal itself on fire? Can he bind its feet, slit its throat, remove its bones, and grind them up as medicine for his own use? None of these acts is physically impossible. The owner "can" clearly "do" them all.

Once again, verbiage threatens to tangle our analysis. Fortunately, there is once again an alternative vocabulary, supplied this time by the conservation community. In chapter 4, the fundamental principle of control was coaxed from behind the term "ownership" for the sake of illuminating the concept of wildness. Now, with respect to the concept of captivity, "ownership" obscures yet another fundamental principle. (The words "can" and "do" abet the obfuscation, as highlighted at the end of the previous paragraph.) When discussing ex situ tigers, the fundamental principle at work, in fact, is *use*.

Red flags. "Use" presumes a dominant/submissive relationship between a user and a resource, which, in the discussion at hand, casts tigers as a resource — a role many people consider a priori to be both incorrect and unacceptable. Those considerations are more than valid, and therefore worthy of assessment, despite the fact that humans are already using tigers as a resource. Reevaluating the roles into which players have been cast by default often leads to a script change. For the sake of determining the need, if any, for such a change in the tiger's passion play, let us examine the most commonly employed subdivisions of the term "use" when it comes to conservation:

Consumptive use, as the first word of the phrase implies, refers to processes through which the resources involved are depleted. When you eat a chicken, it goes away. You have used it consumptively.

Nonconsumptive use, conversely, refers to processes that do not deplete the resources involved. When you take a picture of a chicken, it remains available. You have used it, but not consumptively.

Sustainable use (a word highlighted in chapter 6) refers to processes that leave behind sufficient quantities of the resources involved to facilitate their regeneration for further use. Rendered in those terms, it sounds harmless enough, doesn't it? Well, hold on to your chickens.

When it comes to conservation, the idea of sustainable use generates more friction than any other single issue. At first, that may seem ridiculous, since the roots of both words — "conservation" and "sustainable" — spring from the unified concept of endurance. But sustainable use is a "meta"-definition, which, when applied to living things, inhabits a realm one step more comprehensive than either consumptive or nonconsumptive use. Specifically, sustainable use invokes the difference between individuals and groups. An individual chicken, for example, can be used both sustainably and *non*consumptively (e.g., as the subject of a photograph), but it cannot be used both sustainably and consumptively (e.g., as a meal). At the more comprehensive level, however, if the "resource" to be sustained is an entire barnyard full of chickens, *that* resource can indeed be sustained indefinitely even while its individual components are being used consumptively. Depending on how big your barnyard is, you can eat a chicken every month, week, or day without threatening the long-term survival of the group. This process is more readily recognized under its more common name: harvesting.

There are two predominating arguments that drive wedges between members of the conservation community when it comes to sustainable use. The first is that the premise of sustainability, when mingled with the action of continued harvests, just does not work equally well in all cases. Some organisms are resilient enough to endure a continuous take of individuals from their overall population (such as chickens and cows) while others simply are not (gorillas, old-growth forests, the biosphere as a whole ...). Adherents to this argument can buy a Big Mac on the way to a Save the Whales rally without being hypocritical. They will, however, get lots of dirty looks from the people at the rally who subscribe to the second major argument against sustainable use: the rights and welfare of animals.

More red flags, now waving against a sky purple with emotion. Here is the ember that burns on the hearth of sustainable use: the separation of an individual living thing from its collective species for the sake of an isolated act of human domination. (To keep this volume focused on its taxon, let us here take a departure from flora, with apologies to all hortiphiles. In terms of science, concern for plants is certainly no less justified than concern for animals—in terms of emotion, too, many would say. For those in touch with the secret life of plants, all the arguments presented here can be as readily applied to a fern as to a feline.) For starters, rights and welfare must be separated—a distinction made all too infrequently when discussion turns to nonhuman animals. Animal *rights* deals with entitlements, and we have discussed the intricacies of that argument already in chapter 4. Animal *welfare*, on the other hand, deals with suffering, and here we have a new tool to use in our analysis, though it is new only to us.

Jeremy Bentham, an eighteenth-century English philosopher, strove long ago to separate clearly the motivating factors behind various efforts to conserve animals, a pursuit already attracting advocates in his day. Among much intelligent commentary on the conflict between wildlife and humanity, Bentham made one particularly cogent remark that carries as much or more import today as when he first made it. "The question," he observed with respect to all animals, "is not, Can they *reason?* nor, Can they *talk?* but, Can they *suffer?*" This question now is known as Bentham's inquiry into suffering.

This is the point where cold analysis falters. Any number of strong cases can be made to prove that a human being is more intelligent than a kitten, but few will prove him to be more huggable. The protective reflex—the urge to alleviate suffering—lies somewhere outside the latchkey universe of logic, out there with all those other ineffable qualities like happiness, instinct, faith, and love. For reasons impossible to explain, the impulse to console an animal in distress is equally as compelling to many human beings as the impulse to console another human being. To many, it is more compelling. Ask the people lined up in a pet store if the mewing kittens they're stroking have the *right* to be consoled and see what kind of a response you get. The question, in that context, is a non sequitur.

But that is exactly the question, in a parallel context, that one segment of the conservation community is asking the other to consider when it comes to sustainable use. Individual animals must suffer, the argument seems to say, for the sake of the species as a whole. This Solomon's choice pits the deepest of emotions against the driest of hypotheses. Many people characterize the act of inflicting suffering on *any* animal as an act of cruelty. Some don't hesitate to call it evil. Suddenly it's a holy war.

Just because Bentham asks his question doesn't mean there's a handy answer available. Fido and Fluffy can clearly suffer, but what about a goldfish? What about the brine shrimp you feed the goldfish? What about amoebas? Can viruses suffer? Just where do you draw the line? Unless you're a Jain — wearing a breath mask to ensure you don't inhale any living thing and sweeping the ground before you as you walk so you can be sure every bug has been brushed from your path — you're sure to inflict suffering at *some* level. (Even the Jains are hypocrites, technically; all those little mites on their skin and bacteria in their digestive tracts. . . .) If you have trouble drawing a line *any-where*, you'll end up weeping over the sink as you scoop the seeds from your fellow cantaloupe into the disposal.

Back at a manageable level, it's important to note that the animal welfare argument transcends the issue of consumptive versus nonconsumptive use. An overly hasty parallel is often drawn. High-profile nonconsumptive uses tend to take the form of kinder, gentler activities, like eco-tourism and photography, while consumptive uses usually involve a killing. The use of an individual animal can be entirely *non*-consumptive, however, while still inflicting someone's definition of suffering. Animals in pet stores are "imprisoned." Animals in circuses are "humiliated." Animals in laboratories are "tortured." Suffering is relative. One person's use is another's abuse. Pet owners with the best of intentions often feed their animals diets selected strictly on a basis of human tastes, neglecting what the animal itself might naturally prefer. (Is your dog really better off as a vegetarian?) Finally, consumptive uses, even those that lead to or *focus* on the death of an individual animal, can be couched in terms of mercy, as we shall see in a later chapter.

Certain organizations are very clear about their goal to reduce animal suffering. The Society for the Prevention of Cruelty to Animals (SPCA) could hardly be more specific, with People for the Ethical Treatment of Animals (PETA) and the Humane Society only slightly less so. For the most part, however, the lines remain very unclearly drawn, even within the minds of the individual participants. Huge numbers of "checkbook conservationists" respond to nothing more than a loose desire to do something good for animals like the ones pictured on the envelopes in which so many membership solicitations are sent. Such donors have neither the time nor the inclination to research the particulars of how their contributed dollars are spent. If they did undertake such research, and bounced the results against a careful review of their personal predilections, many would stop payment on their checks.

With the exception of a single reference to circuses, the suffering argument has thus far been applied here only to common animals like chickens, kittens, and goldfish. Were those the only applications of the suffering aspect of sustainable use to be considered, we could now move along with a departing wave to Bentham. But the suffering component of sustainable use plays mightily into the endangered species equation, especially when it comes to charismatic megafauna. Living things that are harvested by humans are, by definition, under some form of human control — more commonly referred to, in this context, as "domestication." Controlled things are not wild. Lots of people are perfectly comfortable with the idea of domesticated chickens, but far fewer are comfortable with the idea of domesticated tigers. Why? Are certain animals more worthy of wildness than others? Is there a spectrum of domesticatability, just as there is a spectrum of captivity? Tigers "seem" more wild than chickens, even though just a few thousand years ago both species were equally free from human control. (Indeed, wild roosters still cluck their way through many a forest in India, so precisely similar to their domesticated barnyard cousins that they demand a double take.) It therefore seems more improper — more cruel, if you will — to deny a tiger its wildness than to equally deny a chicken. Somehow, we, as humans, have grown to associate size, power, stealth, carnivorousness, and beauty with a right to wildness.

That's a baseless coupling. Wildness is not an index of sexiness; it's an index of human control. We will never make meaningful decisions regarding the fate of the tiger so long as the following distinctions remain unclear: Is it the goal of tiger conservation to save *the* tiger, or to save *each* tiger? And in "saving" them — either individually *or* as a species — are we striving to alleviate their suffering, or are we striving to restore their wildness?

Different organizations pursue different and sometimes conflicting combinations of those variables, all in the name of tiger conservation. The activity that puts the spark to the fuse by combining the issues of endangerment, use, sustainability, wildness, rights, and suffering all into one process is known as tiger farming.

〜

In a place called Sriracha, some seventy miles to the northwest of Thailand's capital city of Bangkok, a man named Somphong Temsiriphong has built a thriving business. He started many years ago farming pigs, a vocation for which he showed a knack. Years later, acting on a hunch about a rising market and capitalizing on his successful experience with pigs, Temsiriphong modified his farm to accommodate a more aggressive beast: the crocodile.

Crocodiles breed readily, grow quickly to maturity, aren't fussy eaters (pork serves just fine), and they yield valuable products with every derivative their bodies produce, from their teeth to the tips of their tails. Temsiriphong succeeded even more vastly with his crocs than with his pigs, and the reptiles proved so universally interesting he eventually opened Sriracha to the general public, collecting a modest fee at the gate, beyond which the atmosphere is redolent of an amusement park. Visitors are ushered past pens where crocs the size of carpet rolls lounge as though petrified by the sun. Tours of the nursery also are available, where rack after rack of incubated eggs prepare to hatch into a squirming herd. Teams of lab-coated technicians weigh each offspring, assign it a number, mark it externally with a distinctive notch on the tail that will last for the animal's life, tag it internally with an electronic transponder, and meticulously record all the data. Visitors then proceed to a small museum where they learn interesting facts about other forms of life, including everything from bats to the nonpoisonous scorpions available to be picked up and petted by delighted children and horrified adults. Next, there is, of course, a spacious gift shop, where every trinket that can be manufactured from a dead crocodile is offered for sale: purses, shoes, belts, dolls, key chains, stuffed baby crocs dressed up to look like mariachi singers. . . . Finally, what better way to finish off your visit to Sriracha than with a meal. A crocodile meal. Not a meal that would be eaten *by* a crocodile, but, rather, a meal *of* crocodile. Sweet-and-sour crocodile. Crocodile soup. Scrambled crocodile eggs. . . . All served up in a comfortable, clean, air-conditioned restaurant just yards from the gift shop.

Before you gag on either the concept or the fare, consider a few things: No laws of any kind, either domestic or international, are being broken at Sriracha; the animals are slaughtered and processed as conscientiously as any cow on any ranch in America (slaughter is never pretty, we must remember); live crocs are not one of your more huggable pets; they taste great. With respect to the *farming* that takes place at Sriracha, the only grounds on which we can be resentful in any consistent way involve the premise of suffering—which defends the pigs as quickly as it does the crocs. In the coldly practical terms of continuous harvests for consumptive use, a captive population of crocodiles can clearly sustain the take.

But other aspects of Sriracha complicate the issue ominously, especially when considered in combination. Species of crocodile closely related to those bred on the farm at Sriracha are endangered in the wild. Then, there is a second shopping venue at the farm, just beyond the gift shop: a TCM pharmacy, where prescriptions containing crocodile derivatives are especially cheap. Finally, Temsiriphong has taken to breeding a third species of animal on his farm: tigers.

Thailand, beyond even its obvious charms, is an amazing blend of cultural, legal, and natural ingredients. (It is critical to note that many of the distinctions about to be made regarding Thailand grow blurry as the country rushes toward modernization.) The dominant strain of Buddhism discourages the killing, but not the consuming, of animals. The work of slaughterhouses is therefore left largely to the indigenous Muslim and Chinese populations. Two comprehensive rounds of wildlife-protection legislation have ranked Thailand technically among the most progressive of conservationist countries, but enforcement of those laws remains a problem and governmental corruption is a maxim. Finally, as the geographical heart of Southeast Asia, Thailand enjoys one of the richest biotic mixes on the planet. For the tiger, this socionatural stew equals an environment where the animal is simultaneously wild/captive, produced/consumed, protected/poached.

Under Thai law, Temsiriphong is not allowed either to kill his tigers for commercial purposes or to breed them for sale; if he were a strict Thai Buddhist he would be forbidden to kill the animals for any reason whatsoever (in which case he probably would have chosen a different field). He can, however, legally and piously breed his cats as readily as he likes so long as he registers each new birth with the government and uses the animals exclusively for exhibition. Temsiriphong was not strictly aware of these terms when he began breeding his tigers, but the restrictions don't much bother him now. Business is booming with the crocs, and the tigers—housed in a commodious display—simply add an extra attraction for the visitors, who love watching the cats, especially at the exhibit where they can have their pictures taken bottle-feeding a cub. Conveniently, the felines thrive on extra pork and crocodile meat. Despite such a happy balance, the scales at Sriracha might quickly tip. Asked if he would take advantage of proposed changes in Thai law that would allow him to slaughter his tigers and sell their derivatives through his TCM medicine shop just as he does with his crocs, Temsiriphong does not hesitate to answer, "Sure." The question, in fact, seems a bit superfluous to him.

This could spell trouble for our analysis. On what basis is tiger farming prohibited while crocodile farming is made legal? The platform of suffering supports only both or neither animal, with any seeming advantage for the tiger nothing more than a spin-off of its sexiness. In every other respect, right down to the sales receipt, the dynamics of farming tigers at Sriracha for TCM would be identical to those of farming crocodiles. "It's a big question in Thailand," admits Tim Redford, an independent animal-husbandry consultant who has worked with several of Thailand's foremost wildlife organizations, both governmental and non. "A lot of people, both from the government and from universities, have said — some of them unofficially and others officially in print — that they are in agreement with tiger farming, and that by breeding these tigers they believe it would preserve the wild tigers."

There is the rub. The so-called laws of supply and demand seem to support absolutely the argument that the farming of captive tigers will relieve the pressures of poaching on wild tiger populations: Increase the supply, the price will drop, risks associated with illegal trade will become increasingly less worth taking for black marketeers, the black market will therefore wither, and poaching will diminish in turn. Academically, this is very simple math. So simple, in fact, it has been employed eagerly to reinforce the pursuits of Temsiriphong and a handful of other entrepreneurs in Asia who have opened tiger farms. The profitability of a legitimate augmentation to the ever-dwindling stock of wild tiger derivatives becomes progressively *more* likely and attractive under the laws of supply and demand. If the wild tiger will benefit too, great! Everyone will support the practice. (Remember, please, that we have set aside for a moment the morality of slaughter.) This giddy logic filtered up to the level of national lawmakers, and in 1992 at CITES COP-8 in Japan the delegation from mainland China — where tiger farms far more productive and sophisticated than Sriracha already were in operation — introduced a proposal to sanction the *international* trade of derivatives from farmed tigers.

Not so fast. "It's completely misguided," says Redford. "Tiger farming would bring about the immediate extinction of the remnant wild population." To support this seemingly illogical claim, Redford offers strikingly immediate evidence. "There was a wild crocodile population in Thailand once, but it virtually ceased to exist within a few years of the crocodile farms starting."

Crocodiles are not widgets. Nor are tigers. When it comes to tiger TCM, the existing demand so dramatically outstrips the existing supply that standard models lose their relevance. Only one widget per several thousand highly motivated customers is available in this case study, and when the last widget goes away no more can be made — a feature that further tantalizes the already covetous customers. Supply and demand work perfectly in textbooks, and even passably well in practice, but economics was a simpler science in Adam Smith's day, and Scotland is not Asia. This market has dynamics all its own, and refinements to the equations are essential.

"There is no way to differentiate between a farmed tiger and a wild tiger," Redford illustrates one idiosyncrasy. "The bones are going to be the same size, the skins are going to be the same size.... It's just asking for [wild] animals to be laundered." Laundering: the introduction of black-market goods into legitimate markets by masking or removing their links to illegitimate sources. For wildlife derivatives, which do not (yet) come with the equivalent of bar codes or serial numbers stamped into them, this can be done easily by falsifying the paperwork that documents their shipment. "That's what happened in Thailand with the crocodiles," says Redford. "If you read in the TRAFFIC bulletins, it's well documented about [crocodile-like] caiman skins being laundered through Thailand illegally. They've been put down as farm-bred crocodiles. It shows that the crocodile farmers have not really got any qualms about doing things illegally.... How can we tell that these tiger farmers would not do this? What guarantees are there? Who is going to monitor it?" In a moment we will investigate a few suggested answers to Redford's questions, but let us first understand exactly how wild tigers might come to be laundered.

Of the tiger farms now known to be in operation, none is openly sanctioned to slaughter and sell its animals. (Tales of underground breeding and killing are both frequent and well documented, though the high visibility of such operations tends to make them unattractive among businessmen who prefer to operate in secrecy.) For the most part, these farms came together in much the same way as Sriracha — within the last decade and under way well before anyone seriously analyzed the legal implications. As a consequence, several captive tiger populations already had blossomed by the time COP-8 convened in Kyoto.

If tiger farming, including slaughter, were now to be legitimized either through domestic legalization within a consumer country (such as Thailand or China) or through a change in CITES, an open and unassailable market for tiger derivatives would quickly emerge. The legitimate supply would begin to fill the standing demand through the newly legalized trade, to no one's great surprise. Critics of the economics of tiger farming predict that three disastrous consequences of this new cycle would materialize instantaneously and in the following order: First, a tacit endorsement of tiger TCM's efficacy would be presumed by every potential user in the world. (Fear of just such an endorsement, in part, is what keeps the otherwise useless bones of zoo and circus tigers that die of natural causes from being granted a CITES exemption.) Next, the vortex of demand, strengthened by the presumed endorsement of efficacy, would so violently outstrip the legitimate supply that a galactic price would be established. (Even tigers can't breed that fast.) Finally, black-market suppliers — aka poachers and smugglers — would gladly step in to fill the gap between supply and demand by assuming the now affordable risks of drawing from the physiologically indistinguishable wild population of tigers. Enabling these consequences, a well-oiled sales-and-delivery infrastructure for the legitimate market would already have been established, and the only thing required to shunt poached goods into the legitimate market would be an ersatz shipping document or a purchased signature, both of which would become ever more obtainable as the price of the product ever escalated. "Effectively," says Sam LaBudde of the legalization of tiger farming, "you would hang a price tag around the neck of every wild tiger."

Many argue the price tag is there already. "It's been established," says Michael 't Sas-Rolfes. "Go into a medicine shop in China and they will quote you a price per pound right now." The demand already exists, 't Sas-Rolfes observes, as does the (wild) supply. The trade infrastructure may not be either open or well oiled, but clearly it is in place. All the market forces exist, then, to tag a price on every piece of a wild tiger, and itemized price lists are in fact already purported to be circulating among smugglers and poachers. The farming of tigers can only *lower* the price on the tag that the black market already has hung around the necks of the wild animals, 't Sas-Rolfes submits. "The most important point," he repeats, "the crucial point is that whether the trade is legal or illegal, whether the commodification of the tiger has been expressly recognized or not, the price tag is still there. The demand is still there. . . . You can't simply ignore the fact that the demand is there and say, right, we're just going to ban the trade and then hope that it is going to save the tiger. It won't."

Perhaps not. But there is a subtlety to the economic antifarming argument that must not be missed. If marijuana were legalized tomorrow, would you be any more likely to try it? How about if you or a loved one suffered from glaucoma, a disease that's been found to be

curiously responsive to marijuana? Now, if only five thousand cannabis plants still grew on the face of the earth, and they were located
in truly hard-to-reach regions, how much would you be willing to pay
to own one of them? How scrupulously do you think the process of
gathering those five thousand plants together would proceed? How
picky would you be about the paperwork accompanying your private
supply of marijuana if you could not own one of the plants? How
much do you think (reviving Ken Goddard) a speculator might be
willing to pay to make sure every cannabis plant he did not own was
thrown into a fire? Tigers are not widgets.

Secondary aspects of the tiger's unique situation intensify the
jeopardy of their wild contingent still further. "The salaries in this part
of the world are so low that most of the people are quite poor," Tim
Redford continues. "If they see somebody else getting rich, they're
going to want their opportunity as well. Another point added to that
is that a lot of these people have got access to weapons. Southeast
Asia has been an area of war for twenty or thirty years now. There are
so many guns and weapons here it would be easy for anybody to go
out and shoot a tiger and either launder it through [a farm] or just go
directly to a local merchant. There are some people who are still a
little bit scared of the law, but not very."

Other conservationists are lined up to bolster Redford and
LaBudde with arguments even more universal, if a bit less scientific.
"Look at champagne or cubic zirconium," suggests Judy Mills. "Both
are great examples. Anybody can afford champagne, but I'm telling
you the people who live on the peak [in Hong Kong's most exclusive
neighborhood] don't buy just any champagne. They buy Perrier-Jouët
or all those other ones that I don't even know about because I could
never even dream of being able to afford them. With cubic zirconium,
I have beautiful cubic zirconium earrings. I have all sorts of things
that make it look like I, too, can wear diamonds. But I'm telling you
that if I [could afford] diamonds, they would be real. And I'm telling
you that the people who live on the peak, who are very wealthy and

who can afford the best, aren't going to be wearing cubic zirconium any more than the people who can afford the best medicine would be taking the medicine from farmed animals."

Here Mills puts a fascinating spin on the debate by suggesting that farming animals will threaten wild populations even if the market prices indeed drop as the laws of supply and demand imply. "Farming of wildlife has an additive rather than a compensatory effect on the market for their products," she insists. "It adds to demand rather than compensates for it . . . as we have seen from bear farming.

"There are ten thousand bears in captivity, on bear farms, in China," she continues. "I've been there. I've seen hundreds of bears in small cages in China. I've seen them milked of their bile [in a process through which the bile is withdrawn without killing the animal]. . . . The Chinese have told me, 'No wild bears are being poached anymore because there's plenty [on farms]. We have reached capacity. We can satisfy all our country's need for bear bile.' And [farmed bile] is everywhere. You can buy it anywhere. I can take you downtown Hong Kong, you can buy it here. How it got here we're not going to talk about. It's here, and you can get it. But you know what? I've had people come up to me and try to sell me bear gall-bladders from wild bears."

To help the Western mind better comprehend why gallbladders from wild bears can still find buyers in a market surfeited with farmed-bear bile, Mills unspools a parable. "I am a mainland Chinese," she poses. "I have always heard that bear bile is a great medicine to protect my liver from overindulgence in wine. Though I would love to use bear bile, I've never been able to afford it. But I'm getting wealthier now because our economy is growing so well. And now there is farmed-bear bile, which is much less expensive than bear bile from the gallbladder of a wild bear. Now I can afford it. I'm going to start buying bear bile. And, by God, I'm using it and I think I really do feel better. I'm sure that I'll live longer, I can overindulge as much as I want, and I don't have to worry about cirrhosis of the liver. I'm becoming very rich from my entrepreneurial endeavors in China, and the richer I get the more I'm thinking I should get the very best for myself, because I'm a rich person now. So I want a gallbladder from a wild bear, because that's the ultimate."

With this, Mills leads us into yet another dark alley of the farming labyrinth, the so-called "free-range" dilemma. Still in her adopted role, she continues, "I know that these bears that run around in the wild have more bile acids, more of the good stuff, than those that are in these tiny little cages. That makes intrinsic sense to me because they're eating wild foods and it all fits in with the Chinese medicine prescriptions for eating from nature and holistic this and that, right?" Dropping her masque, she concludes, "So what we have now is another consumer who wants parts from a wild animal. I see the same thing happening with tiger bone."

Restaurants everywhere offer "free-range" chicken and "brook" trout to discriminating customers convinced that these "wild" comestibles are in some way superior to their semidomesticated alternatives. Whether or not the wild items are indeed superior is of no consequence. Perception is reality. Markets for many things merely *perceived* to be superior persist almost by definition. Witness the symbiosis between Wall Street and Madison Avenue. Inevitably, these pseudo-superior goods command prices higher than those established in the markets for their inferior alternatives. TCM derivatives harvested from farmed animals will never be accepted completely as replacements for derivatives taken from animals in the wild simply because they are not perceived among the users of TCM to be as effective. This is precisely the same motivation that will inhibit the acceptance of chemically identical TCM substitutes.

And it gets worse. As with the application of Western science to rhino horn in the laboratories of Paul But for the sake of determining the material's medicinal efficacy, modern technology has reinforced rather than refuted TCM in the examination of the free-range dilemma: Farmed derivatives are not just perceived to be different from their wild counterparts, they actually are. "It's scientifically proven," says Mills with a shrug. "Gallbladders in wild bears contain more bile acids [which are the active ingredients] than those in farmed bears."

Speaking of Paul But, the free-range dilemma will corrupt his investigation into the efficacy of tiger-bone TCM before it even gets under way. The product supplied to him through the efforts of Sarah Christie came from a tiger in a zoo. Results from experiments on those bones can *only* reinforce the convictions of a TCM adherent who believes that bones from a wild tiger are the ones that really work: If the zoo tiger's bones are found to be effective, surely the bones from a wild tiger will contain even more of "the good stuff," just as the bile from a wild bear does. And if the zoo tiger's bones don't work, well, of course not. It's a zoo tiger. To settle the dispute, Paul But or a representative of incontestable reliability will have to hunt down and kill a wild tiger, lift its bones from its body, and carry them back to the lab for comparative experimentation. Not likely.

In the face of such seemingly insurmountable competition, a voice or two of support for tiger farming survives, the first of which emanates from what now may seem an unlikely throat. "The answer is tiger farming," declares David Choy of the Hong Kong & Kowloon Chinese Medicine Merchants Association Limited. He and his colleagues see tiger farming as the almost painfully obvious answer to everybody's tiger problems. "We are watching very closely what's happening in mainland China [with respect to tiger farming]," Choy affirms. "And I am absolutely certain the users of TCM will accept medicines made from farmed tigers." To a person, the pharmacists who dined with Choy at the association's 1995 convention in Hong Kong agreed.

With respect to the potential for laundering wild tiger derivatives through legitimate markets, technology offers a bit of hope. Certain chemicals that can be added to the diets of captive felines can be detected in their body parts postmortem. Such additives could reliably and economically mark farmed tigers. Anyone caught thereafter selling derivatives not laced with the chemical badge would have to explain himself. Also, as research into the molecular makeup of tigers proceeds through the work of such scientists as Steve O'Brien, Ken Goddard, Paul But, et al., it eventually might become possible to pinpoint the provenance of every piece of tiger, even without an artificially introduced chemical marker.

Of course, if the concept of treating tigers like an industrial resource bothers you on altruistic grounds, none of the foregoing arguments matters — even if (especially if) your feelings are swayed by the animal's huggability. You simply don't want tigers to be farmed, period. It's inhumane.

Fair enough. You need to prepare yourself to be called a tiger hugger, but your position is no less valid than anyone else's. Regardless of whether your concern is for animal rights or animal welfare or even a combination of the two, you are more than entitled to stand your ground with perfect validity on a moral basis. But *don't* try to justify that position with conservation logic. You can't. More importantly, you don't need to and you don't want to. It will cloud the issue, and if the issue gets clouded the tigers will go away. Everybody will lose, including you, including the tigers.

↩

An illegal drug was cited earlier as a corollary in presenting the intricacies of the economic arguments involved in tiger farming. The subject of drugs serves even better as a corollary for the moral arguments. The cold, hard realities of supply and demand *insist* that the easiest way — perhaps the only way — to win the so-called war on drugs in the U.S. is to legalize, and then regulate, what is now drug contraband. When it comes to cocaine and heroin and hashish we don't even have to concern ourselves with the supply shortage, the efficacy issue, or the free-range dilemma that so confound the tiger's situation. Nevertheless, the legalization of drugs simply is not an option for the overwhelming majority of U.S. citizens. It just carries too damn much moral baggage, sanctioning what many consider to be a vice.

The sexy tiger carries heavy baggage too. When the Chinese submitted their proposal to sanction the international trade of farmed-tiger derivatives at COP-8 in Japan, the opposition was instantaneous, loud, and strong. In particular, the NGOs decried the move, employing a montage of justifications, not all of them based on logic. The validity of individual arguments against the proposal, however, was far less important than their collective mass and volume. A defining moment had taken place: Tiger farming would forever thereafter be recognized as the electrified third rail of international tiger conservation. The startled Chinese delegation retreated, withdrawing its proposal.

That was hardly the end of it. For one thing, dozens, possibly hundreds, of tigers were strewn across Asia on farms whose proprietors had been anticipating an open market. Few could indulge in the same luxury as Somphong Temsiriphong in Thailand and simply keep their cats for show. Most farms were industrial breeding facilities that had neither the means nor the intentions of making money off the tigers in any other way than by slaughtering them and selling their parts. At COP-8 the cats had been converted from potential profit centers into standing liabilities. What should be done with them?

The first impulse among many of the breeders was simply to kill the hungry, dangerous, high-maintenance animals. But that met with opposition almost as fierce as the commotion in Kyoto. COP-8 had brought the farmed tigers into the international spotlight, where they attracted benefactors from far beyond the scope of CITES. Concerned individuals, groups, and institutions everywhere, from within the countries that housed the tiger farms to places that were neither range states nor consuming nations, rallied on behalf of the farmed tigers, much to the further consternation of the farmers. This refined the argument, unintentionally: It wasn't the farming of the tigers that drew fire, it was the *killing* of them. If ever there were a moral position, this was

it. None of the cats was contributing to an official conservation breeding program. Most were, in fact, of untraceable origin. Their value in
terms of the survival of the species, therefore, was not an issue. What
mattered was that lots of people in many countries for a variety of
reasons simply did not want the tigers killed. Period.

This unlikely predicament perfectly illustrates the mercurial nature of the question asked at the beginning of this chapter: Just what
can the owner of an ex situ tiger do with the animal? Tiger farmers
in Asia "own" their tigers, but they "can't" just kill them. Such intense
scrutiny has been focused on the animals that their owners daren't
risk transgressing the will of their detractors lest they incur a wrath of
many colors. The cries of altruists bent on saving the cats from destruction have reached the ears of everyone from journalists to consumers to legislators. The issue has grown into a *cause politique*. Edgy
national leaders have stepped in to make sure the cats are well cared
for, fearing trade boycotts might erupt if they don't. Laws have been
passed in some cases specifically to make sure, or at least to make a
show, that the tigers won't be slaughtered. The result is a weird state
of limbo where the owners of these farmed tigers are now compelled
to maintain the animals at their own expense while simultaneously
being denied permission to realize the values for which they began
breeding up the tigers in the first place — unwilling custodians who
can't abdicate their jobs.

An assortment of interesting options have been floated to resolve
the quandary. Taiwan offered to give, free of charge, 250 farmed tigers
to India for "relocation in the Indian wild," as it was put in the *Jakarta
Post* on March 2, 1995. The offer drew gags from many conservation
biologists and gasps from the rest. Those hostile to the concept of tiger
reintroduction sneered at the thought of setting 250 captive-bred tigers
free in the forests of India. The results, they asserted, would be tragic
for the tigers at least and potentially for adjacent human populations
too. Those adversaries willing to grant that a reintroduction just might
work were appalled because the ancestry of all the cats in question

was suspect. If the reintroduction were successful, the entire wild tiger population of India would fall suspect to hybridization. Taiwan was thanked and turned down.

A few months later, however, India reentered the eye of the storm by signing with mainland China a bilateral protocol on tiger conservation that contained the following clause: "[The Parties shall] encourage, on an experimental basis, captive breeding activities, with a view to release of the species into the wild." Debate erupted both inside and outside the country and across every conservation line, from field versus zoo to science versus politics to NGO versus government. "It shows a lack of understanding of the tiger and its natural history," Valmik Thapar stated publicly. Gripes focused largely on the viability of reintroduction, but the implied fear was that China was merely cloaking its aspirations to farm tigers in a new international language.

"Look," huffed Project Tiger's Arin Ghosh in response. "That's good drawing-room talk. But trust the country. They are managing their assets. They have a much higher national stake in this than any individual has. . . . Some individual can't just stand up and say, 'I don't trust the Chinese.' And you can go to hell if you don't trust me. It's my bloody job to do this, and I promise I'm going to do it sincerely."

⌣

Since you have to kill a tiger to use its derivatives in TCM, the farming of the animal involves a clearly consumptive use. As highlighted earlier, that is the aspect of the practice, not the captivity involved, that electrifies resistance to it among the advocates of animal rights. But what about when captive tigers are put to thoroughly nonconsumptive uses, in a circus, say, or in a zoo? The rights issue goes a little blurry there, but welfare comes increasingly — though not perfectly — into focus.

Happiness is but a molecule or two more logical than suffering, and the two are closely linked. If you're suffering, you're probably not happy. And unhappiness can itself be defined as a type of suffering.

When it comes to ex situ tigers, the relevant question for advocates of animal welfare is this: How happy is the cat? (Humanists may prefer to leave the room for this part of the discussion.) A knotty question indeed, fraught with philosophical switchbacks. Happy in whose terms? The tiger's? Just when, and to whom, did they make their preferences known? Happy in human terms? Few of us get a kick out of sucking on a dead deer. Who's to say a tiger thrills to human predilections?

Despite such ambiguity, Bentham's inquiry still applies. As with the concept of captivity, there is a spectrum of happiness that is vague in the middle but sharp at both ends. A tiger with its paw caught in a steel trap just is not going to be happy in anyone's terms, as will be readily apparent from his posture, attitude, and noise. Likewise, a tigress lounging in the shade while suckling her cubs after finishing a fresh meal will exude an air of satisfaction and contentment instantly familiar to any observer, even though it may be difficult to describe. She's "happy." Probably the cubs are too. Does it matter to her or to her cubs if they're in situ or ex? That's very important to figure out, because it will answer the question of whether or not a tiger's happiness can be linked to its wildness.

In Indonesia, Ron Tilson makes a point of showing off a new captive-breeding facility for which he arranged the funding from a variety of private sources back in the States. The structure measures fifteen by twenty-four meters and comprises ten enclosures used temporarily to house tigers involved in coordinated captive-breeding matchups. Each enclosure contains a log for scratching and a large wooden shelf on which the cats can crouch above the concrete floor. All the enclosures are open to more than sufficient light and ventilation through the wide bars that form the outside wall of the entire facility. A broad central hall grants access to the personnel involved in caring for the cats and managing the breeding operations. One end of the structure is devoted to special maternity dens and a basic laboratory. In all, the new facility is more than worthy of the pride that Tilson takes in it.

A few yards away is another, older structure. It is not much bigger than the new captive-breeding facility, but it is quite different in composition. The outside wall is all but solid, interrupted infrequently by doors and vents. A central hallway also splits this building, but it is so narrow that two people cannot pass casually without risking attack from the animals that line both sides of the hallway, big cats all, each housed in a box of bars small enough to prevent the tenant inside from turning around without brushing its whiskers and the tip of its tail simultaneously against opposing bars. There are no logs or shelves. The concrete floor is uneven and wet. The air is dark and heavy with the odor of feline excrement.

A kilometer or so down the hill lies a public display for tigers. It is a lush enclosure of many acres, through which paying visitors drive in their private cars. The handsome resident tigers lounge or cavort or come to sniff curiously at the occupants of the vehicles, who cower in enchanted wonder behind tightly rolled-up windows. Perhaps more significantly, if the cats don't want to interact with their visitors at all, they can secret themselves behind mounds or trees or clumps of foliage or rocks, invisible from the drive-path for as long as they like.

How routinely are the tigers circulated out from either of the two structures up the hill into the main display? Precise records are either not kept or not offered for scrutiny. But there are always some tigers confined within the old building. Welfare advocates would argue quite reasonably, in their terms, that *any* amount of time spent in such conditions constitutes a degree of cruelty. And although the suggestion confuses Ron Tilson, many advocates would argue that even the tigers kept within his spiffed-up new facility are being mistreated. Indeed, several wild-caught Sumatran tigers have been housed temporarily in the new structure, seething hostages who throw themselves against the bars with such astounding force every time an observer steps within eyeshot that keepers of the cats discourage such visits for fear the beasts will break their bones or teeth against the steel. They're unhappy.

Almost recklessly, Tilson ushers his personal visitors through the old building in a dramatic comparison of how vastly superior the new building is. No question. But the issue of the welfare of the occupants in either structure does not seem to cross Tilson's mind. Even the members of his visiting teams do not make ready reference to what they all admit upon direct questioning are deplorable husbandry conditions in the old building. An almost awkward silence on the topic prevails as the captive-breeding sciences at hand are conducted. Individually, the tigers housed in the old building are simply of less concern, when it comes to the survival of the species, than the species at large. Tilson and his teams are working to save *the* tiger, not every tiger. They pursue that goal in the most sensible way they can. Resources are limited, and if the Sumatran tiger is to survive as a genetically distinct life-form, either in situ or ex, there simply is not time or money or space enough to cater to the comforts of every tiger that walks upon the soil of Indonesia. Under the constraints of his perspective, Tilson's actions are inarguably — even admirably — consistent.

It is a shame, therefore, that he will not be spared the wrath of animal-welfare activists disgusted with the thought that he can sanction conditions like those perpetuated in the old building up the hill. Worse, Tilson is likely to be accused of *contributing* to the suffering of certain individual tigers, especially those whose lineages are not pure, by ignoring them in favor of individuals whose ancestries make them more valuable to coordinated captive-breeding activities. Two things make such claims against Tilson a shame. First, they mingle logic and morality, which, as we know, will be bad for everyone, including the tigers. More significant, however, is the reality that neither Tilson nor Indonesia are by any stretch unique when it comes to working with, or around, tigers housed in less than perfectly happy homes. Choose a country, it's got zoos and circuses. The resident tigers in many of those sites can only dream of living it up like the tigers kept in the old building next to Tilson's new captive-breeding facility, who at least get plenty of fresh kangaroo meat to eat every day. (Which makes for some pretty unhappy kangaroos, just to whip-saw the welfare of one animal against another. . . . The argument is endless.) Even the zoos in North America are not free of transgression. A staff member at one of the most august, respected, beloved parks on the continent testifies that there are tigers kept continuously belowground in small cages where they "never see the light of day."

This is generally where the forces rally to condemn all ex situ operations everywhere. Concerns for both rights and welfare merge in a battle against what seems to be the tyranny of humans over captive tigers. Zoos are cruel. Circuses are cruel. Magic acts are cruel. The only way not to be cruel to tigers is to leave them alone in situ.

Really? What is the life of a wild tiger like? Although we don't know for the most part, research indicates that when a wild tiger dies, the circumstances in which it finds itself are less than comfortable. It suffers. Old tigers are displaced from their territories by younger, stronger individuals, and the evictees are left to make their way as best they can without a home. Typically that leads to death by starvation, unless the cat depredates on the local human population or its herds, in which case it will either be killed or shooed away to continue starving. But let's stick with wildness as purely as we can by keeping humans out of it. Sometimes tigers fight, which leads to injuries, which lead to infections, which lead to lingering, agonizing, septic deaths — or, once again, to starvation because the animal cannot hunt. Wild tigers don't die happy, and there's even evidence they don't live so happy either. Life is tough in the jungle. Wildness, therefore, cannot be equated with lack of suffering, and thus, by extension, not with happiness.

Hmmm. Once again the argument reverts to humanism. Is the

act of inflicting human intervention of any kind upon tigers wrong? We can clearly alleviate the suffering of individual tigers, but we have to "meddle" with nature to do so. Conversely, is it somehow better not to meddle with nature if it means increased suffering for individual tigers? Yes, we often *increase* the suffering of individual tigers by meddling, specifically when we take them ex situ and fail to care for them properly. But what is proper care?

"Enrichment" is a buzzword among the zoo community. It refers to introducing diversity and stimulation into the environments in which ex situ animals are kept. Not so very long ago, it was the norm to see zoo tigers kept in simple box cages. Such exhibits persist, certainly, but sometime during the middle of this century zookeepers and curators started looking for ways to make their animal displays more interesting, for the inhabitants as well as for the visitors. In particular, introducing aspects of the animals' natural habitats was found to satisfy the interests of both contingents. The animals quickly perked up, either abandoning or reducing many of their stereotypical behaviors (such as pacing), and visitors loved seeing the animals in more natural settings doing more natural things. If they'd wanted tricks, they'd have gone to the circus. (This is not meant to be a slam against circuses, incidentally. Many animal behaviorists will argue that the variety and volume of interaction enjoyed by circus animals is far more beneficial than any amount of enrichment attempted by zoos in what ultimately remains a cage.)

Initially, enrichment took simple forms, such as enlarging the enclosure, using moats instead of bars to keep the animals away from the visitors (and vice versa), and installing a bit of creative landscaping. But methods have become increasingly diverse and sophisticated as the science of animal husbandry has advanced. "Some of the techniques we use at the London Zoo," says Curator of Mammals Douglas Richardson, "include trailing a piece of meat through the enclosure to leave a scent trail. Occasionally we'll leave a meat reward at the end of the trail. Sometimes not. That's to mimic a tiger's hunting behavior, where they sometimes make a kill but sometimes the prey gets away. Or we'll hang the food from the top of the cage so the animal has to use more of its physical abilities to actually climb up a pole or leap up to get at it. That also helps in keeping them physically fit, using muscles they wouldn't use if they were in a small cage, lying around, with the food presented on the floor in the same place at the same time every single day." Indeed, one of the most common health problems with zoo tigers is that they get fat.

So how could enrichment be anything but good? Surely it can only benefit ex situ animals, reducing their boredom (i.e., suffering) by putting them in situations similar to their in situ homelands without introducing any of the associated risks (i.e., suffering). Hallelujah! A recipe for happy tigers. Put them in expansive enclosures — wild animal parks, say — and enrich their environments to the hilt. Everyone will like the results.

Or not. Let us revisit our satisfied tigress from a few pages back, contentedly suckling her cubs. The bearing and rearing of young is undeniably one of the most significant, if not *the* most significant, activity tigers perform. Wild females over the age of four spend all but a tiny portion of the remainder of their lives either carrying or caring for cubs. Males may be somewhat less involved once fertilization has taken place, but if you're going to keep males in anything close to an enriched ex situ setting, you're going to have to keep females, too, so the males can at least exercise their natural inclination to attempt fertilization. (The presumption that males have nothing to do with rearing, by the way, is under reassessment. Recent observations in the wild have revealed surprising paternal attentiveness, and many zoos are finding father tigers to be more interested in their offspring than previously recognized.) Unless something is done to avert the consequences — which could only itself be considered an anti-enriching intrusion — baby tigers are going to arrive roughly a hundred days after one of those attempts.

Perfect. A happy little family. "But what you're going to come up against," warns Sarah Christie, "is space for the cubs." This is a refinement of what she was talking about in the very first quote she offered in chapter 1 of this book. As zoos around the world align themselves with accepted norms of conservation, they tend to rely increasingly on the recommendations of tiger-breeding coordinators, like Christie. That means they don't just let their tigers multiply willy-nilly. They can't afford to. Most zoos can only manage a small number of tigers, and the ones they want to keep, for the sake of good conservation, are the ones with viable ancestries.

But ex situ tigers breed readily, and something must be done with the cubs, who will quickly grow into big, hungry, expensive adult tigers eager to produce yet more cubs of their own. "Suppose you were to make up ten pairs of tigers and breed a litter from each," Christie demonstrates. "Average litter size is, say, two and one-half cubs [which is reasonable, if not conservative], so you end up with twenty-five cubs. You've got to find twelve zoos who can take a new pair of tigers. That's not easy. Everybody's tiger space is stuffed full."

As a temporary evasive measure, adult tigers are sometimes separated. But with lack of space at the very root of the problem, segregation rarely offers a long-term remedy. In addition, certain tigers don't get along and therefore cannot be kept together. Others make particularly good matches for a display, but would instantly breed if put together. The techniques used most readily to overcome all these perplexities are contraception and sterilization. Subcutaneous hormonal implants, similar to those now used in humans, prevent female tigers from conceiving, and castration fixes the males — though this is by far the less desirable and less frequently employed option. Regardless of the method, however, the effect denies the tigers their opportunity to rear young.

In what seems to be a contradiction, Sarah Christie herself is strongly in favor of allowing *all* captive tigers to produce and raise their own young for the sake of enrichment. How done? If we allow ex situ tigers to breed for the sake of enrichment, we end up with no place for the offspring; if we don't allow them to breed, we doom them to profoundly unnatural lives. Yes, we can drag their food through the cage and make them jump for it, but denying them the opportunity to bear and rear their young will deflate every other attempt at enrichment. What is the answer?

Here is what Christie suggests: "Euthanize the cubs."

At the risk of being buried in hate mail — perhaps worse — Sarah Christie vigorously defends what she sees as the only option that is both logical and moral when it comes to keeping ex situ tigers. Her idea is to let pairs breed as they may and then rear their cubs to an age when the offspring would naturally begin to disperse in the wild — somewhere around two or three years old. At that point, you take the cubs away and you kill them. "If there wasn't enough room for the cubs in a reserve," Christie notes, "they'd die when they left home anyway." Quite true, and they would suffer more in that death than in the controlled circumstances of a euthanization. But can we stomach it? Which is more cruel, to put the cubs down quickly and painlessly, or to condemn the parents to lives of sterility? We cannot avoid both. There simply is not room for all the offspring. And though it is not readily discussed in public, tiger euthanasia is already in wide practice. When space becomes a problem among zoos, healthy adult tigers — inevitably ones with less than regal bloodlines — are put down readily. This is, in fact, how the tiger for Paul But was found.

If possible, Christie's justification becomes even more unseemly (in some people's terms) as she describes the spin-off benefits that would accrue from her plan. "Every zoo would like to have tiger cubs," she observes. "Zoos need to bring people through the gate, and people like to see tiger cubs. If people were to buy into the idea of euthanizing cubs . . . then every zoo could have tiger cubs all the time." Not only would the lives of many sires and dams be enriched by letting them produce and raise their own cubs, they would also draw paying visitors in hordes. Thus, killing cubs makes great business sense, a commercial connection many undoubtedly will find reprehensible. Even so, Christie does not flinch, pressing ahead with powerful logic. "So much of this money we're spending [on conservation] comes from zoos, right? . . . But there is this difficulty between gate money and conservation. The gate money is to be used for conservation purposes where it can be, but the program you have to follow in the zoo from a conservation point of view [i.e., only breeding genetically valuable tigers] isn't always compatible with great exhibits. Not breeding from your tigers is not such a good exhibit as breeding from your tigers." The paying public, she points out, doesn't give a damn about the ancestry of cubs so long as they're cute. More cubs, more visitors, more money for conservation — of *the* tiger, not of all tigers. To take full advantage of the natural affection people have for tiger cubs by turning their gate fees into conservation dollars, most of the cubs will have to be killed.

Does any of this sound familiar? It parallels, in a way many will find frightening, the dilemma of tiger farming: Raise up and kill off this fecund animal in captivity for the sake of saving its wild counterparts. The only thing that could more closely link the two practices would be to sell the bones from the euthanized cubs into the TCM market, a suggestion that has not gone unstated by conservationists and TCM practitioners alike who've been presented with Christie's plan. (One person enthusiastically pointed out that the more you enrich the habitat of a farmed tiger, the more its bones will be like those of a tiger in the wild, and therefore more likely to be accepted by users of TCM.)

Christie has no delusions her idea will be warmly received. "Most [zoos] — the vast majority — are going to be against it, not necessarily because they may think it's morally unacceptable, although some people may have perfectly justifiable moral problems with it, but because of a fear of publicity backlash." The suggestion has been made that the overabundant cubs could be offered free to circuses or magic acts or private owners who tend to be less concerned with tiger bloodlines, and certainly some such offers would be readily accepted.

But not enough of them. Tigers are just too prolific. And many exhibitors, while unconcerned with the genetic viability of their tigers, are just as picky about the physical appearance of the animals as breeding coordinators are about their ancestry. In a moment we will see just how such lookism works directly at odds with conservation. Finally, an ironic moral concern might work against the giveaway suggestion: "I consider it to be more humane to euthanize a tiger than send it to a circus," Christie states.

⌒

In addition to tiger cubs, there is another type of tiger that exerts a hypnotic draw upon observers: the white tiger. The situation with white tigers is not so viscerally controversial as the prospect of euthanizing cubs, but it cossets a set of problems all its own, the better part of which send conservationists like Sarah Christie into conniptions.

White tigers are amazing things. As if the normal animal weren't sensational enough, these beings offer a variation, as it were, on perfection. Milky fur beneath black or chocolate stripes — sometimes very faint — and icy blue eyes. Just what are these wonders? They are not albinos, and they are not the tigers that live in the snowy ranges of Siberia, as often is presumed of them. Also, as should be evident from the absence of discussion about them up to this point, white tigers are not a distinct subspecies.

Tales of white tigers surfaced in India centuries ago, with reliable accounts coming to light as early as the late 1800s. In 1951 the maharaja of Rewa caught one of the animals alive and brought it home to his palace to live among other wild-caught Bengal tigers, all orange. The maharaja named the new tenant Mohan, meaning "Charmer." Mohan was mated with an orange Bengal female, who subsequently gave birth to a litter of orange cubs. When one of the female cubs had matured, Mohan was bred with her, and four white cubs appeared. (Lest such a pairing seem perverse, father-daughter breeding

is known to occur with surprising regularity in the wild, as are many
of the other forms of incest.) A popular rumor assures us that every
white tiger now in captivity is a direct descendant of Mohan, but it is
not true. Other white Bengal tigers have been captured, and several
have occurred spontaneously from orange sires and dams. The phenomenon is the result of a recessive genetic anomaly that strips the
orange pigment from the skin and fur, and converts the eyes from
golden green to blue. Otherwise, the cats would be like every other
Bengal tiger. . . .

"Would be" instead of "are" because the special fascination concentrated on them by human beings has condemned the line to an
unfortunate legacy. The arrival of the first white tiger to be brought
to America in 1960 created nothing short of a sensation. Mohini
("Enchantress"), a daughter of Mohan, was purchased for the National
Zoo in Washington, D.C., directly from the maharaja of Rewa. Her
acquisition, transfer, and delivery transfixed America and were subsequently documented in a cover story of *National Geographic* magazine (May 1961). No one less than President Eisenhower himself was
on hand to welcome Mohini to her new home, and from that day on
the National Zoo's tiger exhibit drew unprecedented attendance.

Such attention was not unique either to Mohini or to Americans.
Everybody fell in love with white tigers, a fact not lost on exhibitors.
To propagate the popular attraction, owners inbred the family lines
back on themselves in hopes, quickly realized, of producing more and
more white tigers. In very short order, the first edge of the genetic
sword began to cut. Inbreeding depression manifested itself in a variety
of physical afflictions, including pinched pelvises, knocked knees,
swayed backs, and crossed eyes. Despite such deformities, the power
of the cats to draw spectators outweighed good breeding sense for
several generations. (The tiger time line must be kept in mind here
for perspective: Orange tigers were not yet widely known to be endangered; Project Tiger was still a decade away; there was no such
thing as a tiger SSP. The white tiger was considered rare because it

was white, not because it was a tiger.) Token efforts were made to bolster the line by intermittently introducing orange breeding partners, but that cost at least one generation and inevitably produced more orange cubs, which were just as expensive to raise as white cubs but drew fewer fans. New white founders from outside Mohan's line were eagerly introduced as they became available, but the mean kinship inevitably reverted to an unfavorable density.

At the same time, the animals started reaching wider audiences through a greater variety of exhibition venues. Circuses caught on to their profitability, and owners of private menageries considered white tigers the latest must-have chic. As the tigers dispersed, their pairing for reproduction became more haphazard, and eventually the other edge of the genetic sword sliced in: Someone bred a white tiger — theretofore exclusively of Bengal parentage — with a member of the Siberian subspecies. Not illegal, not immoral, not even unjustifiable considering the genetic welfare of the animal. But in terms of the conservation concerns then poised to erupt on the scene as tigers everywhere were discovered to be disappearing, this was the unpardonable sin that produced the unclean spawn: a hybrid.

"Just about every white tiger on the planet is now a hybrid," Christie confirms, shrugging her lips as though the topic leaves a bad taste in her mouth. "There went a whole slew of tiger genes," she frets, "bred out because they wanted the white genes." Her distaste for the subject is hardly unique among conservation breeding coordinators, none of whom would consider for a moment the option of introducing a hybrid of any color into his or her program. The aspect of white hybrids that so tweaks the argument is the tendency among the zoological institutions around the world — who are supposed to house the purebred tigers so valuable to conservation breeding programs — to continue breeding *whites*. They can't resist. The cats are just too damn popular with the public. Every zoo space filled by a white tiger — a hybrid, worthless to conservation — however, means one less space available for a purebred. Cubs are only draws so long as they remain small. Once they've grown up, they lose their charm, and then they'd better have an attractive pedigree or they're going to be so hard to place in a home they might just end up euthanized. But white tiger cubs don't turn orange when they mature. They retain their allure, which, ironically, is the very thing that marks them as a hybrid while simultaneously granting them an exemption to displace tigers more valuable in terms of conservation. This satire, heightened by the reality that the increased gate fees garnered from keeping white tigers will probably support a tiger conservation effort that seeks, more than just about anything else, space exactly like the kind being taken up by white tigers, is what needles Christie and her ken so.

"If it were purebred," she insists, "I would treat a white Bengal tiger exactly the same as I would treat an orange Bengal tiger. If I had a population of forty Bengal tigers, ten of which were white, I would track their ancestry through the studbook and I would run the genetic program on them exactly as I do for the Sumatrans. I would then breed the ones at the top of the mean kinship list. If they were white or orange would not make a blind bit of difference. It's a naturally occurring gene, and it should not be selected either for or against."

So there. The subject makes for awfully interesting table conversation when curators, managers, vets, keepers, staff, and breeding coordinators from different zoos sit down together. Some, inevitably, begin to justify the space they devote at their institutions to white tigers, claiming that the animals not only pay their own way but even provide for the construction of new space for other tigers, including the precious purebreds. Opponents, who cannot completely discount such claims, grumble something about "junk tigers" or "trash tigers" in response — epithets launched against all hybrids by conservation purists.

Two interesting adjuncts of big-cat color and breeding are appropriate here. Far more rare than the white tiger is the so-called blue tiger, whose fur is in fact either smoky gray or partially black. Suspected to be the result of a genetic variation that causes the stripes to merge, blue tigers have been spotted in the wilds of Myanmar, China, and India. One captive tiger with smoky fur is reported to have been kept in Oklahoma City, and a tiger pelt recovered in 1992 from illegal traders in India is almost entirely black. Also, tigers can be cross-bred with lions to produce "tigons" when the sire is a tiger and the dam a lion, or "ligers" when the pairing is reversed. These hybrids are typically born sterile, much to the relief of conservation biologists, though a third generation can occasionally be squeezed from the line to produce "litigons" or "titigons" or "tiligons" or . . . whatever the genealogy dictates. With space for big cats at a premium, such eccentric couplings are generally left to curious private owners.

Speaking of which, what *about* people who own tigers as private pets? Where do they fit into the ethical equation? Sequestered from public display, aren't those tigers subject exclusively to the whims of their owners? The so-called sacredness of private property is much ballyhooed these days, particularly by politicians hoping to tap into the frustration felt by citizens sick of being told by the government what they can and cannot do with things they own. Limitations on external authority are essential to individual liberty, this argument correctly asserts, but there's another half to the equation that rarely gets as much play. Liberty requires responsibility from each individual for more than just what he or she owns. The problem arises when an individual wants everybody *else*'s authority restricted but not his or her own — a state of affairs known otherwise as a dictatorship. Democracies strive for the greater good of a greater number, a number that includes, either directly or by extension, captive animals. If you set your pets on fire in America, you can be put in jail. That's not likely to change, no matter how sacred we make private property. The important question, then, is not what *can* an owner of an ex situ tiger do with the animal, but rather, what is that owner *allowed* to do with it.

Allowed by whom? Guess what: Not only do governments own all the in situ tigers that roam through their jurisdictions, they own all the ex situ tigers too. People may be granted stewardship over one or more of the beasts, and that stewardship might indeed endure without governmental interruption from the moment of a tiger's birth to the moment of its death, but what has been granted is stewardship, not ownership. Stewards are keepers, not captors, not owners. There are limits — different under different governments — regarding how stewards can use what they've been given stewardship over. Tigers are not widgets. Pets are not possessions. Neither is ever truly private property.

∽

CHAPTER 10

How Much Is
That Tiger
in the Wild?

WHITE TIGERS AND TIGER CUBS are big moneymakers, as we have just seen. Almost every ex situ tiger, in fact, makes money for somebody. They are among the most popular animals at every zoo. Spectators will forever pay to watch humans get close to tigers, whether it's to make them jump through a hoop or disappear off a stage. And the breeding of captive tigers for the purpose of selling their body parts may yet turn a legitimate profit.

How about in situ tigers? Do they—can they—make money for anyone?

Oh, yes. Should they? The arguments surrounding the link between commerce and in situ tigers is different from that link with ex situ tigers, but it is by no means less complicated or less volatile in terms of emotion. In fact, while the "exploitation" of captive tigers is loathsome to many people concerned with rights and welfare, the concept of linking dollars to wildness offends a much wider circle. Let us begin by investigating what are surely the two most readily identifiable techniques for turning wild tigers into cash, known these days as "poaching" and "smuggling."

How accurate are those terms? Certainly they are onerous,

inspiring images of skulking fugitives and smoke-filled rooms where dangerous deals go down at gunpoint. But who are the people who actually poach wild tigers? Who then smuggles them? What do the terms even mean? The so-called practices of poaching and smuggling have actually been going on since before the beginning of recorded history. It's just that up until a few years ago we called them "trapping" and "trading." The change that converted the practices from one vernacular into another was the installation of law. Trapping and trading are legal. Poaching and smuggling are not. With that single exception, the two sets of activities are identical.

This is not meant to excuse the people who kill and transport wild tigers. On the contrary, the reason that laws against certain types of trapping and trading are installed (in theory, at least) is because some larger and more compelling logic has been found to stop those practices. In the case of the wild tiger, that logic is aimed at avoiding the extinction of the species. The import of that aim is more than perfectly clear to all the legislators, heads of state, delegates, scientists, and NGO representatives who have worked so diligently to see things like CITES and all the many domestic laws protecting wild tigers installed. None of those folks, however, is among the people who were out trapping and trading wild tigers in the first place. To this day, the individuals most likely to be found right beside the body of a dead wild tiger are locals who probably make their livings in other, legal, ways.

"Most of the poaching is opportunistic," says Dr. John Goodrich, a field researcher who works full-time in the Russian Far East for the Hornocker Wildlife Research Institute. "A guy is driving down the road, there's a tiger, he's got his gun, so he shoots it. People see a tiger standing in the road and they see five thousand dollars standing there, so they take advantage of it." Further discounting the likelihood of organized poaching operations, Goodrich explains how "it's real difficult to go out and hunt a tiger. . . . And tigers are difficult to snare. We snared for two months with thirty traps out over several kilometers and didn't catch a tiger. It took [us] four months to catch Miravana and four months to catch Lena [which are two tigers subsequently tracked by radio telemetry]. So it's just not worth it to try and go out and snare tigers—unless you find a kill and you suspect the tiger is going to return and you've got a good chance of catching it. But again, that's going to be opportunistic."

Dr. Linda Kerley, Goodrich's full-time co-researcher and his spouse, points out that their observations might deserve a bit of tempering. "We aren't fluent in Russian yet," she notes, explaining that she and Goodrich had been in Russia just five months as of the time these observations were made. "The other thing is that this area is gentle compared to areas closer to Vladivostok. . . . There's a lot more crime as you get closer to the city, and there are tigers there too."

Kerley's last point is crucial, and it is supported by evidence from beyond the institute. Only a fraction of the surviving wild Siberian tiger population inhabits the Sikhote-Alin preserve where Kerley and Goodrich work. And, of the available habitat in which to conduct research, Sikhote-Alin is especially prime. As an officially protected area, the preserve is completely off-limits to human traffic except for formally approved researchers and official personnel. There are no roads inside the preserve, and there are no settlements. Sikhote-Alin would be the last place a poacher would go to target a Siberian tiger intentionally. Far more vulnerable are the tigers that inhabit property closer to the two major urban centers in the Russian Far East, Vladivostok and Khabarovsk. Antipoaching patrols established in those areas, such as Operation Amba, continuously discover new evidence of poaching, much of which is more organized than opportunistic.

Nevertheless, the image of a Russia seething with high-powered corruption softens a bit, at least as far as wildlife is concerned, under the testimonies of the Hornocker scientists. "There is corruption here," concedes Dr. Dale Miquelle, who supervises the work of Kerley and Goodrich and who has lived in the Russian Far East almost continuously for four years. "And there is probably more of it than there is in the United States. But I think a lot of it is a misperception of the way things are done over here." With that, Miquelle offers a description of how personal favors count for more than just about anything else in Russian culture. "The way people do business here is through relationships," he explains. "You help each other out. You do something because you know someone and they asked you to help them. It doesn't necessarily involve a payback of any sort. It may just involve giving them a piece of cake or a box of candy."

That doesn't mean everyone's a saint, and favor-banking can work as well for scoundrels as it does for scientists. The single most infamous instance of tiger poaching in Siberia involved the head conservation officer in the Sikhote-Alin region, who lives just down the street from Miquelle. The perpetrator, who claimed to have shot the tiger in self-defense, was arrested, tried, convicted, fined, fired, and sentenced under wildlife-protection laws already in place. "But eight months later he was back at his job," Miquelle says with a shrug. Despite that inequity, Miquelle repeats his attestation of Russian virtues, revealing, in the process, what some might consider to be an indiscretion of his own. "I have paid only one bribe in the three and a half years I've been here," he confesses. "*One*, and it was to an airline official to get more than the allowed baggage on a flight—to get my equipment on—which she'd allowed a dozen times before. . . . The fact that I've only given one bribe in that much time is, I think, a testimony that you don't have to live in that mode of life here." Indeed, the only form of corruption that Miquelle, Kerley, and Goodrich cite as a continuing hindrance to their work on behalf of Siberian tigers is petty theft, which compels them to lock up and guard every ounce of their equipment every hour of the day.

Down on the island of Sumatra, Neil Franklin offers evidence that supports the hypothesis that most tiger poaching is opportunistic. "The time I remember most clearly," he recalls, "was when somebody said they had seen a tiger and tried to get it [with their car]. They did—knocked it out. Then they skinned it and threw it in the boot."

Such stories stand out for Franklin in part because the death of a tiger in Indonesia due to poaching is surprisingly rare. "It's between five to seven individuals a year on the whole of Sumatra," he says, quickly adding, however, that even numbers so seemingly small can have catastrophic impact on tiger populations so fragmented as those on Sumatra.

In India the situation is more grave. The tiger's higher density and visibility in that country attracts the attention not only of benign tourists (next to be discussed) but also of a breed of poacher something more than merely opportunistic. The cats in that country are simply more plentiful and easier to catch. Consequently, poaching practices have become more uniform and widespread there, though the front-line offender is still typically a villager just trying to make a little extra money. Fortunately the increased visibility of wild Bengal tigers also makes them noticeably absent when they're gone, which means the alarm will sound more quickly, just as it did in 1992.

Among the methods used to trap a tiger illegally, the crudely fashioned leghold snare is the device of choice. Steel traps are found on occasion, as are box traps and rigged guns, but those much less frequently. Poisoned bait and water are also sometimes used. Tigers have been tracked with packs of dogs, but the technique was employed mostly in the past to capture animals for circuses; it generates more attention than the average poacher now likes to draw. Neither the carcasses nor any debris from poached tigers are commonly recovered by authorities, due partly to the thoroughness of poachers and partly to the value of every piece of the animal. Skins, bones, and other derivatives are more likely to be found in the hands of middlemen or smugglers.

In hopes of shielding tiger researchers from charges of animal cruelty, a paragraph is hereby devoted to explaining how they employ similar trapping technologies but with much greater care. The snares to which Goodrich made reference earlier in this chapter also are leghold mechanisms, but they have been specially designed and are uniquely employed to avoid injury of any kind to the tigers. Especially thick and flexible cable is used; the snares are set en masse around fresh kills only and then are checked individually several times a day for as long as they remain armed; specific records are kept on the placement of all snares so they can be methodically collected after each trapping session; trapping is not done in the Russian Far East during winter specifically so that no trapped animal will ever be left in the Siberian cold overnight. Other trapping methods are available, though none have been found to be equally well suited to the particulars of Siberian tigers. Ullas Karanth, for example, coaxes tigers into box traps with the help of human brush-beaters and enormous V-shaped runs. Baited box traps have also proved successful on occasion. Once trapped, regardless of the method, the cats are then anesthetized in much the same way described on the first few pages of this book. The whole process is traumatic for the animal, surely, but researchers make every effort to avoid unwarranted harassment of their quarry. Fatal complications due directly to trapping conducted by responsible and qualified tiger scientists are all but unknown.*

While the direct poaching of tigers themselves clearly impacts the species, there are other types of poaching that are frequently overlooked even though they can be equally devastating. Wild tigers must eat, and the animals they eat are also tempting to the human predator. In raw numbers, poaching of the tiger's prey base in every tiger range country is vastly more widespread than direct poaching of tigers ever will be. The effect is the same for the starving cats who are left behind.

There is yet a lower tier to secondary poaching. The animals that tigers like to eat must themselves eat something. Ungulates—

---

*The spurious but oft-cited exception involves a tiger that died in 1990 after having been immobilized by Ullas Karanth. Charges were leveled against Karanth concerning four other tigers that died concurrently in Nagarahole Park, but an investigation revealed that Karanth had noted the advanced age and infirmity of the tiger he was working with and that the other four tigers had died of natural causes.

hoofed animals—form the better part of the tiger's prey base in most range states. (It must be noted, however, that tigers are among the least picky of eaters, readily devouring anything they can catch: monkeys, peacocks, elephant calves, frogs. . . .) Deer, wild cattle, and wild pigs are all herbivores. They eat vegetation. The vegetation they eat, in large part, is simple ground cover—grasses and such—though the pigs are particularly fond of fallen cones and fruit. The surrounding forest of trees protects and rejuvenates this vegetative base. Remove the trees and the ungulates will go away because they will have nothing to eat. The tigers will go away next for exactly the same reason. Lumber poaching is at least as widespread as prey-base poaching, and the two are closely linked. The same people often participate in both, and often for the simplest of reasons. Tigers don't roam near rich communities. Running water and electricity are typically unavailable extravagances for the surrounding human populations, who poach the prey base to feed themselves and poach the lumber to cook their food and build their homes. These people could even be further accused of "poaching" the very ground cover needed by the wild ungulates by illegally grazing their livestock within protected areas. Regardless of the motivation for, or the level of, the poaching, the consequences for the tiger are the same.

In certain areas, trees of commercial value grow, and lumber poaching there involves motivations and modes much more sophisticated. In its most industrialized form, this is called logging. Bulldozers, trucks, and even helicopters may descend upon a forest to remove one or more types of salable trees, or simply to clear the area right down to the dirt. Such activity, of course, never goes unnoticed, but logging seems to be the one type of natural resource utilization that either escapes open indictment, especially in developing nations, or is perpetrated by the government itself. Trees are plunderable. They can't run away, they won't bite, they don't seem fundamentally "wild," and they appear to be easily reintroducible if overharvested. At the same time, their primary derivative is fabulously utile, it's universally in demand, it's durable, and it stacks perfectly for storage and shipping. To a country strapped for cash, trees look especially green.

"A tremendous amount of lumber is being exported," says Dale Miquelle of the Hornocker Institute, referring to the Russian Far East. "A lot of it's going to Japan . . . but I bump into people from Taiwan and China who are buying. I bump into Americans who are buying. . . . Warehouser tried [unsuccessfully] for a long time to start logging in Khabarovski Krai. The Hyundai Corporation of South Korea has a relatively large logging operation . . . and there's been a North Korean logging operation for many, many years up in Khabarovsk." This siege against Siberian trees, Miquelle explains, is neither clearly legal nor illegal. The breakup of the Soviet Union simultaneously depressed the economy and threw resource-use policy into limbo. Certain areas, such as Sikhote-Alin, remain completely off-limits to logging. Laws also have been put in place to protect certain species of trees. But beyond that it's a sawfest.

"I'm sure the poaching of tigers is a problem," says Miquelle's colleague Linda Kerley. "But we don't see that as much as we see the habitat coming down the road [on the backs of trucks]." Asked if any of the forests near Sikhote-Alin are being clear-cut, Kerley, who flies over the area several times each week to radio-track tigers, responds immediately: "Oh, yeah. Right up to the edge of the reserve. And habitat loss isn't the only problem associated with logging. Whenever they go in and make a cut, they leave a road behind. There's another place the poachers can access."

Miquelle emphatically promotes the importance of this second point. "Both for ungulates and for carnivores like the tiger, one of the most detrimental things you can do is put a road into an area," he says. "It opens it up. It provides access. Hunters are just as lazy as any other group of people in the world. If they can drive there, most will go. If they have to walk, only a small percentage will go. . . . You put a road into an area and you open up the opportunity for hunting ungulates, which of course are the prey base for tigers, and for poaching the tigers themselves." Tigers, in fact, fall especially vulnerable to the building of roads: They are known to prefer using man-made routes to patrol their territories rather than blaze through the brush themselves. With tigers, therefore, a logging road points the gun toward the game and vice versa.

"It scares me to death," admits Kerley's husband, Goodrich, "to think about the potential that exists here for people just to go in and go nuts before the government can get on top of things and put the appropriate controls in place so that logging is done in such a way that it's not going to cause the extinction of the tiger. Certainly some logging in this area will be compatible with the tiger, but we've got to figure out how to do it right."

Russia may well be the most dire example of how logging threatens the tiger, but a plane flight over nearly every one of the animal's range countries reveals extraordinary alterations in the landscape due to logging. Huge tracts in Sumatra have been cleared right down to bare soil without so much as a blade of grass left behind. Parts of China, Vietnam, Laos, and Thailand have been laid equally bare. India's deforestation has persisted so perniciously in some areas the process has given way to a new term: desertification.

Even so, a curious phenomenon associated with the aftermath of intense logging can actually compensate for some of the damage inflicted on the resident tiger populations by the removal of the trees. A fully mature forest often stifles the growth of lesser vegetation near the ground by blocking out the sun. When the trees are taken out, the floor of the erstwhile forest explodes into life just a few years later. This surge of new growth fosters ungulate populations, which in turn foster tigers. This is hardly a comprehensive new management technique for tiger conservation, but it impels a reevaluation of future use of land now being heavily logged in the vicinity of extant tiger populations. Neil Franklin, for one, testifies to having seen a single Indonesian forest logged three times consecutively, "right down to the dirt," only to spring back each time lushly enough to lure tigers.

Inevitably, the word "smuggling" is spoken in the same breath as "poaching," but the process deserves a bit of individual attention. In particular, smuggling is far more likely than poaching to fall subject to the influences of organized crime. Professional crooks are wise enough not to dirty their hands with the most culpable of evidence, and they generally cannot make good enough money at the front end to satisfy their grander goals. In addition, smuggling requires experience, financing, and connections. Opportunism plays a small role (otherwise-law-abiding citizens might "smuggle" a bottle of tiger-bone wine onto an airplane and into Seoul for their parents' wedding anniversary, for example), but there is rarely a profit motive associated with such transgressions, they typically will not be repeated consistently by the same people, and the perpetrators almost never have been directly in contact with the poachers. Redirecting resources toward catching opportunistic smugglers in the act, therefore, is inefficient. A public education program aimed at reducing the overall demand will accrue much greater gains. The meaningful target is the industrial smuggler. The illegality of smuggling tiger derivatives (as opposed to "trading" them) has industrialized the practice and moved it into the hands of people either familiar with clandestine commerce or willing to take the associated risks, or both. Evidence in support of that conclusion, presented by Sam LaBudde, Steve Galster, Michael Day, Rebecca Chen, et al., is clear, continuing, and compelling. Efforts to do something about it remain the charter of international trade regulators and law-enforcement officials.

But back at the front line, the work of actually killing wild tigers is more often than not committed by someone who either would just as soon have never seen the animal in the first place or who would have been just as likely to have killed it for profit one hundred, five hundred, or two thousand years ago. Nobody from the outside paid any attention until the practice became unsustainable. Furthermore, with a predatory carnivore that lurks just outside the villages of less-developed countries, the so-called virtue of not driving the thing to extinction might mean your cows, your kids, or even you yourself will get killed. Thus, a motivation not to kill an animal like the wild tiger is especially hard to instill among the people most likely to commit the act. The problem is to make the larger and more compelling logic that drives the establishment of protective laws meaningful enough to *those* people to make them stop. Just putting laws like CITES on paper means nothing, as we have learned, but it has led to cries for enforcement through such methodologies as more personpower at ports of entry to search incoming shipments, higher fines and longer prison sentences for people caught breaking the laws, and, especially in the case of the tiger, antipoaching patrols. Another voice, however, is rising, with suggestions of another kind.

Supply and demand worked quite predictably in the decline of the tiger. So long as there were tens of thousands of the animals roaming the earth, as many as were needed could be taken sustainably for whatever purpose—skins, curios, TCM, to eliminate a problem tiger... whatever. There would always be plenty more. Because there always would be plenty more, the earlier versions of the industries that grew up around wild tigers—trapping and trading—reached what economists call a "steady state" way back when. Tigers were simply one of several large, attractive, unique animals that offered a variety of profit-centered options to anyone interested in pursuing such. Yes, they had unspeakably beautiful coats, but many would have argued the coats of leopards and cheetah were more beautiful still. They threatened the safety of farms and people, but so did elephants (notorious for raiding crops and trampling farmers). They supplied important ingredients to TCM, but so did bears and almost every other animal in the forest. They were worshiped by local peoples, but so were snakes and birds and cows and dragons. Then, with the advent of this century, tigers became scarce and everything changed.

Suddenly they and their derivatives were more valuable than many rivals for the simple reason that they were harder to come by. Who was responsible for that? The people who had for millennia been trapping and trading tigers?

The exploding global human population, the quest among governments for something called progress, the increased capacity of the members of thriving economies to indulge in luxuries and recreation, and the general availability of newly accurate and efficient firearms all combined to wipe out the tiger, its prey base, and its habitat while simultaneously enlarging the demand base. The price per tiger went up, making the risks associated with trapping and trading them surmountable to an ever-larger corps of opportunists that now has come to include everyone from surprised motorists and angry cowherds to reckless tourists and gangsters. But the market created the poachers and smugglers, not the other way around.

To reverse the process, the new voice says, let's fight fire with fire. Greed fueled the decline, let's make it fuel the recovery. Instead of punishing people for doing something they've been doing for millennia, how about if we reward them for not doing it? This is where the flavor of the word "poaching" makes an unfortunate contribution. Many of us don't like the thought of rewarding criminals. Virtue should be its own reward, and all that. But those criminals weren't criminals until the law came down. Up to the early 1970s, people got cash *rewards* for "poaching" tigers in China. They were heroes, not crooks.

A dead wild tiger right now equals lots of money to the people who are most likely to kill it. Estimates range vastly, and they should be ignored for the most part. It's enough to say that there is a current market for dead wild tigers in which the money to be earned by the people at the front line is seductive enough to make them commit the act. Can we, conversely, establish a market for live wild tigers?

"To avoid the extinction of the wild tiger," Michael 't Sas-Rolfes calmly initiates what he acknowledges will quickly work into a radical solution, "you have to prevent them from being killed uncontrollably. To prevent them being killed uncontrollably, you have to protect them in situ." Nothing shocking so far, and it's important to point out that 't Sas-Rolfes's use of the term "protect" is generic—not indicative of protection*ism*. He quickly moves into swifter waters, however. "I believe that CITES and its very philosophies are seriously misdirected. The people [who attend a CITES COP] don't really give a shit whether tiger bone crosses one international boundary to another. That is merely a symptom of the problem. What they really care about is that they don't want to see wild tigers being killed uncontrollably.... Once a tiger has been killed, it doesn't matter if it is traded between Myanmar and Laos or India and China. That's irrelevant. You have lost the battle already [for that individual animal]. CITES is an after-the-fact policy. It doesn't help. It misses the point."

Leaving discussions of CITES's validity to political theorists, let's give Mr. 't Sas-Rolfes his head. The point, as he puts it, is to make live wild tigers more valuable than dead ones to the people most able and likely either to keep them alive or to kill them: local villagers. Since money is the "value" that now drives the killing, money, 't Sas-Rolfes submits, is the logical value with which to drive the protecting. If a dead wild tiger is worth ten thousand dollars, can we make a live one worth more?

Oh, yes. In fact, there are people who will pay ten times that much—even more, by some estimates—for a live wild tiger. Problem is, they will only pay that much if they are then allowed to kill it.

With the possible exception of tiger farming, the most explosive issue ticking away in tiger conservation these days is trophy hunting. To many, hunting is the one institution more antithetical to wildness than a zoo. The practice, to its adversaries, seems barbaric—distasteful in the extreme. The image of a hunter, to them, comes together something like a cross between Rambo and the Marquis de Sade (not entirely without basis, as we shall see). But hunters have a long and respectable tradition of wild-animal conservation. "We contribute twenty-six million dollars a year to pure wildlife conservation projects," boasts Cary Simonds, a former vice president of Safari Club International (SCI). "Twenty-six million. That's a big difference between us and our political opponents, who don't contribute to conservation but oppose our position." Some of those opponents would dispute Simonds's twenty-six-million-dollar tally, but even inflated numbers should not cloud the fact that hunters, as a group, are responsible for raising tremendous sums for conservation. Licensing fees alone dwarf the budgets of most conservation NGOs, and those dollars go directly back into the system by funding park budgets, restocking programs, ranger services, and so forth. "The heart's cause of every Safari Club member that I have ever known," Simonds vows, "is conservation. . . . Because what we want to do is conserve the future for our families, so that we can bring our hunting heritage along with our family future."

Listening to Simonds talk of hunting and family in the same sentence will nauseate some listeners. Just where does bloodshed fit in with wholesomeness, they wonder. But the connection is neither that simple nor that brutal. Hunting, from a hunter's point of view, is an utterly natural, moral, compelling pursuit that reflects many of life's most basic and important lessons. Sit around a cocktail table with a group of hunters sometime and listen as the conversation inevitably turns quasi-religious. For the most part, these people are not simply out to "blow things away." They are, rather, tapping some fundamental impulse closely related to the survival instinct.

That's why it's unfortunate that so many people involved in the sport seem to set themselves up for criticism. When it comes to conspicuous consumption, it's hard to beat a trophy hunter. For starters, it takes an awful lot of money and free time to hunt trophy animals. Not only is this not a poor man's sport, it's not even a rich man's sport. "Several of the tags have gone for more than $250,000," says Harry Dennis, former president of the south Florida chapter of SCI, discussing an auction of rights—"tags"—to hunt bighorn sheep in Colorado. "Is that an auction for the wealthy? No. That's an auction for the superwealthy. Millionaires don't go to that auction." Defining the pastime, trophy hunters then take the fruits of their labors and stick them on walls or encase them in glass or lay them out across the floor so nobody will be able to miss just how super-rich and superleisurely and superbrave they are. Finally, the very thing immortalized by the trophy is the ever-unacceptable-to-so-many-people act of *killing* an individual. Trophy hunters glorify murder, their adversaries say.

Just the opposite, Simonds counters. "If I were that animal and my last alternative was to take a huge blow of a firearm that would instantly knock me out and make me unconscious and euthanize me, that'd be my first choice. I wouldn't want to die, but if I had to die, which I did, I would choose that."

Who can argue? We've already discussed how much suffering is involved in the natural death of a wild animal. A blow from a gun, by comparison, would be merciful. But Simonds goes on to embellish his metaphor with a bit more enthusiasm than seems necessary. "One other choice I would have, because this is my own predilection, is that I would opt to be shot with a modern broad-head from a bow and arrow, because it is one of the humane ways to ethereally slip into unconsciousness. The way that is done is by a razorlike slice through the body, which does not induce a great deal of pain at all. I've even had animals continue eating after an arrow goes through them. Jump, startle, go back to eating. But internally we're oozing out the lifeblood. So what do they know? It doesn't hurt to bleed. They just sit there and they gradually become unconscious, they lay down and go night-night."

SCI is hardly representative of the interests and pursuits of all hunters everywhere, but the organization is both prominent and powerful, and it is perfectly appropriate for analysis of the relevance of trophy hunting to endangered species. Rhinos, elephants, leopards, bears . . . many rare animals have been legally pursued by one or more of SCI's twenty thousand members at one time or another, often with extraordinary—if debated—results in terms of conservation. "There has never been an animal species brought to extinction by controlled sport hunting," Simonds accurately notes. "In contrast, we have had many crises of populations amongst the animal kingdom based on greedy, consumer-driven commercial hunting. We saw it with the bison. We've seen it with the elephant in poaching." Neither of those examples, however, warms the heart of a trophy hunter defending his choice of recreation so much as the case of the white rhino.

At the beginning of this century, the African white rhino population plunged to numbers widely thought to be as low as single digits. (Lest we kick off a second book here, let's forego an analysis of the reasons, as well as a direct investigation of the following statistics.) Through protection, they were bred up to a point where certain animals could be scientifically deemed surplus—useless to the future survival of the species either because they had stopped breeding or they could offer only genes that already were overrepresented. Trophy hunters were allowed to start taking these surplus animals for a price. Today, there are thousands of African white rhinos, and trophy hunting remains part of the equation.

Rhinos are not tigers, but leopards almost are, and the African leopard has survived a scenario almost identical to that of the rhino with respect to trophy hunting. "Leopard are inherent calf killers," notes Dr. Colin Saunders, a full-time rural M.D. who has worked for thirty-five years in remote areas of southeast Zimbabwe and who was chairman of the national parks board from 1975 to 1987. "Every leopard on every ranch was systematically persecuted, shot, hunted almost to extinction. Vermin status, that's the right phrase." However, in 1975 the government of Rhodesia (as Zimbabwe was then known) enacted a controversial new parks and wildlife law that effectively gave custody of the wild animals to the owners of the property on which they roamed. The appetite among trophy hunters for spotted cats was well known, and several of the landholders sought permission to sell the leopards roaming on their land to trophy hunters—as targets. CITES had just recently come into force, and there was significant resistance to granting the waivers that were necessary for hunters to take their trophies back home once they'd been shot. Nevertheless, a small quota was granted once sufficient scientific evidence had been supplied to assure the nondetriment of the take. "It was absolutely amazing what happened next," says Saunders. "Straight away, anybody who managed to sell one or two leopard per year to a safari hunter tolerated the animals.... And now leopards are not just tolerated, they are prized. People look for them and talk about them and say, 'I've got a big tomcat or three big tomcats on my property and I'm trying to sell one to a safari operator.' They protect it. They don't mind if it takes a few of their cattle, because at the end of the day they benefit to a great extent."

Saunders is careful to point out that the program involves only cats outside the national parks system, but that comprises most of Zimbabwe's leopards, just as it would comprise most of the tigers in Asia. "Trophy hunting gives wildlife a new value," he suggests. "Before, it was a nuisance, competing with the conventional subsistence farmer for grazing land and scarce water supplies, and endangering their lives and their crops. Lions and leopards were killing their cattle. Elephant and buffalo were just marching through the fields of sorghum and millet. The farmers only get a crop every three or four years anyway, so they eliminated the wildlife as much as they could. *They* were the poachers. But now they see a huge benefit, and they are protecting the animals from *other* poachers. They catch the poachers and they beat the hell out of them. The government won't do that. The government has got to take it through a court process that is very, very long-winded."

The money earned through trophy hunting in Zimbabwe must be distributed quite particularly, by law. Only 15 percent is allotted for administration. Thirty-five percent must go toward conservation: "Things like restocking of wildlife, paying full-time antipoaching rangers, or augmentation of water supplies," Saunders specifies. The remaining 50 percent goes directly to the local community. "They decide, 'We want a clinic, we want a school, we want a new bridge, we want a grinding mill to grind maize. . . .' The other half they dish out in dollar notes to households." There's another benefit to the system, Saunders points out, though it can't be measured with money. "We've come a long way with the new government. Black people are now being empowered in the stake to have some say over wildlife. The previously white government said that these animals were for [the benefit of] whites only," says Saunders, who is white, explaining that in the earlier era trophy hunters did not pay locals for the privilege of shooting animals on their land. "The huge black majority had no interest in the wildlife. That all changed with the Act of 1975."

Few hunters are proposing that licenses should be granted to hunt wild tigers just yet. Most would-be tiger hunters, in fact, predict that the day will never come when it will make sense to establish tiger trophy hunting. The population sizes just don't look like they're ever going to be able to sustain such takes, most hunters admit. "We do not have any plans to pursue, nor do we have any interest in pursuing, the hunting of the tiger at this time," says Cary Simonds. "My concern, in fact, is so grave for the long-term survivability of the tiger species that I think it's premature for any of us to give any time or attention at all to consumptive uses. We must be very cautious and scientifically aware of every aspect of managing and coping with this crisis situation."

But low numbers are not the only roadblock to hunting tigers as trophies. "It's completely irrelevant for India," Ullas Karanth declares. "It will antagonize the local people. Here we are, right now, saying to them, 'This place is left for [the conservation of] the tiger, so you are out. Your cattle are out.' They don't like it, but you can make them understand it, because the tiger is in the culture here. It's in the psyche as something that has a right to live. And then you get a rich Texan to come and shoot it for twenty thousand dollars or fifty thousand dollars, and you blow that away. You stand morally naked before them." For all their taxonomic similarity, it seems, leopards and tigers remain unique, particularly in terms of the cultural atmospheres surrounding their widely separated ranges. And there are other distinctions. "It is very, very unlikely that a corruption-free system could be set up here," Karanth continues, highlighting what he calls his country's "miserable" record of bureaucracy. "I think the options for abusing it are too great. It's just not worth taking the risk. I just don't think a trophy hunter comes by and hunts a tiger and goes away and the ground gets protected." On this point he may get some sympathy from the other side. Everyone who promotes trophy hunting agrees that the key to success is an immaculate system for returning the benefits directly to the local communities. The connection between the money and the hunted animals must be tangible and immediate to the surrounding human population. If they sense someone is taking advantage of their efforts to protect the animals, they will stop. They may even turn on the system by attacking the animals.

Then, while rhinos are visible and leopards abundant, tigers are neither. Trophy hunters willingly agree to limit their hunts to animals identified by scientific authorities as surplus, but such individual scrutiny of tigers simply is not possible. One potential solution is to allow trophy hunting of known problem tigers, which almost inevitably will be shot anyway, but the unsavory connection between dead villagers and trophy-hunting dollars has so far repelled both sides from pursuing such deals. Critics of the sport also scoff at the idea that a hunter paying those kinds of prices would willingly shoot anything less than the most perfect specimen he could lay his crosshairs on. "But he doesn't have to have ears for me to take him," Harry Dennis disagrees. "The idea is that you are hunting in a wild, uncontrolled condition. You're not shopping. You're in the damn jungle, schlepping around in the mud and the leeches and whatever. If you get this grand beast and he's got a rough spot on his butt, as a hunter you don't see that rough spot. . . . That lends the beast character. He's been kicking butt in that jungle for the last fifteen years, and now it's time for him to retire."

In fact, wild tigers aren't all that ferocious. Except for very few situations, when a tiger is faced with a human, it would much rather just sneak away (a bashfulness cleverly exploited by tiger-wary wood-cutters who, with limited but intriguing success, sometimes wear face masks on the backs of their heads). There are only six cases when a human is likely to be charged, and only in half of those are the tigers likely to have stalked the person first: 1) Coming between a tiger and its fresh kill is a bad idea, as is 2) coming between a tigress and her cubs. Also, 3) inadvertently surprising a tiger will put you on its bad side. In all three situations, tigers are known to have charged intruders. Typically, however, the move is just for show—an extremely *effective* show, by all accounts—and the cat will veer off to one side or the other at the last second. Unless the intruder is stupid enough to stick around for another bout, the tiger will be perfectly satisfied to have scared him off and will then return to whatever it was doing before being bothered. However, humans unfortunate enough to be 4) crouching in the presence of a hungry tiger might be mistaken for a smaller animal. The most common activities of people who've been stalked by a tiger are harvesting crops and going to the bathroom. Also, 5) tigers that are injured, old, or recently displaced from their territories do tend to stalk people, whom they find awkward and slow in comparison to much of their other prey; these are the cats that become problem tigers. Finally, 6) there are the tigers of Sundarbans, who truly are, by all accounts, man-eaters. Hence, unless the episode occurred either in the Sundarbans or during a bowel movement, the only tale any honest trophy hunter will be able to tell over brandy in the drawing room is that the cat above the hearth so viciously posed by a taxidermist in fact was scared as hell and trying its level best to get away when it was shot.

We want the wild tiger to survive, but are we willing to let a few of them be killed by human beings so the rest can endure? Note that once again, as with tiger farming or euthanizing cubs in a zoo, the suffering argument holds no water; death from a gunshot or a broadhead is going to cause the animal no more suffering than a natural death. Probably less. It's the *killing* that so many of us just can't take—the deliberate, isolated, consumptive act of an individual human being ending the life of an individual wild tiger. It just feels too damn much like murder.

All right, then. Let's take a look at that other, kinder, gentler, non–human-supremacist, nonconsumptive use of wild tigers: eco-tourism. We don't have to kill the tigers; we can just look at them and take their pictures.

Trophy hunting has yet to be considered even potentially viable with respect to tigers, but the business of simply looking at the animals already booms in one country. Several factors render the Bengal sub-species particularly watchable. First, there are more of them. The odds are good. The optimum natural density of the Bengal tiger is also much higher than that of any other surviving subspecies. Next, the natural topography and landscape that define much of the Indian subcontinent are flat, even, reachable, and relatively clear, and much of the remaining tiger habitat occurs in moist or dry deciduous forest—wide open in comparison to the vegetation of Sumatra. A number of artificial elements also contribute to the Bengal's viewability, including open politics and a stable economy. (All this is relative, remember. Think Russia, China, Cambodia, Laos....) Finally, though this is perhaps more sad than praiseworthy, even the most "pristine" parts of India are thick with human habitation and criss-crossed by trails and roads. The Bengal tiger is accessible, and that has fortified a thriving eco-tourism industry.

Rugged adventurers can make arrangements to visit the Nagara-hole State Park and watch for tigers from the porch of their basic, but thoroughly serviceable, shelter for the whopping sum of U.S. $1.75 per day (meals included, at your own risk). Bus tours through the local portion of the park leave every ninety minutes or so for a slight additional charge. Views of sambar and muntjac deer, wild bison, langurs, macaques, peacocks, and elephant are all but guaranteed on every round. Attentive passengers will see a leopard or a sloth bear if they stay more than a day or two. Tiger sightings are reported every couple of weeks.

For those with softer skin and thicker wallets, the Kabini Lodge at the other end of the park offers outright luxury for less than a middling hotel room in Manhattan. Jeeps, each manned by a driver and a dedicated game spotter, patrol the forest and the banks of the Kabini River each dawn and dusk, cruising past uncountable elephant, bison, sambar, muntjac, peacock, crocodile, langur, macaque . . . a show of wildlife so rapturous it repeatedly stops the breath of every person in the vehicle, including both the staff. Sloth bears trundle past every now and again. Leopards reveal themselves from time to time. Tigers, of course, are found only with luck, but rarely do two full weeks in a row go by without at least one Jeepful of effervescent visitors rushing back to the lodge with whispered tales of an encounter with the great Shere Khan.

However, just as the seemingly perfect answer of display enrichment has its failings for ex situ animals, eco-tourism falls short in many ways of the criteria necessary to make living wild tigers explicitly more valuable than dead ones. "The logging revenues from the park were on the order of ten million rupees [which is more than U.S. $320,000] a year," notes Ullas Karanth. "There is no way tourism can bring that kind of money into an area like this. . . . Even trophy hunting wouldn't get that kind of money into five hundred square kilometers of land. The numbers don't add up."

Let's run those numbers. We'd have to round up something near two hundred of the thrifty version of eco-tourists to visit Nagarahole per day, year-round, each spending, say, U.S. $5.00 per day, just to compensate for the logging losses. That's far more people than the bargain facilities could ever hope to handle. So let's be generous and use the Kabini Lodge as our multiplier. At U.S. $100 per day we'd only need about ten people per day year-round to compensate for the logging losses. Kabini itself can handle about sixty visitors at a time, and there are other lodges in the area. If we also throw in an extra U.S. $20 per day per visitor for souvenirs and tips and transportation to and from the lodge and whatnot, and if we overlook the monsoon season, we can almost get to a point where eco-tourism looks as attractive as logging in economic terms.

But how much raw sewage will those visitors flush down the toilet every day? How much trash will they discard? How much gasoline will be burned in their Jeeps, and how deep will the ruts in the dirt trails be gouged from repeated passes by those Jeeps? How much food, clean water, electricity, and soap do eco-tourists require? How much toxic bug spray will they wash from their skin down the drain in the shower each night? What, or who, is at the other end of those drains? Just how many eco-tourists can a five-hundred-square-kilometer park tolerate?

The Safari Club relishes such considerations and makes a point of exalting the ruggedness of their members, who snub the wasteful luxuries required by eco-tour pansies. The economic ego of trophy hunting compounds that advantage by reducing the multiplier. With bighorn sheep in Colorado going for up to a quarter of a million dollars, a single tiger safari could generate more cash than a sellout season of eco-tourists at the Kabini Lodge. "If you got a one-time permit on a tiger," says Harry Dennis, presenting an admittedly extreme calculation, "and you told the bidders it was going to be the one tiger to be hunted, taken under fair-chase conditions, forevermore, I don't hesitate to say that license would sell for at least a half a million dollars. It might be seven figures." In terms of more sustainable tiger hunts, even foes of trophy hunting admit the average safari would bring tens of thousands of dollars into the range country, at least.

OK, so we'll bump the lodge prices and install a few safeguards to make sure eco-tourists inflict as little damage as possible on the environment they've come to see. (A list of just such suggestions has in fact been compiled by the National Audubon Society into what they call a code of ethics for nature tourism; the guidelines include such things as making sure the animals and their habitats are not disturbed by the visit and disposing of waste in such a way that it will leave neither environmental nor aesthetic impacts.) Unfortunately, however, there's another problem, and it is exemplified by tigers better than any other animal eco-tourists are likely to be seeking on an Indian adventure.

At several of the parks in India popular with tiger tourists, some of the cats have become so docile they lounge absently while visitors are jockeyed into position to have their pictures taken with a tiger in the background. In particular, people on the backs of elephants seem to bore the tigers, but Jeeps also can sometimes get within just a few yards. In certain parks, guides scout out tigers that have settled on a kill and then shuttle batch after batch of tourists out to watch the unconcerned star eat, then sleep, then eat some more. At first such access seems fantastic! What an *opportunity*, to see a wild tiger in its native habitat doing exactly what it has been designed to do by nature. But is that tiger really wild, or is it merely in situ? The difference is crucial, because it is the *wildness* that attracts a significant portion of the eco-tourists. They didn't travel thousands of miles and spend thousands of dollars just to see *a* tiger. They can do that at the local zoo back home. They've come to see a *wild* tiger, and one of the complaints fielded most frequently by guides who shuttle groups out to park and watch tigers eat their kills is that there are too many other chatty, camera-clicking tourists on the scene. The experience has lost its authenticity, its wildness.

Certainly there are still large numbers of people who will gladly pay a lot of money for such an experience, regardless of how many other tourists are beside them. And often such an encounter is only a tiny piece of an otherwise fulfilling eco-tourism experience that includes encounters with dozens of other species. But there is unquestionably a relationship between the seeming wildness of the tigers available to be seen and the likeliness of people to come seek them out. If the experience becomes common—less wild—it will lose a portion of its appeal and revenues will drop correspondingly. Few people return from an Indian eco-tour without being asked the question: "Did you see a tiger?" And many go with specific hopes of being able to come home and answer in the affirmative. Lodge managers are wise to such aspirations, and they specifically tout the likelihood of seeing a tiger on their premises. "The forests around Dhikala support one of the highest densities of tiger ever reported," boasts a flier for a reserve north of Kabini. Overeager booking agents, working out of offices far from the lodges, sometimes offer "guarantees" of a tiger sighting, and clandestine live-baiting is not unheard of.

Eco-tourists certainly can't or won't pay as much as trophy hunters to execute their form of use, but since it is nonconsumptive, each tiger can be multiplied by the number of tourists who would pay to come and see the animal over its entire ten- to fifteen-year-long life span. The raw economics are close enough, or at least sufficiently ambiguous, to call the preliminary comparative economics of trophy hunting and eco-tourism a wash and to at least discount Ullas Karanth's economic pessimism. Are there other wild tiger industries? A few, but none that work out so clearly in terms of money. Academic research of wild tigers is a valid and noble pursuit, but students and scientists are too few and too poor to be financially influential. Some governments are turning conservation itself into an industry by offering direct financial rewards for the nurturing of wildlife. "There is a new regulation for the renting of hunting areas," explains Dr. Victor Gaponov, head of the Animal Resources Department of the Primorsk Territorial Administration in Russia. "We are trying to make hunters interested in preserving a minimum number of animals in their hunting areas. We have a flexible schedule of rent payment, and in the case the hunter achieves this level his payment will be less. If the number of the animals in this territory is lower than required, then hunting is prohibited. He will be interested in making this land rich with animals ... and if he helps to protect the tiger, he almost won't pay rent." The details of the program have yet to be worked out, however, and there are concerns that Russia's central Ministries might complicate the plan.

Beyond economics, the huggability factor seems to taint eco-tourism the same way it does tiger farming, favoring more attractive animals. Eco-tours that promise up-close-and-personal encounters with snakes or scorpions just are not going to compete with those that offer one or more of the charismatic megafauna. The effect is mirrored in the way the tiger's seeming ferociousness makes it more attractive to trophy hunters than friendlier game. Bentham's inquiry into suffering also goes a little haywire in trying to balance the two pursuits: Tigers may suffer more as they die under natural circumstances, but it's easier for many people to overlook the apparent inconsistencies of Mother Nature than it is to sanction the superefficient intrusions of human competitors. The alternative for which so many people seem to hope is a world in which some unknowably correct number of tigers will be able to govern their own existences while continuously spawning new generations until each of the animals passes away without suffering. Call it Eden, call it Oz, call it a wildlife Utopia, it's never going to exist. We must deal with the real world, or the wild tiger itself is most surely destined to fade into a fantasy. Happily, something called the flagship-species phenomenon, which is unique to in situ animals, largely compensates for this emotional confusion: Save wild tigers, for whatever reason, and you will also save the humbler occupants of the neighborhood ipso facto, even if nobody wants to gaze upon them or hunt them as trophies. Conservationists also call this the "umbrella" effect. Wild tigers are the flagships of their ecosystems. Their umbrellas are huge. That's why either watching them go away or helping them stick around is so significant. "It's not about saving the tiger in cages either in the West or the East," says Ullas Karanth. "It's a question of saving tigers, prey, the habitat, the whole complex of biota that supports the tiger."

Ultimately, it supports us, too.

↩

We've talked about the earning power of a wild tiger, but what is the "value" of one? A soft concept, to be sure, but it must be determined. The perceived value of wild tigers will drive the selection and implementation of a variety of conservation actions that are potentially counterproductive and possibly even mutually exclusive. Only after the value of a wild tiger has been determined can the amount anybody will either have to, or be willing to, "pay" for its survival be calculated with any degree of accuracy, meaningfulness, or utility. Fortunately, value can be expressed in terms of a process we have already investigated.

Use value: Whether we use a resource consumptively or non-consumptively, sustainably or exhaustively, we still *use* it. The reason we use it is that it yields something in return for its use—ergo, it has "use value." The yield may come in a form as concrete as cash, or it may be as ethereal as delight, but something is yielded in return for the use of the resource, and that is why it is used.

Nonuse value: As the prefix denotes, the antonymical dynamic applies here. Certain resources yield something in return for *not* being used. The ozone layer, for example. These resources yield things when they're left alone—they have value in "nonuse."

A concession to philosophical perfectionists (please skip to the next paragraph if the mere thought of more semantics makes you sick): Pure reason and set theory compel us to admit that even nonuse is a use when we ourselves are identified as the users. When we, for example, don't use the ozone layer, we are, in effect, using it nonconsumptively for the sake of realizing its nonuse values—breathable air, survivable levels of radiation, and so forth. The same paradox reveals a weakness in a statement made earlier in this book: In chapter 9, "use" was identified as the fundamental principle at work when discussing ex situ tigers. In fact, use is equally fundamental to discussion of wild tigers. Technically, we cannot *not* use wild tigers. Were we to back out completely from Sundarbans and ring the area with armed guards to make sure no one could get close to the tigers inside for any reason whatsoever, we would still be using them to realize a variety of nonuse values, several of which are about to be presented. Such enigmas have more to do with words than with tigers, but they accurately reflect the perplexities involved in conserving the animal.

Many resources—wild tigers, for instance—have both use and nonuse values, which are inevitably at odds with one another because we cannot both use and not use a resource. This is the very heart of the wild tiger conservation problem. A large group of people accurately recognizes the various use values of wild tigers and they want to realize those yields in the best interest of the human race by taking action to harvest them. Another large group of people accurately recognizes the nonuse values of wild tigers, and *they* want to realize *those* yields by *not* taking any harvesting action. At the risk of generalizing yet again, we can be relatively sure of finding *con*servationists in either group, but preservationists will be found only in the second. This triggers the next inquiry in the cascade: Value to whom?

Well, the "obvious" response is "Value to us." People. Human beings . . .

By now we all should recognize the folly in presuming that answer. Whether or not we embrace the concepts of animal rights personally, we *must* acknowledge the collective influence of individuals who do, as well as the role their influence plays now, and will forever play, in the destiny of the wild tiger. If we plan to address that influence meaningfully, we must not only acknowledge it, but understand it. Thus, a second potential beneficiary enters the picture: Value to the tigers themselves; they "deserve" to be wild, to be free from human control. Clearly this position eliminates any option for use. If tigers have rights, the animals cannot be used justifiably in any way by humans. Consider the Analogy of the Superior Alien: A spaceship lands, and a superior alien steps from it to announce that humans will now be subjected to the control of its race. On what grounds? If we try to justify our control of tigers on the basis that we are innately superior to them, we would ourselves have to agree to be controlled by some yet superior life-form. What most humanists actually promote, though they are not aware of it, is the position that we—*humans*—are supremely endowed with rights above and beyond those of any other life-form that exists, no matter how smart or powerful. Our rights are unique, inalienable, indivisible, unassailable, self-evident, and maybe even divine. We are the measure of all things This is the very definition of humanism.

Let's examine a flaw or two in this position before we move beyond it. Are there "wild" human beings? There are most certainly captive ones, in prisons, concentration camps, nations with closed borders. Anthropologists are keen to identify "endangered" human beings in the forms of indigenous or aboriginal tribes and cultures. Humans, as a race, do not even agree among themselves on the rel ative values of one another, let alone tigers. Whose definitions are uniquely, inalienably, indivisibly, unassailably, self evidently, and maybe even divinely entitled to prevail? Are some animals indeed created more equal than others?

The antihumanist argument—the basis of pure preservationism —suffers from its own inconsistency. Anyone who professes to promote the well-being of the wild tiger more than anything else is a hypocrite, with only one clearly consistent choice: suicide. No amount of crusading will compensate for all those miles you will drive, all those toilets you will flush, all that trash you will discard. In fact, you'll really do the tiger a favor if you take out a few extra people before you go. There is, ultimately, but a single current threat to wild tigers, and that is the human being. Remove us from the equation and the animal will do just fine. There are very few things on which all conservationists agree, but, with the possible opposition of the most ardent humanists, this is one of them: There are too many people in the world for the good of the wild tiger.

Let us admit, therefore, despite such subterranean game-playing, that the destiny of the wild tiger is within human control, whether or not that is either uniformly applicable to the human race or justifiable in terms of Truth and Moral Justice. We must, to repeat our new mantra, deal with things as they are, not as we wish they were. (Cervantes was a romantic, not a conservationist.) Otherwise, the decisions will be made through default and inertia. For the sake of determining the tiger-conservation path to be taken, then, each of us must ask ourselves why we, individually, want tigers to survive in the wild. What is their value to *us*, personally? Consider the following before offering an answer.

How might you use a wild tiger? Consumptively, you might want to hunt one down. You might want to eat the derivatives of one in hopes of curing your ills. You might want to hang its skin on your wall or across your shoulders. These are among the potential consumptive use values of a wild tiger to you, personally. Some people will offer lots of time or money or some other resource in exchange to realize one or more of these values. Some will offer nothing at all. Some will compromise by accepting similar values from captive tigers in return for having to offer fewer exchange resources. And some will offer money or time or other resources to see that other individuals are not allowed to realize any of these values, but we'll get to that in a minute. Nonconsumptively, you might be willing to offer lots of money or time or resources to see or photograph a tiger in the wild. Or perhaps you'd like to study its behavior. But you may be willing to sacrifice a degree of that wildness in return for fewer exchange resources, or you may even settle quite happily for seeing a tiger in a zoo. All the above exemplify the *use* values of tigers to individual human beings.

Unless you are super-rich (in global terms), young, unencumbered, very highly motivated, or all four, you will have tallied up an absolute zero so far when it comes to figuring out the value of a *wild* tiger to you personally. Only an infinitesimal speck of the human population will ever come close to having anything resembling a chance to use a wild tiger in any way whatsoever, consumptively or non. That is precisely what makes such opportunities so expensive and enviable. The motivating forces behind almost *everybody's* efforts to save the wild tiger lie, in fact, in *nonuse* values.

Asked the question of why they want wild tigers to survive, a significant number of respondents will answer something like, "I just sleep better at night knowing they're out there." This is about as defined as the value of a wild tiger gets for a lot of us. But just because it's ill-defined doesn't mean it's invalid. The metaphor of sleeping well at night gauges the morality of many of our most important pursuits. With tigers, it means we just don't want the wild ones to go away, and many of us will offer money or time or some other resource in exchange just to make sure they *don't* go away, even though we know we'll never be able to use them. This concept is referred to as "long-distance" value. It is active, widespread, and potent when brought together in large quantities.

There are other nonuse values that are equally common and much easier to define in specific terms. Premier among them is something expressed as a fear that we don't know everything there is to know about the value of wild tigers yet, and that by doing away with them we will inadvertently be sabotaging our better interests down the road. This is known as "option" value. We want the option of using wild tigers in the future, even though we're not sure right now why or how we're going to use them. "If we destroy it all right now," Ullas Karanth observes, "it's like a man burning up his insurance policy."

Another reason many of us sleep better at night just knowing wild tigers are roaming around out there somewhere is that we find satisfaction in preserving all the use and nonuse values, both known and unknown, for future generations. This is an extension of option value known as "bequest" value. It soothes us to know we are being good stewards, not selfishly using up all the wild tigers. Guilt avoidance plays into this, in response to which people will readily pay heavy prices.

Avoidance of other undesirable consequences also factors into the value of not using up all the wild tigers, in some ways that are concrete and others metaphysical. Tigers are among what biologists call the "crown" predators: They eat everything but nothing eats them. (We speak here in terms of naked animals facing one another without tools, which knocks the highest crown from off the human head.) Removing a crown predator from an ecosystem can trigger all sorts of biospherical complications, some of which are quite predictable. In certain areas where tigers have been extirpated, the ungulates on which those tigers preyed have thrived and subsequently grazed the open land down to bare dirt. Grade school geology tells us what happened next: Rain washed all the topsoil downstream, not only screwing up the next year's supply of vegetation for all those ungulates but also trashing everything else that depended in any way on any portion of the entire watershed. This is the same cause-and-effect ladder we saw kicked off by lumber poaching, only in reverse, with the tiger going away first instead of last. Biologists call this a "disruption syndrome," from which the biosphere eventually will recover, but all kinds of radical swings may come to pass over lengthy spans of time—millennia, at least—before it does. And the final steady state just might not include human beings. A variation on this is called a "pulse" of extinction, in which an ever-widening circle of linked biota goes away very quickly and forever, irrevocably diverting the future of the entire planet. The dinosaurs went away in a pulse of extinction. We still don't know exactly why.

Before such apocalyptic imagery gets conscripted in the name of tiger conservation, it is essential to point out that ecosystems are surprisingly resilient despite their apparent delicateness. Leopards, for example, would just love to see the wild tiger go away so they could step in and control the ungulate population. A host of other predators, not all of them with crowns, would benefit at each successive stage of the disruption, along with omnivores, herbivores, scavengers, et al. The seesaw action of the syndrome itself handily demonstrates how the biosphere is auto-regulated. Also, scientists suspect that pulses of extinction require heavy-duty jump starts, like an asteroid the size of a mountain or a volcano fifty times more powerful than Krakatoa. Nevertheless, we don't exactly know what the removal of the wild tiger from the biosphere will instigate, and that alone should give us pause. Humanists often pit the tiger against the human race in an oversimplified equation of either/or. Reality is probably much closer to something like both/neither.

Suppose that the wild tiger is in fact expendable to the biosphere. Crown predators, after all, are not necessarily "keystone" species, which scientists identify as those animals and plants that individually support, either directly or by extension, enormous numbers of other species. Almost by definition, these life-forms are situated farther *down* the food chain, and they come in humbler packages than crown predators; starfish, for example, or mangrove trees. Certain types of rodents are among the more exotic of the keystone species. Losing a keystone species is significantly more likely to trigger a disruption syndrome or a pulse of extinction than the loss of a crown predator, and the wild tiger is not considered a keystone species. In terms of human sentiment, however, the tiger *is* arguably the most charismatic of the charismatic megafauna, the most huggable of huggables. You can build grassroots movements and sports teams and political parties and corporate images around the tiger. When it comes to conservation, the tiger is *the* flagship species. If we can't save the tiger, how much hope is there for the pupfish? Eventually, we're going to face the loss of a keystone species significantly less sexy than the tiger. How much enthusiasm will we be able to generate? "[Conservation] is a matter of selling an idea," says Ullas Karanth. "Selling the idea to common people. Selling the idea to voters. Selling the idea to bureaucrats. Selling the idea to lots of interests. People can be made to give up some of their facilities, the resources they are enjoying, provided you are able to sell the idea to them that something is worth saving." The tiger, he notes, is an easy idea to sell, "but it is very difficult to sell the idea of a biodiversity index. It simply goes over people's heads."

And what will it do to our collective psyche to lose, by our own hand, one of our most vivid natural metaphors for power, beauty, stealth . . . wildness? What will it mean thereafter to be told, "You fight like a tiger," or "She's a real tigress," or "Put a tiger in your tank?" Substitute the word "dinosaur" in each of those phrases and see what happens to the implications. The unavoidable irony of the extinction of the wild tiger is that it will prove the vulnerability of an animal driven into extinction because it seemed invincible.

In large part, it is fear of exactly such a loss of metaphor that produces the most visible of all nonconsumptive use values for the wild tiger: public relations.

❧

Early on the morning of September 28, 1995, at the National Zoological Park in Washington, D.C., a unit of motorcycle police cordoned off the tiger and lion display—a man-made mountain (tigers on one side, lions on the other) surrounded by a moat from beyond which visitors view the resident cats. Television crews began arriving shortly thereafter, representing everyone from the CBS network in New York to Television Taiwan and a host of local stations. Next came a team from Fleishman-Hillard, the public relations firm whose offices are strewn around the globe and whose client list reads like ticker tape. Managing the scene as though it were a military operation, the Fleishman-Hillard team deployed throughout the display area, consulting one another via walkie-talkies as they advised the television crews concerning suitable angles and likely interview sites while simultaneously directing the zoo staff in setting up tables, chairs, risers, a podium, and a lectern directly in front of the tiger display, inside

which a Bengal-Siberian hybrid named Varuna paced, entirely unconcerned by the commotion.

Next came representatives from the National Fish and Wildlife
Foundation, offering the Fleishman-Hillard team whatever assistance
was necessary. The foundation is a nonprofit NGO originally set up
by Congress in 1984 to assist the U.S. Fish and Wildlife Service by
collecting, administering, and distributing funds in the form of grants
to organizations and individuals who pursue conservation activities
aligned with the objectives of the service. (The foundation's role has expanded to include several federal agencies since it was originally chartered by Congress.) Shortly after sunrise, the caterers arrived, delivering
silver urns and china, and food they would spend the remainder of the
morning protecting from interloping swarms of yellow jackets.

The event was being called a press conference, but it was open
only to persons who had received invitations in advance. Such exclu-
sivity is less than typical of press conferences, which are more often
than not designed to generate as much exposure as possible, and therefore are open to all who care to attend. In this case, however, the
client was more comfortable maintaining control.

Around 7:30 A.M. the invitees started showing up: Ron Tilson
from the Minnesota Zoo; Howard Quigley from the Hornocker Wildlife Research Institute; John Seidensticker, curator of mammals for
the National Zoological Park (whose office was just yards away from
where the podium had been placed); Sydney Butler, executive director
of the AZA; Ginette Hemley, Director of International Wildlife Policy
with WWF-U.S.; Gilbert Grovesnor, president and chairman of the
board of trustees of the National Geographic Society.... Among those
scheduled to attend but unable to make it due to last-minute appoint-
ment conflicts were Marshall Jones of the Fish and Wildlife Service,
Mohd Khan bin Momin Khan of the IUCN in Kuala Lumpur, Ulysses
Seal of the CBSG, and the Honorable Newt Gingrich, Speaker of the
U.S. House of Representatives—who sent a letter drafted that morning
via his staff to apologize for missing the conference.

What, and who, in the world could attract such a crowd to a zoo on a Thursday morning? The answer to both questions arrived just before 8:00 wearing glasses and a dark blue suit: Charles R. Sitter, president, Exxon Corporation.

Four years prior to this Washington press conference, a gentleman named David Schmalz—a shareholder in the Exxon Corporation—had flown to Dallas, Texas, from his home in the Netherlands, at his own expense, to attend the company's 1991 annual shareholders' meeting. When the opportunity had been offered, as it is at each such meeting, for shareholders to address management directly, Mr. Schmalz had stepped to the microphone and asked what the company was doing to support the conservation of the tiger, which the corporation had adopted as its symbol almost a century earlier. Management conferred briefly, then explained to Mr. Schmalz that they were involved in a few miscellaneous tiger-conservation efforts. Schmalz's question caught the attention of the chairman of the board, who promised that the matter would be given further consideration.

He was quite as good as his word. When Charles Sitter took his turn at the mike in Washington four years later, he explained that Exxon was about to donate $5 million over a five-year period to something called the Save the Tiger Fund, a newly organized financial vehicle to be administered by the National Fish and Wildlife Foundation. "It's very hard to imagine a world without tigers roaming somewhere free and wild," Sitter told the audience, gesturing, with forgivable irony, toward Varuna. "We don't want that to happen, and it's not just because it's our symbol, but because the loss of this regal beast would diminish us all." Before the day was over, news of the Save the Tiger Fund aired on national and international television, a toll-free telephone hot line (set up by the foundation) began taking calls, and a Save the Tiger Fund home page opened on the Internet's World Wide Web.

This was indeed very big news for tiger conservation. Not since WWF had announced its contribution of $1 million to Operation Tiger more than two decades earlier had anyone assembled anything close to so vast a sum from a single contributor to be used exclusively on behalf of the tiger. In terms of hard-dollar contributions from a single private source, Exxon's bequest dwarfed all the monies formerly committed to the salvation of the wild tiger combined.* Exxon had, in fact, been vigorously increasing its involvement in tiger conservation since the moment David Schmalz had retaken his seat in Dallas. The company and its wholly owned subsidiaries—the ESSOs—had established themselves as generous contributors by supporting everyone from Sarah Christie in England to Paul But in Hong Kong to Dale Miquelle in the Russian Far East. All this earlier largesse, however, did not add up to anything nearly so grand as the commitment pledged to the fund by Exxon at the press conference on the morning of September 28, 1995, at the National Zoo in Washington.

Nor did it spare the company from charges that it now was using a tiger to sop up the oil spilled by the Exxon *Valdez* six years earlier in the single biggest eco-blunder ever. "Help or Hype from Exxon?" asked the headline of an article that ran in *Business Week* shortly before the press conference. "Even when Exxon Corp. tries to do good," the piece opened, "it has a knack for riling conservationists. In an attempt to spill up an image still stained by the 1989 Exxon *Valdez* spill...." Then, during a live interview with CBS *This Morning* on the day of the conference, host Harry Smith told Edward Ahnert, president of the Exxon Education Foundation, "You know what a lot of people say. 'Exxon, that's a name that's tied with one of the worst ecological disasters in memory.' Is this anything more than image rehabilitation?" Well ready for that question, Ahnert replied, "Harry, I don't think that anything that we could do with the tiger would make the public forget the tragic accident that was *Valdez*. This is a

---

*This fact still should not diminish the recognition due many NGOs, governmental agencies, and corporate sponsors of tiger conservation who had been funding the likes of Ron Tilson and the Hornocker Institute for several years, including the Ralston Purina Big Cat Survival Fund, the National Geographic Society, and the U.S. Fish and Wildlife Service, among many others.

totally separate endeavor." Later, in a separate interview, Ahnert added, somewhat wearily, "We would be doing this project whether or not the *Valdez* had taken place. That was a tragic accident, and everybody in the company is deeply sorry and regretful of that.... We can't rewrite history. Regrettably, there are a lot of cynics out there who, no matter what we say and no matter what we do, will criticize our efforts to save the tiger as simply a cover-up for the *Valdez*."

Exxon had suffered earlier slings and arrows as well, flung by none other than Michael Day of The Tiger Trust. "ESSO Dumps Tiger Campaign," a banner headline in the winter 1994/95 issue of *Tiger News* declared. According to Day, ESSO U.K. had approached him with plans to help the wild tiger by selling tiger-shaped coin banks at their U.K. filling stations and then donating the money to The Tiger Trust. For reasons undisclosed, the company backed away from the deal at the last minute, infuriating Day. Ed Ahnert, asked almost a year later if he was aware of the situation, responded, "We know Mr. Day." Asked if he cared to comment further, he said, "No."

Then there is the issue of tiger farming. While conducting a "tiger master-planning workshop" in Thailand just a few months before the press conference at the National Zoo, Ulysses Seal and Ron Tilson had ushered the workshop attendees—a group that included representatives from China, Laos, Myanmar, Malaysia, Singapore, and Vietnam in addition to the Thai and U.S. contingents—on a field trip through the tiger farm at Sriracha. A specific reason for the visit was never presented, but it was clear upon arrival that Seal and Tilson were by no means hostile to the operation. The workshop group partook of every service and display, beginning at the restaurant and concluding at the TCM pharmacy. Several workshop participants petted the tiger cubs. Some bought souvenirs at the gift shop. The master-planning workshop was financed in part by Exxon. The gate fees at Sriracha were included in the workshop. Is Exxon funding tiger farming?

"The question hasn't come up," Ahnert said just days after the press conference in D.C. "The council hasn't met to discuss this, and

I'd rather not anticipate their position. But I will say that I would be surprised if, when this comes up, if it ever does, that there will be any interest on the part of the council in supporting projects like that."

No, Exxon is not deliberately funding tiger farming, and anyone who uses the information presented here to attack the company as if it were will be guilty of misrepresenting the facts. Absent an analysis such as the one presented in this book, the company cannot be blamed for looking through the prisms handed to it by its many eager and competing potential beneficiaries. Who could guess that giving lots of money to tiger conservation could be interpreted by anybody as a bad thing? Nevertheless, an astounding if inadvertent degree of coziness has developed between the Save the Tiger Fund and the practice of tiger farming. Ulysses Seal is the chairman of the eight-person council set up by the Fish and Wildlife Foundation to administer the fund, of which Ahnert also is a member. Seal, perhaps more than any other individual, will influence the decisions regarding how the money in the fund will be spent. As should be clear by now, he does not represent the views of everyone involved in tiger conservation. Standing on the grounds of Sriracha, he was unfazed by inquiries regarding whether or not Exxon was prepared to be linked in any way with the third rail of tiger farming. His perspective remains utterly scientific, for which he cannot be criticized. To him, if there are tigers somewhere, they need to be found, analyzed, documented, and managed. That's the nature of his science. Just how completely that science will be adopted by Exxon customers, shareholders, and employees hostile to the concept of tiger farming remains to be seen.

Tilson, too, is not shy about touching on the subject of tiger farming. "The reproductive potential of tigers is enormous," he told his audience in an address he delivered at the 1995 convention of AZA in Seattle, Washington, just ten days before attending the Exxon press conference in D.C. "Outside of Chonburi [in Thailand] there is an ongoing and rapidly increasing tiger industry that is being very professionally done," he continued, referring directly to Sriracha. "It is not a difficult issue to captive-breed tigers for slaughter for the market. It can be done. It can be done cheaply, and it can be done in the tens of thousands of animals." As several of his cospeakers (a panel that included Ginette Hemley, Judy Mills, and Paul But) squirmed in their seats, Tilson made little more than a token effort to distance himself from an outright endorsement of tiger farming. "Will it stop the loss of wild populations?" he asked. "It's a difficult issue. I don't have the answer.... Ethically, is this correct? I think on this we're outvoted. It's not for us, from North America, to overlay a cultural template of ethics on countries of other origin. It's up to various countries to come to their own decisions as to whether they're going to be developing these kinds of supplemental programs or not."

⤚

The PR value of tigers pays political dividends as well as commercial ones. The fact that Newt Gingrich failed to attend the Exxon press conference (the welfare debate was raging that day) should by no means be construed to indicate a lack of interest on his part. On the contrary, Gingrich is more than hip to the cause. Just a few kilometers down the road from the National Zoo in Washington, D.C., lies the nation's Capitol. Eleven months before Exxon's press conference, the U.S. Congress had passed a piece of legislation called the Rhinoceros and Tiger Conservation Act, establishing thereby what was intended to become, more or less, a public version of the private Save the Tiger Fund. (This is a gigantic simplification, but it is not inaccurate. Extra volumes would be required even to attempt a full explanation of the American legislative process.) The act authorized the U.S. government to set aside public money—tax dollars—specifically for projects aimed at conserving rhinos and tigers. Authorization, however, is quite separate from action, and eight months passed before any money was budgeted for the act. When it was, Newt Gingrich was among the congressional bloodhounds who sniffed it out and promoted its allocation. "This is a very small amount of money," he said, referring to the $200,000 initially appropriated, "but it is symbolically very important, and symbolically important in part for the signal it sends to people, particularly in Africa and Asia, about whether or not the United States is prepared to reach out and be helpful."

Those weren't the only symbolic signals being sent. As Gingrich spoke, the newly Republican Congress was embarking on one of its most divisive tasks: reauthorizing the Endangered Species Act. Conservationists were screaming that Congress was emasculating the ESA rather than reauthorizing it, and unquestionably there were efforts under way by some of the Speaker's closest allies to retool the ESA to the right. Funding for the Rhinoceros and Tiger Conservation Act supplied an irresistibly cheap and timely opportunity to tout Republican concern for endangered species.

Gingrich's simultaneous devotion to both the Conservation Act and the Save the Tiger Fund ("I want you to know of my enthusiastic support for the creation of the Save the Tiger Fund," his letter assured the crowd at the Exxon press conference) demonstrates a couple of curious overlaps between the two. Both have been designed specifically to accept tax-deductible donations directly from the public. Which, then, is a "better" choice for someone willing to write a check for tiger conservation? The only obvious distinction between the two is that the act includes rhinos while the fund does not. Beyond that, things get fuzzy. Neither organ decides in advance precisely how its monies shall be spent. Proposals are considered, and those deemed worthy get funding. There are not two distinct agendas or directions, though the fund has received a bit of criticism for what seems to many like favoritism for zoos. Ironically, among the features intended to balance that favoritism, the fund manifests its most direct linkage to the act: Marshall Jones, who holds the purse strings for the Rhinoceros and Tiger Conservation Act, is a member of the eight-person council that directs the activities of the Save the Tiger Fund. It's not inconceivable that a check written to the act could end up being spent through the fund, and vice versa.

"Fine," says Amos Eno, executive director of the National Fish and Wildlife Foundation, which administers the fund. "The more people who contribute, the better." His point must be well taken. Those interested in tiger conservation should not close their checkbooks either to the act or the fund simply because an accounting in advance for precisely how the donation will be spent is unavailable. Nobody involved with either entity wants the wild tigers to go away. Their assembled know-how represents an impressive chunk of all the tiger expertise available anywhere in the world. Letting just such a group hash out how the money should be spent may be exactly the option many donors are seeking.

Finally, with respect to the PR value of the wild tiger, we must not be seduced into thinking it is only meretricious politicians and corporate executives who seek to take advantage. NGOs, as we have seen, are at least as likely to enlist the image of the tiger in their quests for members, donations, and general support. Few print up greeting cards or calendars that feature pictures of the critically endangered cape stag beetle or the red rump tarantula. Few miss the chance to use a tiger.

⤸

There are other values of wild tigers, to be sure. Economists are out there making up new ones all the time. (Assume a wild tiger . . .) But each one gets increasingly esoteric, and to discuss them further would diffuse whatever strength has been generated by those analyzed thus far. Academia has already played what many will consider to be too big a role in this book, and leaning upon it further will do little for the tiger, with one lingering exception. . . .

Thus far, we have presumed that everyone considering the values of wild tigers is interested in seeing the species survive—the species has plenty of positive value, in other words. Poachers, TCM devotees, and trophy hunters may be willing to tolerate the deaths of individual tigers, but certainly they have no interest in the extinction of the species. Just the opposite. Poachers and smugglers would lose a lucrative product line. Trophy hunters would lose a target and a potentially thrilling story. TCM adherents might lose their lives. Is there anyone who actually wants the animals to go away? Do living wild tigers have any negative values?

Sure, and we have discussed almost all of them. But they have been largely disguised as consumptive use values. A roundup of them will be of special utility here because it will supply an isolated contrast in an economic context. If market dynamics are to be relied upon to promote the survival of the wild tiger, we must first identify the opposing forces (hereby done) and then strive to accentuate the positive while eliminating the negative.

If there are indeed tiger-bone speculators operating anywhere in the world, they clearly have a keen interest in killing off wild tigers. Next, anyone living in the neighborhood of problem tigers certainly looks forward to seeing them either taken or extracted. Then, working our way down the ranks of conspicuousness, people who would like to graze their livestock or raise their crops in an area where a wild tiger might be tempted to help itself either to the domesticated animals or to the harvester would probably be thrilled to see the animal go away. Finally, governments and corporations interested in alternative uses of tiger habitat will need to be compensated in some way for sacrificing whatever opportunity cost the tigers represent. (Just how rich an oil field would have to be discovered beneath the island of Sumatra or in the Russian Far East for a petroleum company to be willing to displace the resident tiger populations overhead?) It is in precise opposition to these negative values, economists suggest, that the positive values of wild tigers now must be lined up toe-to-toe, after which the collective stronger of the two will automatically prevail. The reason wild tigers now find themselves in such a plight, this argument posits, is that the negative values have been allowed to dominate the equation. Reverse the polarity and the problem will be solved. To free-market philosophers, it is literally as simple as that.

❧

CHAPTER 11

Thinking Small

REDUCING THE TIGER to mere genetics, philosophy, politics, and economics insults the animal and preposterously glorifies the analyst. Tigers are a wonder. It doesn't matter what language we use to explain that. Nevertheless, dull equations and high-flown rhetoric have their place in making such wonders at least seem more understandable to us.

In working toward a conclusion, let us simplify. Certain things associated with the conservation of the wild tiger are both doable and unencumbered by serious conflict. Tiger farming is not suddenly going to become palatable to advocates of animal rights, and a billion-plus potential users of TCM are not suddenly going to discard their convictions. Zoos are never going to enrich their environments sufficiently or correctly enough to satisfy staunch supporters of animal welfare, and a grieving mother is never going to understand why some people consider a marauding tiger more important than the child it has killed. Those battles will continue to rage long after the fate of the wild tiger is decided either by us or by inertia. The animal's conservation is a big problem. For at least this one chapter, let's think small.

If the wild tiger doesn't have a place to live, the case is closed. The animal will go—already will have gone—away. First things first, then: a bit of habitat. Lest we get swept back into the discussion of conflicting uses of land, we can agree that there are already a bunch of places set aside for tigers and their kin. Let's start with those, by-passing for the time being the question of whether or not they will turn out to have been sufficiently large or connected enough to sustain the species a thousand years from now. Laws are already on the books to protect these areas and their inhabitants, so further legislation—in terms of these existing habitats—is not needed. (Different laws are a different story, to be discussed in a moment.) What desperately *is* needed is enforcement of those existing laws, but how can that be done?

The answer may be deceptively simple. "Quite the best case of it," says Neil Franklin, beginning an object lesson, "was when we had a study site which we monitored continually for eleven months. It was a small area of three hundred and fifty kilometers square. When we started the project up, the first time we went in we found people logging, taking wood, collecting this, that, and the other. But from that point on, we never had another person come inside that three hundred and fifty square kilometers for the next ten months."

At first it may seem as if Franklin has left something out of his homily. Just what was it, we wonder, that scared off the intruders? In this case, the messenger is the message: Franklin himself frightened them away. "We've found that this has just knocked the number of intrusions we've come across," he continues, listing other instances of his unlikely fearsomeness. "It just wiped it out in some areas. The first time we go into an area we might come across ten or fifteen people. The second time we go back, for the next two or three months there just won't be anybody. And word has gotten back to the villagers."

Wait a minute. Word of *what?* Are Franklin and his team ter-rorizing the villagers? Do they dress up like local deities and howl in the night? Are they hiding in the bushes making tiger noises? What special thing are they doing to drive all intruders from their research areas? "Nothing," Franklin says. "We're just a scientific team collecting data.

"Basically, they are quite scared we're going to report them," he continues, a bit mystified by the phenomenon himself. "We always take photographs of everybody, even if we don't have film in the camera. And we often make a show of talking into our radios. Of course we don't carry guns, or anything like that. . . . It just scares people. You can see the worried looks on their faces. The last thing they want, like anybody else, is to be put into prison. They've still got families on the outside. They're basically trying to support families by doing this."

Can it really be that simple? Just placing figures of apparent authority in the parks, armed with nothing more than a walkie-talkie and a camera? As far as the Sumatran tiger is concerned, who would know better than Neil Franklin? We can talk all we like about how we think trained patrols, bristling with weaponry, are needed to counteract poaching, but Franklin is out there walking around in the jungles of Sumatra, speaking to the natives in their own tongue, seeing for himself how they react. Anybody offering contrary advice is theorizing.

Furthermore, Franklin's observations are supported by the other researchers around the globe who actually walk where tigers walk. "When people know that these tigers have radio collars on them and they know that people are following them all over the place," says John Goodrich of the Hornocker Institute, "they're going to be a little bit reluctant to poach." His colleague, Dale Miquelle, endorses the observation with a personal experience. "We talked to the police extensively about capturing the person who did it," he says, referring to the poaching incident that involved the wayward conservation officer cited earlier. "They felt pressure. There was an American [involved]. They felt something needed to be done." Something was done. Two months later, Miquelle was called back to the police station to discuss the matter with two gentlemen in suits who did not speak in direct terms. "I finally realized we were talking to the KGB."

The story is much the same in India, minus the obeisance to Westerners. Researchers indicate that a simple human presence in India's parks—even of tourists and their guides—makes locals more wary of entering illegally, and scientific authorities such as Ullas Karanth are almost as effective as guards in that respect. Sadly, some of India's best tiger reserves harbor an even more powerful deterrent: Militant rebel factions have moved in and taken over, plundering the territory in the process.

In most of the other range countries there is so little full-time tiger research either published or taking place it's impossible to calculate its impact on illegal intrusion. But that also means the field is wide open to benefit from such an effect. Perhaps we can save tigers in situ simply by studying them. Personpower is the problem—not so much that there's a shortage of willing research candidates or money to sponsor them, as there is a shortage of administrative mechanisms to match the needs with the resources.

This is the same obstacle that thwarts the effective enforcement of CITES. Those laws are clear. The lists in the appendices are specific. The penalties are discrete. There simply are not enough people in place to catch the violators. "But there's a real boon to this problem," says Judy Mills. "Sniffer dogs." Travelers who enter the U.S. through the international terminal at the San Francisco Airport (at other airports, too) are welcomed to the country by both man and beast. As you wait in line to have your passport checked, a dog on a lead—usually a beagle; particularly good nose—is trotted out to sniff cheerfully at your carry-on baggage and at you. You don't want him to sit down in front of you. If he does, it means he's found something that's going to make the person on the other end of the lead very angry, like a kilo of cocaine, or a bomb. These dogs are extraordinarily accurate, outperforming human inspectors by several orders of magnitude, particularly in terms of efficiency. One sniffer dog can cover hundreds of bags in moments without needing to open a single one, and almost without ever being skunked. They work for kibble. They don't require a pension. They don't go on strike. In Canada, Mills explains, such dogs already are being used with great success to sniff out bear gallbladder. Each dog is capable of detecting several scents, so the original targets of drugs and bombs need not be forgone for the sake of introducing a few wildlife aromas onto the no-no list. "The dogs are capable of sniffing tiger bones and other endangered species parts," says Mills. "That capability has not been taken advantage of except in Canada."

Next on the low-tech list, a bulldozer. "If you want to log, go ahead," says Dale Miquelle, in a suggestion as likely to surprise timber executives as it is to infuriate protectionists. "Put in your road to get in there. But when you're done and you come out, destroy a section of that road so it's impassable. That's all you have to do. For a logging company that's a minor investment. A half-day's work with a bulldozer would do the job." As Miquelle pointed out earlier, it is the logging *road* as much as the logging itself that threatens the tigers by making them accessible to poachers, both professional and opportunistic. Snip that road at its mouth when its legitimate purpose comes to an end, and, with respect to future poaching of tigers, it's almost as though the road was never built. With respect to logging, there's even a residual benefit. "Half a day's work would open the road up again in thirty or forty years if they want to go back in," notes Miquelle. In terms of compromises between industry and conservation, this one is going to be tough to beat.

For those less inclined to compromise with loggers, there are other small but meaningful opportunities. "Nobody has got their infrastructure together," laments Valmik Thapar, referring to the most basic of business basics. "There is no copy machine, no filing cabinet, no computer. There is no office to function from. You can't expect to run an international strategy like this." Indeed, you can barely expect to run a country. The most rudimentary means of communication, taken completely for granted in developed countries, are wildly extravagant luxuries in every single one of the fourteen tiger range nations. Anyone who's tried to send a fax of more than a single page into India or make a long-distance phone call out of Indonesia will commiserate with Thapar. "Get that bloody basic infrastructure there," he frets.

Transportation also lags. "To be perfect," says Rudolph Youdt, vice chief of the Sikhote-Alin antipoaching brigade, "we need a truck. To be mobile. To go everywhere. Not only to ride along the streets, but also to go up the small roads. We know the places where the poachers are, but we cannot get there." Disabled or nonexistent vehicles are the bane of tiger researchers and conservationists everywhere. The same lack of technology that hobbles basic communications in the range countries also cripples transportation, producing vehicles that are decrepit the moment they roll off the production line and that will be stalled for months while their replacement parts are ordered from the factory. When a reliable, economical vehicle makes its way to a research or antipoaching site it is cherished, shown off, and protected. Inevitably, it boosts morale as steeply as it elevates the efficiency of the work.

Concerning that work, and moving a step up the ladder of complexity, it is imperative that the scientific community agree upon, and then standardize, a means of counting tigers. If precise numbers are destined to be demanded forever by the general public, a better censusing technique must be devised. If the general health of wild tiger populations will suffice, then let a unified methodology of assessment be adopted. Camera trapping has specific values, it is doable, and it's cheap. So are line-transect prey surveys. So is the collection and analysis of tiger scat. No single technique answers all the questions, but all answer some. Combined and standardized, they will answer enough.

Still more ambitious, let's find out once and for all if captive-bred tigers can be reintroduced into the wild. This project will be relatively complicated, time-consuming, and expensive, but it is discrete—it is a doable experiment that can be scientifically monitored and that will yield specific, identifiable, repeatable results. The implications justify the effort. The path of wild tiger conservation will forever be diverted in one of two directions depending on the outcome of such an experiment. Promethean resources, including money, technology, personpower, and time, which are now being pitted against one another due to uncertainty regarding the reintroducibility of the wild tiger, would finally line up to complement each other. This question can be answered.

So can others. Does tiger-bone TCM work? Paul But is ready, able, willing, and poised to tell us. His answer won't settle the issue, but the lack of an answer leads to exactly the same kind of speculative wheel-spinning as the reintroduction quandary. When his research is complete, this question mark will go away and we can proceed on a basis of knowledge instead of belief. We also can then either dispense with or continue the search for a substitute. Yes, that search is fraught with secondary complications all its own, but the only thing we can be sure of by not looking for a substitute, if one is needed, is that we'll never know if one exists. Another question mark, at least, can be eliminated.

Hand in hand with the work Paul But is doing in his laboratory goes the work done both in Ashland and in Steve O'Brien's laboratories at the National Cancer Institute. Regardless of where the genetic baseline for tigers surfaces first, all will benefit from the shared information. In particular, the Ashland lab will spin off conservation benefits by complementing the law-enforcement measures mentioned earlier in this chapter, as well as those yet to be described. So long as Ken Goddard and his staff are left with only calcium as evidence, the wild tiger gains nothing from their work.

Each of these projects, in isolation, is cheap in global-conservation terms. Several are outright bargains. A determined individual could buy a truck and give it to Rudolph Youdt. The costs are so low, the projects so doable, so absent of conflicting logic, and so visible in terms of results that governments and NGOs should be tripping over one another in the rush to undertake them. (Some already are.) Those sponsors won't be able to buy better advertising. Go ahead, stick an NGO logo on the side of that truck, or saddle that sniffer dog with a jacket that bears your company's logo and an explanation of how the animal has been trained to look for derivatives from endangered species. Do we really care who capitalizes on the PR value of conserving the wild tiger so long as they're telling the truth? At last, a competitive aspect to the problem of wild tiger conservation that cannot hamstring the hoped-for goal. Too *many* working trucks for Rudolph Youdt and his colleagues? Please, let's give him a chance to work that problem out. Too *many* sniffer dogs in one airport? Considering the volume of work available, that's unlikely. More than forty-three thousand baggage-laden passengers entered the U.S. through Los Angeles International Airport alone every single day during the month of August in 1995—almost two thousand per hour—and that does not include what arrived through air cargo. What's the downside of trying? Let's find a way to fill up those empty guard posts in Nagarahole State Park for a year and see what happens. If it doesn't work, well, we're out a little over U.S. $20,000. That's not good, but it's survivable. And the evidence suggests success, not failure. Will undertaking these projects be easy? No, but the tiger is worth it. There will be all kinds of start-up headaches involved in even the simplest of the suggestions made here, and apt administration will be crucial. Good ideas are a dime a dozen; well-implemented ideas are one in a million. A mediocre idea that's well implemented will be infinitely more effective than a terrific idea that is implemented poorly.

At the risk of breaking our pledge to think small in this chapter, there is one more area for improvement that cannot be left unaddressed. Domestic laws regarding tiger bone need to be clear, simple, and uniform. The state of California comes very close to a standard, but Hong Kong does better. The essential wording involves something like "... products claiming either to be, or to contain, derivatives from tigers, and products found in fact either to be, or to contain, derivatives from tigers...." Between that and CITES, the stuff will have no legal sanctuary. Only then will meaningful international enforcement be possible. Laws such as these, unfortunately, will preempt the argument regarding TCM validity, but only for a while. And we cannot move on to that bigger question until everyone has a level legal playing field and the efficacy studies are complete. Exemptions are granted to CITES; they can be granted to domestic laws too, if deemed appropriate. At the moment, however, we have a hemorrhage, and we need to apply a tourniquet. If we don't, TCM containing wild tiger bone will go away for good no matter what. Our options don't include continuing the status quo.

This discussion of law leads conveniently toward a conclusion. One particular theme, expressed in two words, crossed the lips of the people interviewed for this book more frequently than any other. Marshall Jones: "There has to be a political will on the part of the countries that are range states for tigers and the countries that are the consumers of tiger products." Judy Mills: "Active political will must be marshaled on behalf of medicinal species in consumer countries as well as in range states." Valmik Thapar: "It requires a vast amount of political will...." Any number of similar quotes from additional sources could continue this list.

Political will. Governmental representatives of the people, in action. The prevailing majority of people don't want to see the wild tigers go away. So why are they? A secondary theme emerges in the three quotes just listed, and it was popular in many others. Both Jones and Mills directly mentioned range states and consumer countries, and Thapar was heading that way. A sensible collection on which to focus. There are fourteen wild tiger range countries, and about half again that number recognized as primary consumers of tiger derivatives. Some are both. What good sense it makes to start with them.

That observation is hardly new. In March 1994 representatives both governmental and non from all the wild tiger's range and consumer countries were invited to attend the inaugural convention of something called the Global Tiger Forum (GTF) in New Delhi, India. Most everyone invited showed up. Much valuable information was exchanged. Political associations crucial to the survival of the wild tiger were either established anew or reaffirmed. It was an exciting international innovation, hatched by India and supported by UNEP— a worldwide political forum aimed at saving a single endangered wild species. A mini-CITES, just for tigers. By all accounts, the event was a ripping success, destined to revolutionize every approach to tiger conservation. Just one small formality remained to activate the forum once it had adjourned. The representatives were to return to their respective countries and instruct their governments to ratify participation in the GTF. This sounds more complicated than it is. Ratification, sometimes called by different names, is simply the means through which a government makes known its willingness to comply with regulations outside its domestic jurisdiction. All CITES signatories have "ratified" their ascension to the treaty. Members of the UN have "ratified" their membership in that organization. In terms of international politics, this is very pedestrian stuff. The need for formal ratification stems from a variety of diplomatic protocols (which are far too complicated to get into here), and it also involves a commitment of funds. As with the UN and CITES, the GTF requires administrative operating capital, to be supplied primarily through dues paid by ratifying nations. At the inaugural meeting in New Delhi an interim secretariat was assembled, scheduled to be replaced by a permanent one as soon as five countries—just five—ratified their participation in the forum. Everyone waved good-bye and headed home to start the process.

As of the time this book went to press, only three countries had ratified participation in the GTF: Myanmar, Bhutan, and India. The others were offering an assortment of political doublespeak in their attempts to explain reasons for not ratifying. This is lunacy. A forum in which common interests can be discussed by the people both affected and empowered to enact relevant change is prerequisite to the solving of every problem. The concept forms the basis for how we interact as human beings, from the boardroom and the PTA to the congress and the parliament. It's part of what we call civilization. The GTF is exactly the correct forum from which to launch at least an *auxiliary* to all tiger conservation. It's not a matter of power or control. The GTF could no sooner force any single country to follow an external law regarding how it uses wild tigers than CITES could force one of its signatories to adopt the domestic policies of another. The GTF is a forum, not a police force. It's necessary, and it's sensible. If it dissolves for lack of ratification, what then? How else do we propose to bring all the interested parties together to discuss the conservation of the wild tiger? No second attempt will be different in any significant way.

This is not, by any means, to claim that the GTF will solve all the wild tiger's problems. None of the suggestions in this chapter will. But the GTF is worthwhile. It's a fine little place to show some political will.

Afterword

〰

WILDNESS CANNOT BE EXPRESSED IN WORDS. It can be talked or written *about*, but the element itself must be witnessed to be appreciated.

Before I began researching this book, my only exposure to tigers had been in zoos—looking at them from long distances, separated from them by bars or glass. I had never heard a tiger roar. Even in my work to complete this book I have sought out people more than animals. But many of the people I have sought out were inevitably found in close proximity to tigers, and I gained extraordinary exposure to the cats.

From San Diego to Thailand, from Indonesia to Russia, I was granted access to captive tigers that many keepers would envy, partly due to my connection with the researchers, partly due to lax or non-existent safety regulations. Several of the captive-bred tigers were so docile and curious they were amusingly similar to house cats—ears snapping forward at the slightest noise, noses sniffing tentatively at the tip of a shoe, cheeks and jaws nuzzling and nibbling at littermates. Paws would stamp down on moths and roaches, which would spring to life the moment the paws were lifted, only to be stamped again.

Tigers, though they do not purr, make a delightful array of endearing noises. It was all I could do not to reach out and scratch them beneath their chins.

That impulse was cured by my first exposure to a wild-caught female. Physically, she was not a large cat. In terms of presence, however, she was colossal. When I approached her enclosure, she crouched and pinned her ears flat. She thrust out her chin, drew back her lips, and partially closed her eyes. Her posture, combined with a sound that mixed steady hissing with low, surging growls, presented a being far more like a snake than a tiger. She did not look directly at me for some time, peering, rather, at some unfocused-upon point a few feet to my side. Then, slowly, she turned her head to lock eyes with me. She exhaled heavily. Ropy saliva spilled from the side of her mouth. Here before me was the Alien that Hollywood has attempted, but failed, to produce on film.

I backed away, inadvertently moving toward another enclosure in which another wild-caught tiger was being kept. He charged the bars and roared at me. I confess that I originally had prepared myself to be quite disappointed by a tiger's roar. Surely, the jaded journalist in me felt, the phenomenon had been aggrandized by the writers who preceded me, all seeking to capitalize on an experience their readers most likely would never be able to share, nor thereby discount. But I testify that a tiger's roar is an amazing thing. It shakes your rib cage from several yards away. The animal extends the sound uncannily by producing it both on the exhale and the inhale. It is a thrum, a howl, a whistle, a cry. . . . All at once. It made my skin crawl, and I loved it.

I later had the opportunity to witness the immobilization of that tiger. Even anesthetized he had an awesome presence. I touched his teeth, dull but deadly sabers. His unsheathed claws were sharp as pins. His tongue was a rasp, his eyes liquefied limes, his tail a steel cable wrapped in fur. His coat I found to be surprisingly stiff, very different from the fluffy domestic models that patrol my neighborhood back home.

But all these tigers were captive, ex situ, though their homelands were but a few kilometers away. This was not wildness.

A few months later I was hiking through the Sikhote-Alin preserve in the Russian Far East with Dale Miquelle as my guide. A "walk" was what he had proposed. Three hours later I was up to my hips in unblazed foliage, brushing ticks from my clothes and wondering what the hell I had gotten myself into. We came across the bed of some large animal on our walk, a six-foot oval tamped into the grass. We passed the dens of several wild pigs. We spied a flock of ravens perched atop a stand of trees—a telltale indicator of a kill. For all those close encounters, the only beasts we spied aside from birds were a frog and a field mouse. Plenty for me. That night at dinner, however, John Goodrich and Linda Kerley mentioned they had spent their afternoon tracking Geny, their largest radio-collared male tiger, who weighs more than six hundred pounds. "Where was he?" Miquelle asked casually. "Blogadotna," Kerley answered. Blogadotna was exactly, precisely, where Miquelle and I had walked that afternoon.

Was it Geny's bed we had inspected? Was he watching us from just yards away, as scared of me as I was of him? I know Siberian tigers typically don't stalk human prey, but why tempt fate? Just a few months earlier Goodrich and Kerley had inadvertently startled a tiger they were tracking and had been charged. The animal came within fifteen feet before veering off and allowing them to back away. (Their goal, it should be noted, is never to see or be seen by a tiger they are tracking so as not to influence its behavior.) I'm not sure whether it puts me more at ease to imagine Geny as fully aware of my presence in his territory or as oblivious. But when Kerley told Dale and me that Geny had been with us, it made my skin crawl. And I loved it.

The only time I saw a tiger in the wild was in India. My companions and I were returning to the Kabini Lodge after having feasted our cameras on herds of elephant, flocks of birds . . . animals of every origin, type, and description. "Tiger!" called the guide. Our Jeep came to a quick stop. The animal stood some twenty yards away, considering us warily. Moments later, she slipped into a nearby stand of foliage, silently dissolving as her stripes switched places with shafts of bamboo.

I loved it.

Acronym Glossary

AI   artificial insemination

AZA   American Zoo and Aquarium Association (a North American NGO for zoos and aquariums)

CBSG   Conservation Breeding Specialist Group (one of the IUCN/SSC specialist groups, of which Ulysses Seal is the chairman)

CITES   The Convention on International Trade in Endangered Species of Wild Fauna and Flora (a trade treaty drafted in 1973 that now has more than 120 signatories)

COP   Conference of the Parties (the biannual convention of CITES signatories)

EEP   Europäisches Erhaltungszucht Programm (the European Endangered Species Breeding Programme, for which Sarah Christie is the Siberian and Sumatran tiger captive-breeding coordinator)

ESA   Endangered Species Act (the American domestic legislation that, among other things, empowers CITES)

ESP   Endangered Species Project (an NGO coordinated by Sam LaBudde)

GASP   [Tiger] Global Animal Survival Plan (formulated under the direction of CBSG, who renamed it "the Tiger Global Conservation Strategy" in August 1995)

GEF   Global Environmental Facility (an auxiliary of the World Bank)

GTF	Global Tiger Forum (an IGO comprising all fourteen wild tiger range countries and all major tiger-derivative consumer nations)
IGO	intergovernmental organization
IUCN	International Union for the Conservation of Nature and Natural Resources (a scientifically oriented IGO formed in 1948)
IVF	in vitro fertilization
MFN	Most Favored Nation [trading status] (granted by the U.S. to countries who thereafter have enhanced trading privileges)
NGO	nongovernmental organization
PHPA	Perlindungan Hutan dan Pelestarian Alam (the department of Forest Protection and Nature Conservation in Indonesia)
PHVA	Population and habitat viability analysis (a technique for assessing animal habitats)
SCI	Safari Club International (an NGO for trophy hunters)
SSC	Species Survival Commission (one of the six IUCN commissions)
SSP	Species Survival Plan (a charter organized under the direction of the AZA and implemented by its member-specialists)
SWAN	Society for Wildlife and Nature (an environmental NGO formed in 1982 in Taiwan)
TCM	traditional Chinese medicine
TRAFFIC	Trade Record Analysis of Flora and Fauna in Commerce (an investigative NGO funded by WWF and IUCN)
UNEP	United Nations Environmental Program (the body within the UN chartered with addressing environmental issues)
UN	United Nations
WCS	Wildlife Conservation Society (a New York–based, scientifically oriented NGO with which Ullas Karanth is associated)
WWF	World Wildlife Fund (a fund-raising NGO formed in 1961 by IUCN; aka the World Wide Fund for Nature)

Acknowledgments

MANY PAGES WOULD BE NEEDED TO CONTAIN a list of just the names of all the people who have assisted and encouraged me, without so much as a thought regarding their own benefit or recognition, as I conducted my research for this book. Gestures ranged from the grand to the humble, including everything from advice on a career in writing to proofreading the words on this page. In all cases, I have striven to be generous and timely with my thanks. Here, I take an opportunity afforded exclusively to authors to express my gratitude in print to several people whose contributions have been, for reasons either personal or professional, extraordinary:

To my editor, Vicki Austin-Smith, for her keen eye, her strict but polite pen, and her common sense in the face of my occasional exasperation; to my agent, Peter Rubie, for his presumption from the very beginning that this book was a good idea; to Georgeanne Irvine and Linda Coats, at the San Diego Zoo, for granting me access to the zoo's private professional library; to Jan Percival Lipscomb, at Scribe Communications, for sharing her insights on traveling through India—except for the one about getting spiders caught in my hair; to Steve Hood, at Ursinus College, for his speedy and detailed replies to my queries concerning Asian politics; to Mary Maruca, at the U.S. Fish and Wildlife Service, for her glee in proving there is no fact she cannot either verify or correct; to Michael Dee, at the Los Angeles Zoo, for taking the time to supply me with a book that no one else could be bothered to sell me; to John Aquilino, for being frighteningly well connected; to Cynthia Botteron, for her willingness to share information with someone she might have considered a competitor; to Laura Kunkle, for extending a crucial dinner invitation; to my travel adviser, Frank Baquero, for assembling complicated itineraries, rearranging them repeatedly at my caprice, and then changing them back after fielding a frantic incoming fax or garbled phone call from me in the middle of the night from the other side of the planet; to my erstwhile assistant, Laura Schmitt, for deigning to be underemployed by me before moving on to pursue her own writing career; to Charlie Elster, for offering the kind of advice authors hate to hear but need so badly; to Alan Russell, for treating me as an equal from the day he met me and for leading me to Peter Rubie; to Sue Horton, Bella Stumbo, and Andrea Herman, who taught me anything important I know about journalism; and, finally, to Amy Tan, for an acknowledgment she once wrote, which led to all this.

Selected
Bibliography

MUCH OF THE INFORMATION DISPENSED in this book has been gleaned from obscure written sources, some of which remain unpublished, others unavailable in translation. In addition to such recondite references, I have consulted numerous periodicals, both popular and professional. While I keep copies of all such material on hand for fact-checking purposes, I do not see the value in detailing it here. Instead, I have compiled the following list of books that I found uniquely insightful, provocative, utile, and/or enjoyable. Between that and the accompanying list of "Organizations and Resources," the reader will have ready access to a rich and variegated stockpile of data concerning tigers and the conservation of endangered animals.

Barnes, Simon. *Tiger!* New York: St. Martin's Press, 1994.
Bonner, Raymond. *At the Hand of Man: Peril and Hope for Africa's Wildlife.* New York: Knopf, 1993.
Day, Michael. *Fight for the Tiger: One Man's Fight to Save the Wild Tiger from Extinction.* London: Headline, 1995.
Desai, J. H. and Malhotra, A. K. *The White Tiger.* New Delhi (India): Ministry of Information and Broadcasting, Government of India, 1992.

Gee, E. P. *The Wild Life of India*. New Delhi (India): HarperCollins, 1964.

Gray, Gary G. *Wildlife and People: The Human Dimensions of Wildlife Ecology*. Urbana (and Chicago): University of Illinois Press, 1993.

Hemley, Ginette, ed. *International Wildlife Trade: A CITES Sourcebook*. Washington, D.C.: Island Press, 1994.

Hoage, R. J., ed. *Animal Extinctions: What Everyone Should Know*. Washington, D.C.: Smithsonian Institution Press, 1985.

Hoyt, John A. *Animals in Peril: How Sustainable Use Is Wiping Out the World's Wildlife*. Garden City Park (New York): Avery Publishing Group, 1994.

Ives, Richard. *Of Tigers and Men: Entering the Age of Extinction*. New York: Nan A. Talese (Doubleday), 1996.

Jackson, Peter and Nowell, Kristin, eds. *Wild Cats: Status Survey and Conservation Action Plan*. Gland (Switzerland): IUCN, 1996.

Mann, Charles C. and Plummer, Mark L. *Noah's Choice: The Future of Endangered Species*. New York: Alfred A. Knopf, 1995.

McNeely, Jeffrey A. and Wachtel, Paul Spencer. *Soul of the Tiger: Searching for Nature's Answers in Exotic Southeast Asia*. New York: Doubleday, 1988.

McPhee, John. *Encounters with the Archdruid*. New York: Farrar, Straus and Giroux, 1971.

Montgomery, Sy. *Spell of the Tiger: The Man-Eaters of Sundarbans*. Boston: Peter Davison (Houghton Mifflin), 1995.

Richardson, Doug. *Big Cats*. London: Whittet Books, 1992.

Sankhala, Kailash. *Tiger! The Story of the Indian Tiger*. New York: Simon and Schuster, 1977.

Schaller, George B. *The Deer and the Tiger: A Study of Wildlife in India*. Chicago: The University of Chicago Press, 1967.

———. *The Last Panda*. Chicago: The University of Chicago Press, 1993.

Singh, Arjan. *Tiger Haven*. New York: Harper & Row, 1973.

Singh, Billy Arjan. *Eelie and the Big Cats*. London: Jonathan Cape, 1987.

Thapar, Valmik. *The Tiger's Destiny*. London: Kyle Cathie (Trafalgar), 1993.

———. *Tigers: The Secret Life*. Emmaus (Pennsylvania): Rodale Press, 1989.

Thomas, Elizabeth Marshall. *The Tribe of Tiger: Cats and Their Culture*. New York: Simon & Schuster, 1994.

Tilson, Ronald Lewis and Seal, Ulysses S., eds. *Tigers of the World: The Biology, Biopolitics, Management, and Conservation of an Endangered Species*. Park Ridge (New Jersey): Noyes Publications, 1987.

Ward, Geoffrey C. with [sic] Ward, Diane Raines. *Tiger-Wallahs: Encounters with the Men Who Tried to Save the Greatest of the Great Cats*. New York: HarperCollins, 1993.

Zwaenepoel, Jean-Pierre. *Tigers*. San Francisco: Chronicle Books, 1992.

Organizations
and Resources

American Zoo and Aquarium
  Association
(AZA)
7970-D Old Georgetown Road
Bethesda, MD 20814-2493
USA
Phone: (301) 907-7777
Fax: (301) 907-7980

Cat Specialist Group
c/o IUCN/SSC
1172 Bougy
Switzerland
Fax: 011-41-21-808-6012
E-mail: peterjackson@gn.apc.org

The Chinese University of Hong
  Kong
Chinese Medicinal Material
  Research Centre
Science Centre East Block
Shatin, N.T.
Hong Kong
Phone. 011-852-2609-6140
Fax: 011-852-2603-5218

Conservation Breeding Specialist
  Group
(CBSG)
12101 Johnnycake Ridge Road
Apple Valley, MN 55124
USA
Phone: (612) 431-9325
Fax: (612) 432-2757
E-mail: cbsg@epx.cis.umn.edu

U.S. Fish and Wildlife Service
1849 C Street NW, #3447
Washington, D.C. 20240
USA
Phone: (202) 208-1459
Fax: (202) 219-2428

Earthtrust
25 Kaneohe Bay Drive
Kailua, Hawaii 96734
USA
Phone: (808) 254-2866
Fax: (808) 254-6903

Endangered Species Project
(ESP)
Fort Mason Center, E-205
San Francisco, CA 94123
USA
Phone: (415) 921-3140
Fax: (415) 921-1302

Global Tiger Patrol
The Basement
253 New Kings Road, Fulham
London SW6 4RB
U.K.
Phone: 011-44-1717-364525
Fax: 011-44-1716-106828
E-mail: tigerpatrol@gn.apc.org

Hornocker Wildlife Research
    Institute
c/o University of Idaho
P.O. Box 3246
Moscow, ID 83845
USA
Phone: (208) 885-6871
Fax: (208) 885-2999

Humane Society of the United
    States
(HSUS)
2100 L Street, NW
Washington, D.C. 20037
USA
Phone: (310) 258-3002
Fax: (310) 258-3007

IUCN — a.k.a. The World Conser-
    vation Union
Washington Office
1400 16th Street, NW
Washington, D.C. 20036
USA
Phone: (202) 939-3416
Fax: (202) 797-5461

Ranthambhore Foundation
19 Kautilya Marg
Chanakyapuri
New Delhi, 110 021
India
Phone: 011-91-11-301-6261
Fax: 011-91-11-301-9457

Safari Club International
K (SCI)
Washington, D.C. office
445 Carlisle Drive
Herndon, VA 22070
USA
Phone: (703) 709-2293
Fax: (703) 709-2296

Save the Tiger Fund
c/o the National Fish and Wildlife
   Foundation
1120 Connecticut Avenue, NW
   Ste. 900
Washington, D.C. 20036
USA
Phone: (202) 857-0166
"Tiger Info. Center:"
1-800-5-TIGERS (584-4377)
Internet: http://www.5tigers.org

SWAN International
1st floor, Number 25
Alley 5, Lane 79
Hsiu-Ming Road, Section 1
Wen-Shan District
Taipei 116
Taiwan ROC
Phone: 011-886-2-937-6455
Fax: 011-886-2-936-2791

The Tiger Trust
Chevington
Bury St. Edmunds
Suffolk, IP29 5RG
U.K.
Phone: 011-0284-851001/3
Fax: 011-0284-851002/4

TRAFFIC International
219c Huntingdon Road
Cambridge CB3 0DL
U.K.
Phone: 011-44-1223-277427
Fax: 011-44-1223-277237

Wildlife Conservation Society
(WCS)
185th Street and Southern
   Boulevard
Bronx, NY 10460-1099
USA
Phone: (718) 220-5155
Fax: (718) 364-4275

World Wide Fund for Nature
(WWF/World Wildlife Fund)
1250 24th Street NW
Washington, D.C. 20037
USA
Phone: (202) 293-4800

Index

~